THE NONPROFIT
GUIDE TO THE INTERNET

NONPROFIT LAW, FINANCE, AND MANAGEMENT SERIES

THE NONPROFIT
GUIDE TO THE INTERNET

ROBBIN ZEFF

John Wiley & Sons, Inc.

NEW YORK • CHICHESTER • BRISBANE • TORONTO • SINGAPORE • WEINHEIM

This text is printed on acid-free paper.

Copyright © 1996 by John Wiley & Sons, Inc.

All rights reserved. Published simultaneously in Canada.

Library of Congress Cataloging in Publication Data:
Zeff, Robbin Lee.
    The nonprofit guide to the Internet / Robbin Zeff.
      p. cm.—(Nonprofit law, finance, and management series)
    Includes bibliographical references.
    ISBN 0-471-15359-1 (pbk. : alk. paper)
    1. Nonprofit organizations—Management—Computer networks—Handbooks, manuals, etc. 2. Nonprofit organizations—Computer network resources—Handbooks, manuals, etc. 3. Internet (Computer network) I. Title. II. Series.
HD62.6.Z43 1996
025.04—dc20   96-5937

Printed in the United States of America

10 9 8 7 6 5 4 3 2 1

About the Author

Robbin Zeff, Ph.D. (robbin@zeff.com), is president of THE ZEFF GROUP, a consulting firm that brings technology and culture together. An experienced fundraiser and trainer, Robbin conducts seminars nationwide on Internet strategic planning for nonprofits and cyber-fundraising. She holds a Ph.D. from Indiana University, spends her spare time jumping horses, and believes the key to good writing is a cat by every computer.

Contents

8. Cyberspace Law for Nonprofits 149
Tova L. Zeff, Esq.

Appendix A Internet Resources for the Nonprofit 165

Appendix B Reference Material   227

Appendix C Glossary   233

Index   239

Foreword

To the surprise of many the Internet, created as a cold war defense strategy, is not just creating a generation of antisocial surfers. Instead it is also fostering the growth of "cyber communities" in ways no one could have ever imagined. The Internet has greatly expanded our individual ability to communicate by removing the traditional barriers of time, space and physical attributes. In 1835 Alexis de Tocqueville, a French statesman and philosopher, characterized the new American republic as a nation of joiners. Today Americans are still creating and joining the over 900,000 voluntary associations that now exist in the United States—and they are also the overwhelming majority of the estimated 30 million Internet users worldwide.

Community building is the underlying rationale for the creation of all nonprofit organizations. Nonprofit managers are increasingly recognizing the value of the Internet as a powerful new tool in this arena. By using the Internet a nonprofit organization can both expand access to its services to new, underserved and/or isolated clients and build its community of donors.

Perhaps an even more compelling reason for nonprofit organizations to become more knowledgeable about the Internet is that it has stimulated a reexamination of issues such as freedom of speech, equal access, and privacy. These issues shape the daily operation and delivery of services of many nonprofits. As experienced community builders, nonprofit organizations should be aggressively sharing their expertise in policy discussions of these crucial issues.

As important as the Internet is for the nonprofit sector it is only one of many major challenges facing nonprofit managers today. Busy nonprofit managers are looking for a concise and clear guide that will both provide a solid overview of what the Internet is, and, more importantly, how it can help their organizations survive and grow into the 21st century.

Robbin Zeff, who is both an experienced fundraiser and an excellent trainer, has assembled the practical handbook for which nonprofit managers have been searching. I first met Robbin at the Foundation Center library in Washington, D.C., when she asked me to teach the section on foundations for her United States Department of Agriculture (USDA) fundraising course. We have gone on to teach other foundation and corporate fundraising classes together and to develop a series of workshops on the Internet for Washington, D.C., nonprofits. Much of what I learned about the Internet I have learned from her.

Convinced of the potential the Internet has to promote the many missions of the nonprofit sector, Robbin has volunteered countless hours to promote the use of the Internet by nonprofit organizations. This informative book's only failing is that cannot possibly capture Robbin's boundless enthusiasm for this topic.

After reading *The Nonprofit Guide to the Internet* nonprofit managers will realize that, in order to preserve and build the communities needed to help society into the next millennium, they must lead their organizations onto the information superhighway sooner rather than later.

Patricia Pasqual, Director
Foundation Center, Washington, D.C., Library

Preface

As a society we are fully engaged in the technological age. This technological revolution is not only changing the way America does business, but the way the entire world communicates, exchanges information, and purchases goods and services. By not incorporating new technology into daily operations, your organization risks not only being outdated, but also being unable to function in today's computer-centered work and home environment. The information superhighway is here to stay. Computers are a key aspect of communication—locally, nationally, and internationally.

The nonprofit community continues to evolve and struggle with the pressing issues facing society today: We must work harder; we must work smarter. On-line (a computer connected to one or many computers) access is a tool that will enable your organization to be more efficient and effective. In short, going on-line will make your organization work smarter.

The press today bombards the public with *whiz bang* articles about the Internet and the activities of the on-line revolution. There is no question that on-line activity is destined to increase. For the nonprofit organization, the decision to go on-line is no longer an "if" but "when" and "how." While the Internet may drastically change over the next few years, an organization that takes initial steps towards involvement today will ensure success.

AN OVERVIEW OF THE GUIDE

This guide addresses the needs, concerns, and potential of the Internet's use for nonprofits. It is directed toward anyone involved in the nonprofit community, whether an association executive or a grassroots volunteer. This guide is not a "how to" primer covering the technical nuts and bolts of the Internet. Rather, it examines the specific interests and organizational considerations of the nonprofit community to show how the Internet can be a positive addition to your organization's operations from programming to outreach to fundraising. In short, this guide addresses the fundamental question of how the Internet can benefit your organization.

Structure of Guide

This guide consists of the handbook itself and extended appendices. The goal of the handbook is to answer the questions surrounding why and how a nonprofit can maximize its use of the Internet. The appendices are a collection of Internet resources compiled especially for the nonprofit community.

The handbook consists of eight chapters, each focusing on the specific means by which a nonprofit can employ the Internet. The first chapter "The Story of Cyberspace" introduces the cyberspace culture and addresses some of the questions involved in understanding the Internet. Chapter 2, "Making the Technological Leap" surveys the hardware, software, and connection needs in getting on-line. Chapter 3, "Why a Nonprofit Should Go On-line" presents the arguments for connecting your organization to the Internet. Chapter 4, "Communication, Outreach, and Public Awareness in Cyberspace" examines how the Internet can serve as a communication vehicle for your organization. The following chapter, "Research Tools and Tricks on the Information Superhighway" looks at how to conduct research on the Internet and what information exists on the Internet that is of particular value and interest to the nonprofit community. Chapter 6, "Cyber-fundraising" explores how a nonprofit organization can use the Internet as a medium for raising funds. Chapter 7, "Making it Happen: Establishing Your Presence on the World Wide Web" explains how to formulate a strategy for building your on-line presence. And the final chapter is written by attorney Tova L. Zeff and presents the issues involved in "Cyberspace Law for Nonprofits."

There are three appendices. Appendix A is an extensive, annotated list of Internet resources—primarily Web sites of particular interest and value to nonprofits. All Web sites discussed in the guide are listed in this appendix. Appendix B consists of reference materials: books, periodicals, and on-line manuscripts. I realize that many readers may not have much experience with the Internet and that the terminology may seem technical and hard to grasp. To help make it easier for you to understand and converse in this new world, you will find a basic glossary at the end of this book (Appendix C). Words that are defined in the glossary appear in italics in the text.

The Internet is an ever changing forum, which makes including current examples a complicated task. All screenshots included in this guide are current as of February 1996. Because many organizations change their Web pages frequently, you will need to explore the Internet on your own. To give you some direction, Web addresses are included in the text. They appear in brackets and in bold face type.

Steve Glikbarg of Impact On-line hears all the time that nonprofit organizations get on-line for two important reasons, "One, they think it's really cool and two, they're afraid not to." *The Nonprofit Guide to the Internet* was written to provide nonprofit organizations—from the largest, national group to the smallest grass roots entity—with the questions and answers and tools and tricks to knowledgeably go on-line with a solid, strategic plan.

I OWE IT ALL TO SIBERIA

My involvement with the nonprofit community goes back 15 years. I spent ten years as a volunteer and staff member in both small, grassroots groups in Indiana and national technical assistance providers in Washington, D.C. For the past five years, I have serviced the nonprofit community as a consultant and trainer, specializing in innovative fundraising strategies. Working with nonprofit organizations from these various vantage points has taught me many things and has helped me to identify three basic truths about any organization. First, there is always more work than people to carry out the tasks. Second, just as the issues and concerns that inspire the formation of an organization change and evolve, so too must the organization itself change and evolve to serve the needs of society. Finally, there is never enough money to do all the work that needs to be done.

I wrote this book with these truisms in mind so that all suggestions are within reach of even the smallest organization's limited budget. The greatest feature of the Internet is that its assets are accessible for a minimal amount of money. Many speculate that the Internet will be the great equalizer because a small company or group can have the presence of a giant corporation on-line.

In all my years in the nonprofit community, I have always been an advocate of maximizing computer capability to maximize the effectiveness of the organization. Whether maintaining a mailing list database, publishing a newsletter, or conducting corporate research, smart use of an organization's computer only enhances its ability to get the job done.

It was not until I lived in Siberia in 1993 that I experienced first hand the power and importance of e-mail and the global reach of the Internet to the four corners of the world; I was living in one of those corners at the time. Because of my work with environmental NGOs (nongovernmental organizations) in the former Soviet Union, I knew there was e-mail in Russia through Glasnet, the Association for Progressive Communication (APC) affiliate Internet service provider (ISP) in that area of the world. With laptop in tow, I moved to the quaint town of Irkutsk near Lake Baikal to teach at the University of Maryland–Irkutsk State University Joint Faculty of Management.

Once in Irkutsk, I began my quest to get on-line. It was not easy to get hooked up; the telephone lines barely worked, and when I did get a line it often was of a quality too poor to use. I was unable to connect to Glasnet from Irkutsk and found a local Russian ISP. The service was run by Evgeni, who spoke excellent English and ran his business from a room deep in the bowels of the old mainframe computer center at Irkutsk State University. Evgeni was a Russian entrepreneur who made a business selling access to the Internet. He charged me $10 a month plus a fee per kilobyte. I quickly became his biggest client, racking up a $20 to $30 bill per month, which I paid in U.S. cash dollars.

As far as I could tell, the biggest roadblock to Internet access growth in Irkutsk, and all of Russia for that matter, was lack of good telephone lines. I once asked Evgeni how he acquired such a good, clear telephone line for his service. Evgeni smiled and said, "Simple, everyone in Russia is hurting for money today. I rent the KGB line. They always had good phone lines and now they need money more than they need the telephone line."

When I returned from Siberia six months later, I continued to use e-mail. It was about this time that the World Wide Web stormed on the scene, and I wasted no time learning about this new feature of the Internet. Shortly thereafter, I started to incorporate my ideas about the potential of the Internet to nonprofit organizations into my fundraising training workshops.

Soon I was being asked to do workshops specifically on nonprofits and the Internet. In these workshops, I learned a lot about what nonprofits were doing on the Internet and problems they faced in entering the cyber-space arena. I decided to put my ideas down in an article "Navigating the Internet for Nonprofits" that appears in *The Nonprofit Manager Handbook* edited by Tracy Connors and published by John Wiley & Sons, Inc. The more workshops and seminars I facilitated on nonprofits and the Internet, the more I addressed and learned about the dynamic cyberspace area and the greater the potential I saw for the nonprofit community. It is through the ideas, examples, and discussions with my many workshop and seminar participants that the genesis of this book emerged.

Robbin Zeff
Arlington, Virginia
June 1996

Acknowledgments

There are many people who helped make this book possible. First, I want to thank my editor at John Wiley & Sons, Marla Bobowick, for sharing my vision in this topic and being the force behind turning the idea into reality. I would like to also thank Michael Detweiler for helping me keep a sense of humor throughout the production process.

I also want to thank the many people whose comments, suggestions and input helped me turn my cyberspace research into this book: Dan Bricklin, John Passacantando, Pat Pasqual, Joshua Baucher, Charles Bennington, John Richards, Jim Clark, Andy Goldman, Jami Love, Sheree Parris Nudd, John December, Steve Glikman, Steve Gladis, Howard Sartori, Sheryl Rosenthal, Ed Stern, Abby Goodwyn, Ronnie Levin, and Jill Barancik.

In doing research on and about cyberspace, my best source of information came from the cyberspace community itself. I want to thank everyone who participated in the Nonprofit CyberSurvey for sharing their thoughts and experiences with their nonprofit Web site with me: Kimberly Adams, John Bancroft, Putnam Barber, Scott Barnett, Valerie Blassey, Jacek Bochenek, Ray Boomhower, Andrew Bradley, Sandi Brockway, Kelly Christiansen, Mike Clark, Bill Cox, Jennifer Doctor, Steven Durland, Susan Ellis, Gina Faber, Miles Fidelman, Steve Gibson, Judith Hengeveld, Peter Ide, Jennie Inglis, Cindy Johanson, Beth Kanter, Stephen Karnes, Carlyle Kyzer, Howard Lake, John Longhurst, Jeffrey MacKie-Mason, Thomas March, Cortney Martin, Ray Mitchell, Brian Moura, Elaine Needham, Sarah Nesbeitt, Karen Ostgard, Mark Olweny, Jillaine Patterson, Gilly Rosenthol, Jerome Scriptunas, Steve Kris Shearer, Joan Shildneck, Kirk Glenn Smith,

Selena Sol, Ellen Spertus, Michael Stein, Peter Tavernise, Robert Tewes, Richard UpJohn, Philip Walker, Jens-Erik Weber, and Jay Whittle.

Every writer needs a place to write. For me, Metro 29 diner in Arlington, Virginia, served as my early morning source of inspiration.

I would like to thank Sharon Hodgdon and Jim Wise for their moral support in writing this book.

A project like this cannot be brought to completion without the support of good friends. I owe a great deal to my cohorts in the Tuesday and Thursday night jump classes at the Potomac Horse Center, and especially my professional trainer, Brian A. Gruber, for always "keeping me on my job" whether on horseback or on-line.

There are three people who helped me with this book over and above the call of duty. I was extremely lucky to find such wise and witty readers and editors as Curtis Wong, Jasmin Holmstrup, and Catherine Swanson. I could not have completed this book without them.

And finally, I want to thank my family, Debbie, Jack, Zanni, Brick and especially Tova (the author of Chapter 8) for their constant encouragement and support.

CHAPTER 1

The Story of Cyberspace

INTRODUCTION

The story of the *Internet* is not one of machine over man. The Internet poses no threat to traditional communication processes, but rather it expands them beyond time and space, physical and geographical barriers, and social and economic standards that are the present determinants of most communication.

The story of cyberspace is not the story of the rapid speed at which use of the Internet has spread since it was opened to commercial use. It is not merely the expeditious nature with which pages have emerged on the Web, or the elaborate graphics on the *World Wide Web*. The story of *cyberspace* is the development of a virtual community, one with no geographical barriers, one that challenges our concepts of time, space, and reality. It is a community where the voice of the chairman of the board of a Fortune 500 company is on equal footing with a junior high school student from Paducah, Kentucky. Cyberspace is just another form of communication, joining the ladder of communication that includes face-to-face interaction, telephone conversation, faxes, letters, and reports.

The Internet is neither owned nor managed by any one person, company, or country. Some would go so far as to say that the Internet is anarchistic by nature, and yet the computers networked on the Internet communicate in a consistent manner. The Internet is not a thing or a place, rather it is a cooperative networking effort that spans the globe.

Cyberspace is a multilevel communication medium where it is as appropriate to conduct global research as it is to reply quickly to a message; a place where it is just as appropriate to view the great works of art as it is to play a game. Moreover, there is an immediacy in the interaction of communication in cyberspace. Messages are received and answered within minutes from anywhere on the globe.

One of the fundamental principles in cyberspace is sharing. People share information, experience, advice, even software. A large percentage of the information on the Internet is in the public domain. It is not uncommon for the author of a piece of information on the Internet to encourage readers to use the material freely; this rarely happens in other places in society.

In cyberspace, people are known and acknowledged based on their ability and on the product they give to the cyberspace community. For example, one of the early directories of resources for nonprofits was compiled by **Putnam Barber [http://www.eskimo.com/~pbarber/]**. This single individual took the initiative to find resources of value to nonprofits online and made them available to anyone and everyone with Web access. A person in Los Angeles, California or in Irkutsk, Siberia may not know Putnam Barber as the president of the Evergreen State Society, but they can all access and benefit equally from his contribution to the body of knowledge on nonprofit management.

In cyberspace physical disabilities are invisible. The disabled community encourages the use of universal design (a concept borrowed from architecture, where a design incorporates special need considerations in the initial plan rather than as later modifications) whether one is building a skyscraper or a Web page. In cyberspace no one knows if the user is in a wheelchair or stutters or is deaf. In cyberspace a person with chronic fatigue syndrome can work at a comfortable pace. Cyberspace is already a welcome community for the disabled, but much more can and should be done to enhance accessibility for people with all types of disabilities.

CYBERSPACE CULTURE

The profile of people on-line is changing and diversifying as on-line opportunities expand and the average computer comes set up for on-line connections. What was once only the domain of those affiliated with universities and research institutes is now found in homes and offices around the globe. The Internet Demographics Survey—a poll conducted by Nielsen Media Research (a division of Dun & Bradstreet Corp.) and released by **CommerceNet** in October 1995 [**http://www.commerce.net/information/ surveys/exec_sum.html**]—concluded that roughly 37 million people in the United States and Canada alone have access to the Internet. The survey found that average Internet users are 16 to 34 years of age and that two-thirds of users are male. If one factors in that there are Internet connections in almost every corner of the globe, the true reach of the Internet is mind boggling.

Moreover, the ages of Internet users is expanding in both directions. In a few years, the demographics of Internet users will include almost everyone who can read and write. There are some that predict that the limiting factor will be access to equipment rather than age or gender. Time will tell.

The cyberspace community is growing at a phenomenal rate. When the Internet was formed in 1971, it consisted only of four connected computers. In the first half of 1995 alone, according to InterNIC, the official Internet registration service in the United States, the number of *hosts* (i.e., servers) connected to the Internet grew 37 percent to 6.6 million worldwide with each host representing hundreds if not hundreds of thousands of users. The number of people with Internet access is certain to increase at this astonishing rate.

Information on the World Wide Web is expanding exponentially as well. There are anywhere from 35,000 to 50,000 home pages in existence. A true number is impossible to know because new sites are appearing hourly as old sites are moved and reconfigured.

No one really knows where the Internet is going or where it will be in five years because even predictions for six months into the future are out of date once they are proposed. One thing is certain, however, the Internet is and will continue to have a dramatic impact on society.

UNDERSTANDING THE INTERNET—QUESTION AND ANSWERS

While many first time users find the Internet confusing, understanding the background and environment of the development of the Internet will make some of its quirks more comprehensible and maybe even endearing.

Why Does the Internet Appear Disorganized?

With all the commotion over the Internet, it may seem puzzling that information on the Internet is not neatly organized. The reason is tied to its original conception. The concept of the Internet was born as part of the quest to find a solution to one of the major strategic military dilemmas of the nuclear age: how to ensure that communication could continue during and after a nuclear war. In the early 1960s, the RAND Corporation (a prominent think tank) made public the concept of a communication network with its vulnerability factored into the design. The idea was that if a network in its entirety is innately unreliable, then each contributing part of the whole must be able to function independently in the tasks of sending, receiving, and storing information. In this way, each packet of information would travel the network like a giant game of hot potato, the packet always staying airborne so that the dismantling of any host computer (or server) would never impact the traveling packet's ability to reach its destination.

In 1969 the Pentagon's Advanced Research Projects Agency (ARPA) decided to provide funding to test this packet-switching concept of communication networking with a small, select group of computers. The first host computer was at UCLA; later that year three more hosts were added (Stanford, University of California, Santa Barbara, and the University of Utah), comprising the newly formed ARPANET. Each server was a completely separate and independent body joined together in a network by their agreement to follow the same packet-switching protocol. ARPANET grew to 15 hosts in 1971 and doubled in size the following year.

The decentralized structure of ARPANET aided its rapid expansion throughout the 1970s because the network could handle different kinds of machines as long as each followed the agreed upon standard for a communication called Network Control Protocol (NCP), later changed to Transmission Control Protocol/Internet Protocol (TCP/IP). By 1984, there were over 1000 hosts and growing on the Internet. In 1986, the National Science Foundation joined the network with the development of NSFNET. At the end of the following year, the number of hosts broke 10,000. The massive growth of the network resulted in the formal termination of ARPANET in 1989–1990 to allow its new form—the wildly successful Internet—to officially and independently take the helm.

Hence, the same design strategy that allows each part of the Internet to function as an independent whole, is the same aspect of the Internet that makes it virtually impossible to determine the precise number of users. As Charles Bennington, Manager of Network Services at Essential Organization, points out, "The root of the Internet's design makes knowing anything quantifiable about the Internet unnecessary, because the Internet was designed to be a network of pieces."

How Was E-mail Developed?

The scientists and researchers using ARPANET could transfer data and share computer facilities for running massive statistical applications. However, what quickly became apparent was that the primary traffic on ARPANET was the exchange of personal messages. The exchange of electronic mail became fundamental to the growth and notoriety of the ARPANET, so much so that in 1976, with much fanfare, the Queen of England sent an electronic message. The following year the University of Wisconsin provided over 100 researchers with electronic mail. It was precisely the exchange of information that attracted researchers and other academics to ARPANET, thereby aiding its rapid growth and expansion. In fact, one of the early applications of ARPANET, in addition to e-mail, was USENET (topic specific discussion groups) and the mailing list (a technique whereby an identical message could be automatically broadcast to a list of subscribers).

Who Can Use the Internet?

For most of the Internet's first 20 years, it was primarily used by educational and scientific institutions. Up until that point, the only way to get access to the Internet was as a government agency or through a university or research facility; one needed government agency approval to connect. All this changed in 1990 when the Federal Networking Council modified its membership policy from only organizations with sponsorship by a U.S. government agency to anyone who wanted membership. This opened the door for commercialization of the Internet and resulted in exponential growth, especially in the United States. In 1990 commercial service providers developed, and today anyone can have access to the Internet.

How Does the World Wide Web Fit into the Internet?

Have you ever wondered, "What has particle physics done for me lately?" Today you can point to the development of the World Wide Web and thank the researchers at CERN (*Conseil Europeen pour la Recherche Nucleaire*) in

Geneva, Switzerland for developing a means for physicists to actively collaborate with other physicists around the world in real time.

This involved the concept of a hypertext system in which a document contained live and active links to other documents. The sending and receiving of these hypertext documents required its own protocol and in 1989–1990, CERN launched *HyperText Transmission Protocol* (*HTTP*). To aid in the reading of hypertext, software needed to be developed that allowed the user to read hypertext documents; CERN developed the first prototype Web *browser*. Without a doubt, it was the development of the browser that made viewing of the linked text and graphics easy and accessible. By 1992, browsers were available on the Web free of charge to the general public.

These developments resulted in the World Wide Web phenomenon. This phenomenon is an Internet application consisting of a diverse environment of interconnected text and graphic-based sites joined together in an interactive webbed conduit for information exchange.

In just five short years, the Web grew from conception to become the most popular application on the Internet with well over 35,000 sites and a staggering growth potential; in fact, even the **White House** premiered a Web site in 1993 [**http://www.whitehouse.gov**]. By 1995, the commercial on-line services such as America Online, CompuServe, and Prodigy began offering Web access.

How Can a Nonprofit Compete with a Well-Financed Business on the Internet?

Nonprofits, specifically universities and research institutes, were part of the very foundation that shaped the Internet. They were the first users of the Internet and were the first to grasp its potential as a multidimensional communication vehicle. The commercial potential of the Internet undoubtedly sparked its current rapid growth, but nonprofits led the charge to push for the Internet's use as a global communication vehicle.

As far back as the 1980s, organizations were using computer networks and bulletin boards to communicate and exchange data. For example, PeaceNet was established in 1986 to connect organizations and individuals involved in issues of peace. A year later the idea behind Peacenet was used to form the Institute for Global Communications (IGC), a networking service for social change organizations. In 1990, the Association for Progressive Communications (APC) was founded to coordinate global networking with IGC as its U.S. partner. Today IGC links over 13,000 member organizations and 20,000 individuals in its networks—PeaceNet, EcoNet, ConflictNet, LaborNet and WomensNet—all providing access to the Internet.

For the past ten years, high technology has helped document the course of social conflict. The revolutionaries at Tiananmen Square used faxes to inform the world as events unfolded. The fall of communist Russia was documented through e-mail messages. Global communication mediums such as the Internet will make political communication blackouts more difficult, if not impossible.

In 1994 commercialization of the Web began to operate in full swing, years after the nonprofit community had been using the Internet for information retrieval and exchange. Nonprofit organizations and related entities hold the second largest number of domains, second only to commercial domains. Undoubtedly, the phenomenal growth of commercial domains is directly related to the financial potential of the Internet being touted throughout Wall Street.

The Internet is friendly territory to nonprofits. There is no inherent value in one Internet address or another. The root domain of .org or .edu holds equal weight with .com or .net. Content, not money, determines the value of a Web site.

Does Anyone Monitor the Quality and Accuracy of Information on the Web?

There is no overseer or gatekeeper that monitors information on the Internet. Without a doubt, the sheer volume of material available on the Internet is staggering. John Passacantando, Executive Director of Ozone Action, feels that the volume is connected to the fact that no one governing body oversees the Internet to determine appropriate content or to administer credibility of sources. "Without those traditional gatekeepers we need to edit ourselves," says Passacantando. "One thing you see all over the Net is just piles and piles of stuff because there are no editors. But this will change as people become more sophisticated." At this point, one has to judge the quality and accuracy of the information based on the source. Equally as unstructured is the fact that there is no authority to go to with complaints on content. For now, the test for accuracy and validity of content rests on the source of the information. The more credible the source, the more reliable the information.

What Are the Security Concerns on the Internet?

Security concerns have been around since the very earliest days of the Internet. The first real security problem was the spread of a *worm*. A computer worm is a program that can run by itself and duplicate itself. In 1988 a worm infected 6,000 of the 60,000 active hosts on the Internet. Known as the Internet Worm, it was actually an experiment by Robert Morris, Jr. to see how many machines a program could operate on without causing problems. The worm ended up running out of control, bringing many machines to a halt, and Robert Morris was eventually sentenced for his action. The Internet Worm resulted in the formation of active Internet security measures as well as the formation of the Computer Emergency Response Team (CERT) by the Defense Advanced Research Projects Agency (DARPA).

A *virus* differs from a worm in that a virus consists of a piece of software programming code that adds itself to an existing computer program. A virus requires that a host program be run or activated and then attaches itself to a file. The type of damage a virus can cause ranges from altering of data to displaying of messages to crashing the computer. Viruses are common in the personal computing community because of weaker security.

Many wonder if it is possible to get a virus from surfing the Internet. One cannot get infected by a virus from viewing Web pages or filling out forms. A virus is contracted from the installation of a program, the use of a file on disk, or from downloading an executable program from the Web. The more respectable the source, the less likely it is to contract a virus. In any case, prevention is the best solution for viruses. The installation of antivirus software is recommended for all computers to check for viruses every time a computer is turned on and periodically while in operation. This way, if infection occurs, disinfection can take place immediately, before any damage occurs. There is now antivirus software on the market that checks files downloaded from the Internet.

How Can I Make My Computer Experience Less Frustrating?

Without a doubt, computers and frustration are synonymous. It is inevitable that at some point something will go wrong with any computing effort. Fortunately, with each modification of software and hardware, the bugs and other points of aggravation are smoothed over.

Learning to use the Internet takes patience and time. A million things can go wrong and all it takes is one glitch to start out on the wrong foot.

Take things slowly and follow installation instructions. Read the manual; it can be a great help. Most on-line services and access providers supply technical support as do commercial software companies. There is often a fee associated with the use of technical support, but there can be a great advantage. A five minute phone call to technical support could save hours of trial and error. Equally important, investing time in learning the Internet through training is time well spent. With computers, the more you know the more satisfying the experience.

CHAPTER 2

Taking the Technological Leap

INTRODUCTION

Technological change can be scary to any organization. This guide provides you with information to answer the questions you will face in making the decision to go on-line.

Building the technological infrastructure of an organization enhances it in every aspect. A good internal computer system connected to a strong on-line presence does not mean that the organization is losing touch with those it serves. Rather, it is maximizing its available communication tools to better serve its constituents. An on-line presence is just one part of an organization's overall outreach strategy. Good use of the Internet does not mean eliminating other forms of communication from an organization's approach, but rather enhancing channels of communication and complimenting programs already in operation.

The Internet will never replace the personal side of organizing and outreach. Instead, the Internet helps amplify outreach. Robert B. Tewes, Webmaster of Taxpayers Against Fraud finds that, "The Internet allows nonprofit organizations, or any organization for that matter, to disseminate their message to a potential audience numbering in the millions." The expansive reach of the Internet to a global audience provides unprecedented exposure for the nonprofit community. Moreover, this outreach vehicle is immediate and inexpensive in relation to the short- and long-term benefits.

TECHNICAL AUDIT

The reason on-line activity has grown so rapidly over the past few years is the ease of access. Very little is required to go on-line, send e-mail, navigate the Web, or set up a site on the Web. The primary piece of equipment required to go on-line is a computer.

The following section describes specifically what you will need to go on-line in terms of hardware, software, and connection services (see Exhibit 2.1). The price of hardware could be either more or less than your general office needs. Keep this in mind when reviewing the equipment recommendations made in this chapter.

Hardware

Computer

Many computer manufacturers are designing computers with the Internet in mind. With today's computer applications, the faster the computer the better. Files on the Internet contain thousands of bytes, and the faster the computer the more quickly it will be able to read and download information. The graphical nature of the Web means that tens of thousands of bytes may be dedicated to just one graphic within a site. Although graphics take time for the computer to read them and are often purely cosmetic, they are also part of what makes the Web so attractive and easy to use.

The majority of new desktop computers are designed for multimedia use. This means they include speakers and a graphics and sound card, as well as a high-speed processor and at least 8MB of RAM. Many also include an internal modem. The design of these computers takes into consideration the graphically enhanced visual nature of the Web and its many large-size files. They are usually sold in packages with a color monitor, keyboard, and mouse, as well as some basic software.

In buying an office personal computer, think about the applications for which the computer will be used. This is especially important considering the average life span of a personal computer is 2 to 3 years. The price of

Required

Hardware
Computer (minimum 486 and 8MB)
Monitor (color recommended)
Modem (minimum 14.4K bps)
Phone Line

Software
Communications software—dialer
　　Merit Network's MacPPP 2.0.1 (ftp://ftp.merit.edu/internet.tools/ppp)
　　InterCon Systems' InterSLIP (ftp://ftp.intercon.com)

Browser software
　　Netscape Software (http://home.netscape.com/comprod/mirror/index.html)
　　NCSA Mosaic (http://www.ncsa.uiuc.edu/SDG/Software/Mosaic/
　　NCSAMosaicHome.html)

E-mail software
　　Pegasus Mail version 2.01 (ftp://ftp.let.rug.nl/pub/pmail/winpm201.zip)
　　Eudora Light (http://www.qualcomm.com/quest/light.html)

Internet Software
FTP application software
　　Cute FTP version 1.4 Beta 6 (ftp://papa.indstate.edu/winsock-1/ftp/CuteFTP.Betas/
　　cftp14b6.zip)
　　WS FTP32 (ftp://ftp.usma.edu/pub/msdos/winsock.files/ws_ftp32.zip)—This is the
　　32-bit version

Usenet News software
　　Trumpet News Reader (ftp://ftp.trumpet.com.au/wintrump/wtwsk10a.zip)
　　Free Agent version 1.0 (ftp://ftp.forteinc.com/pub/forte/free_agent/fagent10.zip)

HTML editing application software
　　HTML Assistant and HTML Assistant Pro (http://fox.nstn.ca/~harawitz/index.html)
　　Mel Park's Plaintext (*E-mail address:* mpark@nb.utmem.edu)

Optional (Partial List)
Printer (recommended)
Stereo speakers

Exhibit 2.1 On-line checklist: Hardware and software requirements.

computers seems to stay around $2,000 to $2,500 with more features being added with each passing year.

Monitor

No specific monitor is required. A black and white or monochrome one will work fine. However, a color monitor is best for easily recognizing links and display graphics. While the cost of monitors varies greatly, the better the monitor, the clearer the presentation. The prices for color monitors start at around $200.

Modem

Because of exponentially increasing on-line use, major developments are being made to improve *modems.* As of this printing, 28,000 (28.8 KB) baud rate modems are commonly used. The *baud rate* determines the speed of the modem in reading and transmitting data. Many new computers include modems in the package. A 14.4 KB modem costs about $75, while a 28.8 KB can be found for around $200.

Printer

A printer is not required but is quite useful for downloading and printing information to read at a later time. Some on-line services charge a per hour fee for usage, commonly referred to as connect time. Printing of documents can save connect time and reduce on-line costs. Laser printers are becoming the standard for quality printing. Prices vary considerably with the price of a personal laser printer starting at around $400.

No other hardware is required, although there is a great deal of other equipment that can be purchased to accentuate Internet use. Stereo speakers enhance the sound quality of audio files. Large screen monitors are available for easy viewing, especially of graphics. Scanners, cartridge drives, sound cards and everything else that is available for a computer enrich its use, but come at a cost and are not required.

Software

Many computer packages contain start-up *software,* including a basic operating system, a word processor and other applications. The first piece of software necessary to go on-line operates the modem. Communication software usually includes set-up procedures that enable the communications software to work with most modems on the market.

Browser

The most discussed piece of software for the Internet is the *browser*. A browser is a user or client program that interprets and provides the environment in which the user navigates the Web. It allows the user to access and search the Internet by inputting different addresses. It also saves, prints, places bookmarks, sends e-mail, and performs numerous other tasks. Netscape and Mosaic are among the most popular browsers. Specifically, browsers are designed for the Web. Each browser displays the Web differently, and choosing the best browser depends on its intended use. Commercial on-line services provide their own Web browsers.

Freeware and Shareware

Freeware and *shareware* are software that may be downloaded onto the hard drive and used for a trial period. With shareware, if the user likes the program, he or she is expected to send a check in payment (usually $5 to $10, although some programs cost more). Freeware is free software just as the name implies. Freeware and shareware are very convenient and easily obtained; there is no need to visit the computer store. Commercial versions of shareware programs are also available and usually include additional options, but all for a higher price. Browsers, *File Transfer Protocol* (*FTP*), e-mail programs, *HyperText Markup Language* (*HTML*) editing applications, and more are all available as freeware or shareware.

Commercial Software

Recently, commercial software for the Internet user has appeared on the market. Just a year ago, most Internet software was shareware but now such packages as *Internet in a Box* are available in stores for under $100. Often, for the first time user, this product may be easier to implement because detailed instructions are included and everything necessary is provided.

GETTING ON-LINE

Jumping onto the on-ramp of the information superhighway may seem incredibly complex. Technologically it is; however, Internet applications exist to make the jump an easy and accessible process.

There are many components to the Internet. One can use the Internet to send electronic mail called *e-mail,* and look at text-based directories of sites called *gophers* or the graphically enhanced World Wide Web. Each has a specific function and offers unique advantages. An individual or organization can access a wide variety of services on the Internet, the vast majority of which are free.

The following sections provide a general, technical overview of the elements of the Internet, and how an organization can tap into them.

FEATURES AND APPLICATIONS OF THE INTERNET

E-mail

One of the first Internet applications and one of the most used features is electronic mail commonly referred to as e-mail. E-mail is sent over a computer network such as the Internet. It allows messages to be sent from one computer user to another anywhere in the world, usually within minutes. If a user is not at his or her computer, the mail is stored and can be read at any time. It is so fast and convenient that users refer to regular mail as *snail mail.* It is estimated that over 30 million people across the world have e-mail and it is by far the most utilized element of the Internet.

Many e-mail software programs, such as **Eudora Light,** are available as freeware [**http://www.qualcomm.com/quest/light.html**]. There is also a commercial version called Eudora Pro. Many freeware versions are samples of more elaborate commercial programs.

E-mail addresses vary considerably. The most common Internet address includes the individual's first initial and up to seven characters of his or her last name. This is followed by the @ symbol meaning *at,* which gives the domain name, the location of the individual's e-mail account. For example, the President of the United States address is president@whitehouse.gov (Exhibit 2.2). Another format for e-mail addresses consists of a series of numbers, such as the commercial on-line service CompuServe uses for its customers (e.g., 12345.6789@compuserve. com).

A domain name is a unique name assigned to a computer connected to the Internet. The root domain, the suffix after the domain name, distinguishes the characteristics of operation of the domain holder. There are six primary root domains:

president@whitehouse.gov

$$\underline{}_{1} \quad \underline{}_{2} \quad \underline{}_{3}$$

1. Name of specific person or machine to receive the e-mail. This is the user's ID.

2. Name of company or entity to receive e-mail

   2 and 3 make up the domain name

3. Top-level domain

.gov—government	.edu—education
.org—organization	.net—network
.com—commercial	.mil—military

   There are also 106 two letter country codes, such as
   UK = United Kingdom
   US = United States
   SU = former Soviet Union

Exhibit 2.2 The anatomy of an e-mail address.

☐ .com—commercial

☐ .gov—government

☐ .edu—educational institution

☐ .org—organization or association

☐ .mil—military

☐ .net—network

The *domain name system* (*DNS*) came into being in 1983. As of October 1995, there were 12,000 registered .org domains according to InterNIC Registration Services, the official domain registration entity for Internet users in the United States, which handles the registration of domain names of the Internet. Until 1995, domain names were free; however, the explosion of Internet use has resulted in the adoption of a domain name registration fee.

FTP

In addition to short e-mail messages, entire files can be transferred over the Internet. *File Transfer Protocol* (*FTP*) is a means to transfer files from an off-site database or server to a user's computer.

Gopher

This Internet tool simplifies using and finding networked information by creating menus that list the files available at a specific location. The menu or file is in text only format.

The World Wide Web

The Web has become the premier feature of the Internet. It offers vast amounts of information in easily accessible text and graphics format. For this reason, it is very appealing to almost any user, regardless of purpose.

The Web is viewed through a browser. A browser is software that allows the user to gain access to the Web. The language used to design a Web page is HyperText Markup Language (HTML) and is designed to allow any computer with a browser to read and interpret material on the Web, as opposed to most software that can only read documents composed with that particular software.

Understanding a URL Address

The addressing system for the Web is similar to a street address. Each address has a *Uniform Resource Locator (URL)*. The URL tells the computer what type of *protocol* (an understanding on how to communicate between different computers) is being used, where the site is located, and its type. For example, the address [http://www2.whitehouse.gov] would bring the user to the White House Web site (Exhibit 2.3). A Web address is made up of several parts, the first piece tells the computer what type of protocol to use to access the site. It is similar to a long-distance access code for the telephone. Many Web sites, such as the White House, begin with http (which stands for HyperText Transport Protocol). The "www" stands for World Wide Web. "Whitehouse" is the name of the site and the suffix ".gov" is the domain for a government site.

Home Page

Home page is the name given to the first page of a site. It usually welcomes the user to the site and offers basic information regarding what the site has to offer. From the home page, the user can travel to other pages by using links. For example, a home page that covers the topic of cooking may pro-

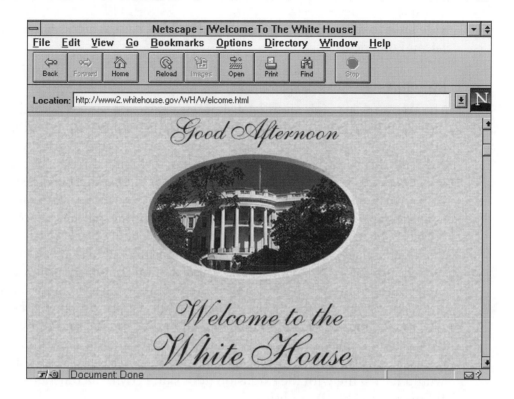

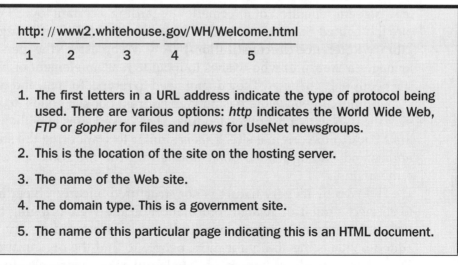

1. The first letters in a URL address indicate the type of protocol being used. There are various options: *http* indicates the World Wide Web, *FTP* or *gopher* for files and *news* for UseNet newsgroups.

2. This is the location of the site on the hosting server.

3. The name of the Web site.

4. The domain type. This is a government site.

5. The name of this particular page indicating this is an HTML document.

Exhibit 2.3 The anatomy of a URL address.

vide links to other pages with cooking tips for Cajun, American, continental, and other cuisines.

Hyperlinks

The Web consists of thousands of sites with each site consisting of a home page and additional pages with text containing embedded hyperlinks to other sites. A *hyperlink* or *link,* as it is commonly referred to within a Web page, is easily distinguishable from other text on the page because it appears in a different color and format, such as blue, underlined text.

When the user points to a link and clicks with the mouse, the computer is instructed to go to the address embedded within that link. Each page within a site has its own specific address and clicking on a link will call up the specific page within that site. For example, the address [http://www2. whitehouse.gov/White_House/Publications/html/Publications.html] is a page linked to the White House Web site that allows you to request a specific document page that houses official White House press releases. The www.whitehouse.gov site is contacted and asked to find and retrieve the document "Publications.html". This is a page on the site with press releases in HTML format. Just as those using Microsoft Word software would have a file with the extension (.doc), an HTML document often has the extension (.html) or (.htm).

Links relating to a site's topic allow the user to seek out new and different information on another site with just the click of the mouse. It also may prevent repetition of information regarding a certain topic. For example, the United States Constitution is on the Web **[http:/info.rutgers.edu/ Library/Reference/US/constitution/]**. Any Webmaster (the person who manages a Web site) who wishes to include it as an element of his or her site needs only to link it. They do not need to retype, format, and upload it.

Additionally, since there is no Web address book, a good site will provide the user with a list of related links. The linked sites may then provide links back to the original site. This is similar to wandering the stacks at a library and finding related books located next to the book one originally came to find.

The Web by its very nature is not structured linearly. Hyperlinks help to connect similar or related information on the Web, bringing a unique form of homeopathic order to a multidimensional expanding structure. An added bonus is the ability for more people to find the organization's site. The user may not have known it existed until he or she traveled to a related site and hyperlinked to the organization's site without intentionally looking for it. By establishing mutual links in this way, the site will attract more users through this necessary, and free, hyperlink publicity.

For example, if one is interested in breast cancer, one could go to the **American Cancer Society's** Web site [**http://www.cancer.org/**] (Exhibit 2.4). At the site you would learn that the American Cancer Society has a special breast cancer network [**http://www.cancer.org/bcn.html**]. In addition, from the American Cancer Society's site, one can link to other breast cancer sites such as the **Breast Cancer Information Clearinghouse** [**http://nysernet.org/bcic/**] maintained by the New York State Education and Research Network. Users can travel throughout the Web visiting sites with similar interests. There can be numerous benefits to creating hyperlinks. Many sites already exist and an organization may discover another nonprofit with similar goals and interests in servicing clients.

GETTING CONNECTED

The Internet is the backbone of the on-line world. To get directly connected to the Internet, you can subscribe to a service called an *Internet Service Provider (ISP)*. There are also commercial on-line services—series of computers connected by phone lines—that, in addition to providing Internet access, offer proprietary services and material unavailable elsewhere on-line. This section reviews the options and services of both to assist you in developing your organization's Internet connection strategy (Exhibit 2.5).

Internet Service Providers

ISPs are companies that provide dial-up Internet access, which means you can access the Web, send and receive e-mail, transfer files, and establish Web sites. In addition to access, *ISPs* provide the basic software needed to conduct these functions on the Internet. The software packages are usually shareware or freeware Mac and Windows versions of software and consist of communication software (i.e., a dialer), e-mail, and a Web browser.

There are different types of ISPs and most are commercial enterprises. However, a few have emerged that are designed specifically for the nonprofit community. Examples are **Impact Online** [**http://www.impactonline.org**] and **Essential Organization** [**http://www.essential.org**].

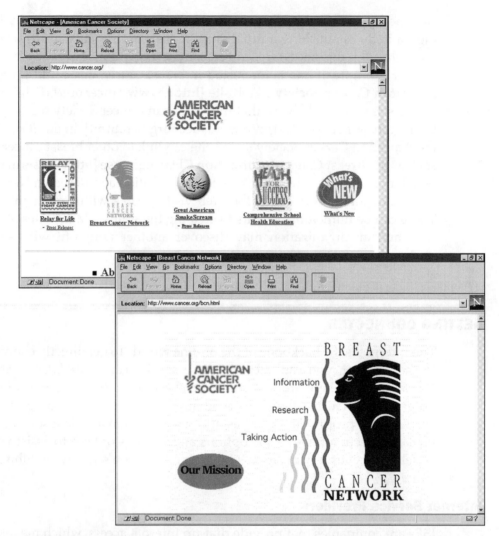

Exhibit 2.4 Hyperlinks—American Cancer Society and its Breast Cancer Network. *Reprinted with permission.*

In general, ISPs have either a national or a regional focus. Nonprofit ISPs usually service a national clientele. National ISPs have local access numbers that allow you to connect to the server from anywhere in the country, and in some cases internationally. Examples of national ISPs include **Performance Systems International, Inc. (PSI)** of Herndon, VA [**http://www.psi.net**] and **EarthLink Network** of Los Angeles, CA [**info@**

Internet Service Providers
1. National
   Nonprofit ISP
2. Regional

On-line Services
1. Commercial
2. Nonprofit

Exhibit 2.5 Internet service connection options.

earthlink.net]. Regional ISPs offer Internet access to users in a limited geographical area such as **Capital Area Internet Service (CAIS)** of Arlington, VA [**http://www.cais.com**] and **LA Internet** of Los Angeles, CA [**http://www.lainet.com**]. If your organization uses a regional ISP, consider their limitations if you have chapters or affiliates scattered about the nation.

The costs involved in using an ISP consist of a set up fee, a monthly user fee and an additional fee for the ISP to house a Web site on its server. ISPs and nonprofit networks offer competitive rates for access.

On-line Services

On-line services refer to large computer interactive bulletin boards such as America Online, CompuServe, eWorld, Microsoft Network, and Prodigy, as well as the nonprofit on-line services such as HandsNet and Institute for Global Communications (IGC). These services offer proprietary information to members, such as newspapers, magazines, shopping, and chat features, as well as e-mail, the Internet, and Web access. There are many worthwhile value added features for the nonprofit from these services. For example, both America Online and CompuServe have special nonprofit resource areas that will be described in the following section.

Though there is some variation in service fees, most on-line services charge a monthly fee of $9.95 for 5 hours of access and $1.00 per additional hour. This fee can add up, especially if you are using these services for e-mail as well as for surfing the Web.

Commercial On-line Services

As a commercial entity, these on-line services go after a broad audience and have discussion forums for such diverse communities as dog owners, equestrians, gourmet cooks, and members of AARP—and have other on-line features to service different segments of their ever expanding market. Currently, America Online (AOL) and CompuServe are the only commercial on-line services with specific forums dedicated to servicing the needs of the nonprofit professional community. As two of the largest commercial on-line services, AOL and CompuServe see the nonprofit as a growing and dynamic aspect of their consumer base and are showing a commitment to serving this community. Ted Leonisis, President, American Online Services Company says, "America Online is committed to civic involvement and the growth of the nonprofit sector."

America Online [http://www.aol.com], the nation's largest commercial on-line service with 5 million members, is the home of access.point Civic Involvement System (Exhibit 2.6), a comprehensive on-line nonprofit resource launched in May 1995. It is available to all AOL members free of charge and can be reached by the keyword, access.point.

The features of the Civic Involvement System include:

❏   Ability to donate to a favorite charity

❏   Advertise or find a job or volunteer opportunity in the nonprofit world

❏   Learn more about the programs and activities of nonprofit organizations

❏   Chat in real time with other members interested in civic involvement

❏   Shop in the Nonprofit Sector Marketplace—a shopping center of reports, products and services for the nonprofit community.

For the nonprofit professional, there is the Nonprofit Professional Network, where anyone involved in nonprofit work (staff, volunteers, board members) can learn about nonprofit issues such as management, fundraising, technology, tax, and legal and public policy.

The overall focus of the Civic Involvement System is "to empower individuals to take action and find information that allows them to make a difference," according to James Clark, founder and President of access.point, Inc. "It is our goal to unite the nonprofit sector on-line. Access.point will allow nonprofits to reach larger audiences and work more easily with each other, as well as make nonprofit professionals more informed."

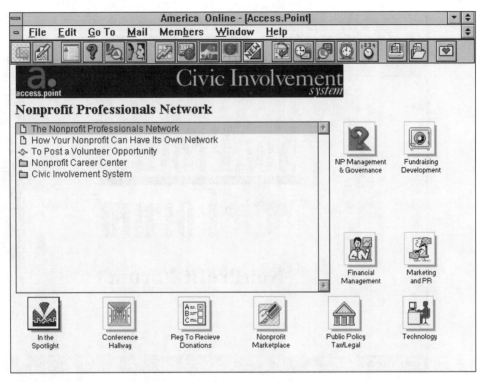

Exhibit 2.6 America Online—access.point Civic Involvement System. *Copyright © 1995–96 America Online, Inc. All Rights Reserved. Reprinted with permission.*

CompuServe [http://www.compuserve.com/index2.html] has 4 million subscribers worldwide. In 1995, it launched the NonProfit Forum™, a private forum service requiring an additional fee for access. The NonProfit Forum system (Exhibit 2.7), can be reached by the keyword, nonprofit.

The NonProfit Forum was founded by veteran nonprofit professional Sheree Parris Nudd, who designed the forum to serve as a professional resource center for anyone involved in nonprofit work: "If somebody needs something and has a question and there is no direct source in the NonProfit Forum library, I will try to find a resource or a next step for them." The administrators of NonProfit Forum feel strongly that the forum should work as a resource as well as a mentoring tool. The forum is run by nonprofit professionals who use their experience as well as their wide personal networks of resources to help others on the forum. For example, you can get feedback on direct mail and grant proposals from members of the forum. The idea is to have a consultant on-line. The three

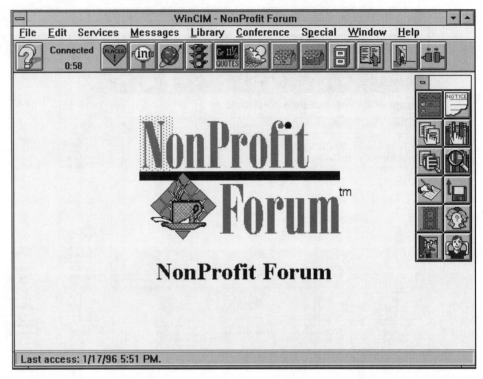

Exhibit 2.7 CompuServe's feature area for nonprofit professions—NonProfit Forum™. *Reprinted with permission.*

main features of NonProfit Forum are a message area, a library, and on-line conference rooms.

The NonProfit Forum is a place where ideas are generated and expertise tapped from service providers such as fundraisers, consultants, software vendors, and so on. In short, according to Nudd, at the NonProfit Forum, "You're finding real answers to real problems by real people."

Nonprofit On-line Services

The age-old adage that information is power has long been a driving force in the nonprofit community, with the gathering and disseminating of information the core mission of many organizations. The value of connecting people through computer networks sparked the interest of the nonprofit community early in the Internet's development. As a result, on-line services focusing on the needs and concerns of the nonprofit community emerged. Two of the largest are IGC and HandsNet. Both services facilitate communication among individuals and organizations involved in social change on a local, state, national, and/or international level by offering a full range of communication networking features for the exchange of ideas and information, as well as Internet access.

HandsNet [http://www.handsnet.org/handsnet] is a nonprofit on-line network (Exhibit 2.8) linking the national human service community. HandsNet services approximately 5,000 public interest and human service organizations in the United States. HandsNet members receive public policy alerts and analyses, notices of legal and administrative actions, abstracts of key studies and reports, Federal Register notices, funding information, and daily updates of crucial human services news. Members have access to more than 150 national clearinghouses along with research and advocacy organizations serving as regular information providers. HandsNet works to build an on-line community with its members. The average member spends $45 per month on membership and access fee costs. Initially, one could access HandsNet only through a separate dial-up service; HandsNet is now accessible through any Web browser expanding

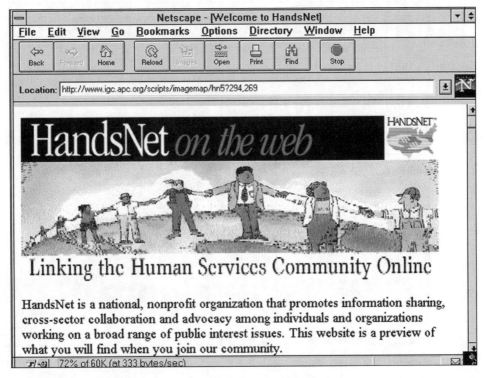

Exhibit 2.8 HandsNet home page. *Reprinted with permission.*

its reach into the nonprofit community. The HandsNet Web site serves as the gateway to the HandsNet network.

The **Institute for Global Communications (IGC) [http://www.igc.apc. org]** is a worldwide computer network system (Exhibit 2.9) servicing the activist community to "create progressive change in the fields of human rights, social justice, environmental sustainability, conflict resolution, women's empowerment, and the equitable treatment of workers." IGC is the United States partner of the Association for Progressive Communications (APC), an international coalition of computer networks that services over 28,000 people in 133 countries. IGC is the home of five networks: PeaceNet, EcoNet, ConflictNet, LaborNet and WomensNet. These networks have served as unifying communications conduits for the exchange of ideas and support for individuals and organizations. When you join one of the IGC networks you become a member of IGC at large and have access to information on all the networks, as well as hundreds of news services and publications of the alternative press, as well as Internet access.

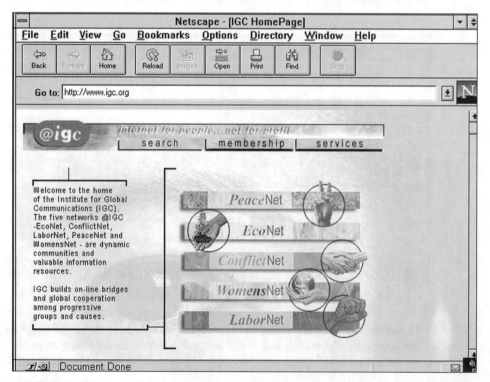

Exhibit 2.9 The Institute for Global Communications home page. *Reprinted with permission.*

CONNECTION OPTIONS: A DIFFERENCE OF STYLE

The question remains: Which connection option best suits the needs of your organization? Today, any service you choose will provide basic access to the Internet. The differences between the types of services rest in the package of resources and customer service/technical support they provide. In fact, the difference between an ISP and an on-line service can be likened to the difference between shopping at a national discount clothing store such as Loehmanns or a national upscale department store such as Nordstrom. At Nordstrom, service is premium, the merchandise is well organized and beautifully displayed, and everything is done to enhance the customer's shopping experience. Nordstrom also has its own line of products available only through their chain of stores. The prices of the merchandise are competitive, but not the main defining feature. Likewise, on-line services are a one-stop shop for Internet access and other on-line activities from e-mail and chat rooms to news and selected merchandise. They offer value-added interactive services that are well organized and presented in a user-friendly environment not available elsewhere on the Internet.

An ISP is like shopping at a discount store. For example, Loehmanns is the home of the bargain shopper. At Loehmanns, you can find designer clothing at bargain basement prices if you have the time, patience, and fortitude to search through the hordes of merchandise. Clothes are loosely organized and displayed on long racks. Loehmanns is a place to shop primarily for the discount price, and maybe for the thrill of the hunt. Similarly, an ISP connects you to the Internet at a low and competitive rate and it is up to you to learn how to explore and use the Internet applications and make order out of the tens of thousands of Web pages.

In formulating an Internet connection strategy, it is important for your organization to determine its intentions in regard to the Internet before signing on with an ISP or an on-line service. This involves determining the following:

❏ Who will have access—a person, a chapter, the entire organization.
❏ What will be done with that access—research, e-mail, establishing a Web site.
❏ What plans your organization has for future growth on the Internet.

Only then will you be able to determine which service will best meet your needs and which is most cost effective in the short and long term.

Because the on-line industry is constantly evolving as new ideas, applications and technologies are developed, the services that companies offer, as well as the companies themselves, come and go and change on a regular basis. Today's upstart may be tomorrow's powerhouse. Therefore, it is important to stay informed of the changes in the industry so that you always get the most competitive rates and services.

PREPARING YOUR ORGANIZATION TO GO ON-LINE

Whether you are a volunteer, a staff member, a board member, or the executive director of an organization, there are three key issues that must be addressed in order to go on-line.

Determining Who Should Get Access.   First, will everyone in the organization have on-line access? In other words, should every computer be fully equipped for Internet access? For many organizations, this will be a financial decision based on equipment availability and equipment purchasing ability. The more people in an organization who communicate on-line and use on-line resources, the faster that communication vehicle will become a part of the organizational culture.

Importance of Training.   Second, training is key for successful incorporation of on-line activities into an organization. Most of us are a little bit wary when we start something new—an unknown destination represents an unknown outcome. The more we know about the Internet and the more comfortable we become with it, the faster the Internet will move from being a scary mystery to a valued communication and organizing tool. Training should be provided to each staff person. Today, a plethora of workshops for the Internet are available at local nonprofit training centers such as the Support Centers of America, local colleges, and computer training centers. Moreover, an organization can look internally to its volunteers and staff for people with Internet skills who can do individualized training.

With computers, as with any skills-building experience, one learns by doing. Whether you are learning a new software program or trying to navigate the Internet, the best way to learn is by practicing. Staff will need time to explore and expand their personal capabilities in cyberspace. This will be time well spent, because a comfortable and knowledgeable Web surfer will be able to navigate the Internet more effectively and efficiently.

Internet Use Policy.   Third, the issue of an office Internet use policy may present itself because of the high entertainment value of the World Wide Web and the tendency for people to exchange personal e-mail messages as well as work related ones. Most organizations have an official or unofficial in-house policy dealing with personal use of office equipment, such as the telephone, fax, computer, and copy machine. In fact, for many nonprofits, the unofficial policy is merely not to abuse the privilege of access and use. A separate policy for the Internet is unnecessary. Issues of Internet use belong under the professional office protocol standards already in place.

CHAPTER 3

Why a Nonprofit Should Go On-line

REASONS TO GO ON-LINE

Perhaps in the past your organization has focused much of its budget and energy on service to clients. You may be asking yourself: Can I afford to divert the time and funds necessary for building a technological infrastructure? This guide will demonstrate that the benefits of going on-line outweigh both the costs and the concerns.

Why are people going on-line? According to Jennie Inglis, reference librarian at The Free Library of Philadelphia, "We were driven by the fact that we are one of the largest public libraries in the country and we needed to be a presence on-line." Why do you need a presence on-line? "One of the greatest problems for any organization has always been lack of communication and information," says Mark Olweny of Friends of Makerere in Canada. "The Internet has to a large extent helped resolve this."

There are three important reasons why an organization should go on-line. First is the fact that the Internet enhances an organization's ability to communicate with its members, its staff, and the general public. Second, the Internet provides incredible access to information from around the world. Third, the Internet is an exciting new fundraising medium. These points are discussed in the following sections.

1. Ability to Communicate

The Internet is a remarkably flexible and diverse outreach vehicle that will expand your organization's ability to communicate both internally and externally. "It is another tool to help us to get our message across," says Ray Mitchell of Amnesty International. "The big difference is that this tool allows us to reach tens of thousands of people very quickly and for very little cost."

Being on-line establishes a 24 hours a day, 365 days a year location where anyone can access information about an organization directly from that organization. Users who may never have heard of your organization before can directly interact with you at their own convenience. "It has raised the profile of Amnesty. We have received many e-mails from Internet users who had never read an Amnesty report or did not know what the organization did until they visited the Web site," says Mitchell. Beth Kanter, Network Coordinator for Arts Wire, sees their Web site as a key aspect of their outreach efforts. "We are in the business of being a network for artists and arts organizations and our Web site is one of the ways we do it."

E-mail messages can be left and answered at any time of the day or night, allowing for a broader outreach. The Internet presents an important vehicle for communication with current members. It also offers the opportunity for new dialogues with potential members, allowing for general organizational marketing. "We have had many new membership inquiries as a result of our Web site," says Steve Kris Shearer, Associate Director of California Odyssey of the Mind. The Internet offers tremendous membership recruitment possibilities. "Any group no matter how small, no matter how geographically dispersed can use the Internet to build a constituency through free electronic publishing," says Richard Upjohn, Associate Director of the Center for Civil Society International. "Nonprofits will be limited only by the strength or weakness of their ideas."

A Web site greatly expands your communication horizon as well: "The story of the Internet is a fantastic one. For computers to reach further into remote places of the world and to enable people to communicate is fantastic," says Karen Ostgard of PagOne Internet Advertising. "The net gives us access to people and places that would otherwise be impossible for a small nonprofit," explains Carlyle Kyzer, Executive Director of Abwenzi African Studies. "Through our Web site we have contact with many Malawians studying or working abroad. Up-to-date information about Malawi (and many African countries) can be difficult to find in libraries. With the Internet we are much more in touch with not only what is going on in Malawi, but how Malawians feel about it." Sarah Nesbeitt, Assistant Librarian at Bridgewater State College believes that the greatest benefit of the Internet to non-profits is the enhancement of communication between nonprofits. When she collaborated with another nonprofit on the development of her Web site **Internet Resources for Non-Profit Public Service Organizations [http://asa.ugl.lib.umich.edu/chdocs/nonprofits/nonprofits.html]** she heard stories about nonprofits learning about each other through the Internet. In one instance, she heard how the Internet had helped an organization establish contact with sister organizations across the country.

Many people who travel the Internet are casual explorers. They are looking for information, fun, and activity. Ray Boomhower, Public Relations Coordinator of the Indiana Historical Society has found that the Society's Internet has increased its profile. "It has positioned the Society on the cutting edge of a new technology especially with our members and Hoosiers everywhere."

Equally important is how the Internet will strengthen your organization's internal communication. E-mail facilitates instant and continuous interaction between staff, for an e-mail message transmits to its destination within minutes. This allows communication to occur daily, even hourly among staff members, volunteers, and board members in the office, at home, in satellite offices, or when staff is traveling without incurring the high cost of long distance phone calls. For example, when out of the office, you can access your e-mail by using a notebook computer with a built-in or external modem and a local call to an access provider. If your computers are not networked internally, on-line access will allow you to use e-mail to communicate with other staff members and interested persons.

2. Ability to Gather Information

Being on-line provides an organization with access to information not constrained by its physical proximity. Once on-line, one can access or exchange information as easily with a person or site in Paris, Texas, as in Paris, France. "It has provided our members with a resource on the Internet where they can obtain the latest country reports, news releases, Urgent Actions and so on," recounts Ray Mitchell. "Not only can they retrieve these documents but they are also in electronic form, allowing the AI member to easily incorporate the information into their local group's newsletter."

The ability to provide information quickly will help you better service your clients. Tom Tate, Systems Manager for the USDA Cooperative Extension Service, was able to help a teenager from a town hit by a midwest flood locate information about water purification. The town's water plant was shut down and the teenager wanted to know the procedure for purifying drinking water manually. Tate e-mailed the teenager telling him where he could find this information on the Extension Service's gopher server. A few weeks later, Tate received an e-mail from the teenager saying that he had become a local hero because he had distributed the information he had gathered on how to prepare safe drinking water to the entire town. The teenager had been able to get the answer to his question within a matter of hours.

There is an immediacy to Internet research. Andrew Bradley, a technical writer at the Universities Space Research Association, has found the Internet invaluable when the answer to a question is needed instantly. "I was in a teleconference mostly listening to some higher-ups talk about the possibility of procuring a certain Boeing aircraft for NASA. A question came up about the plane that no one knew the answer to. I jumped on the Net. Took a lucky guess at Boeing's home page address. Found a link to the history of the 747 and got the information. All in about a minute and a half."

The information available through the Internet includes searchable databases, directories, bibliographies, dictionaries and resource lists. The Library of Congress is on-line as well as most major university library card catalogs. Some are text only, but more and more on-line information appears through the Web with its elaborate text and graphic capabilities. Whether one is doing prospect research on a foundation or a corporation, scanning newspaper articles for a particular policy issue, or gathering data on a specific illness, the Internet allows you to do global research from the comfort of your home or office computer with material immediately retrievable and downloadable.

Researching and gathering information on the Internet can be done faster and more conveniently than through phone or mail requests. Elaine Needham, President of Needham Associates, is a firm believer in the convenience and efficiency of researching over the Internet. Needham explains, "For instance, the U.S. Department of Education makes many of its publications downloadable—it is so much quicker and cheaper to download information you need when you need it and print out only what you need. No wasted storage space! No lost time waiting for the mail and then finding they have mailed the wrong pamphlet!"

3. Ability to Raise Money—Cyber-fundraising

The Internet has the potential to start a revolution in the area of fundraising. With over 37 million people connected to the Internet—and that number growing at a feverish pace—the Internet provides the nonprofit community with the ability to reach a mass audience for fundraising purposes quickly and cost effectively.

Whether sending a solicitation by e-mail or requesting contributions on a home page, *cyber-fundraising* is a medium with vast potential. There are many reasons for this. One important reason is that the Internet offers a captive audience for solicitation. Depending on approach and intentions, visitors to a nonprofit's site can be asked for donations, membership, to take action, or express their opinion on an issue. These activities will bring the individual into the nonprofit's arena and can, in time, promote additional participation and contributions. Whether an organization is the Sierra Club selling merchandise or advertising wilderness adventures on their Web site or the American Red Cross soliciting donations in response to the latest natural disaster, nonprofits are finding that the Internet is a fundraising vehicle that works.

COSTS FOR GOING ON-LINE

Without a doubt, financial concerns are a fact of life for nonprofits. There never seems to be enough money to do good work. Karen Ostgard of PagOne Internet Advertising worked on the Raphael House Web site and is a firm believer in the value of a nonprofit going on-line: "Many nonprofit organizations are very low on funds, and rely only on very limited means of exposure. If a site helps one person, it has paid for itself 1,000 times over." Andy Goldman of the **North American Conference on Ethiopian Jewry** [**http://www.cais.com/nacoej/index.html**] feels strongly that the meager amount of money that was spent to put up and maintain their Web site was far outweighed by the return: "Whether it's new donations or inquiries by journalists, our Web site is making our small organization appear like a giant."

There is no denying that purchasing and maintaining a computer system in an organization is a financial commitment. Computer technology changes rapidly and therefore is not a one-time-only investment. A computer system purchased today will become increasingly out of date with each passing year. Once a nonprofit enters the information age and purchases computers, it has to commit to an ongoing upgrade of the system—both in terms of hardware and software—as the technology and market dictate.

What are the costs one can anticipate? First, there are costs associated with the purchase and maintenance of hardware and software. Second, one needs an account with an Internet service provider or with a commercial on-line service to provide a gateway to the Internet. An overview of pricing is provided in Exhibit 3.1.

Defraying Costs

There are many means to help defray the costs of building the technological infrastructure of an organization. Computer companies like to coordinate their philanthropic activities with their business interests. For example, Apple Computers has a long history of donating computers to nonprofit organizations. Such donations from other hardware manufactur-

Estimated One-Time Setup Costs	
Computer	*$2,000–$2,500*
120mhz Pentium Processor	
16MB RAM	
1000MB Hard drive	
3.5" 1.44MB floppy drive	
15" color monitor	
28.8K bps internal modem	
ISP Setup Costs	
SLIP/PPP account (basic access)	$15–$25
Web site	$30–$60
Total	$2,045–$2,585
Estimated Yearly Fees	
Basic Access (SLIP/PPP account)	
Monthly	$12.50–$20
After 4–10 hours (or unlimited	
access flat rate)	$1 per hour
Yearly costs	$150–$240
Web Site	
Monthly	$30–$60
Yearly costs	$360–$720
Total	$510–$960

Exhibit 3.1 Costs associated with going on-line.

ers should be pursued as well. Software manufacturers have similar programs. There are also organizations in place that work to distribute computer equipment—hardware and software—to the nonprofit community. One such group is the Lazarus Foundation in Columbia, Maryland, that collects working and nonworking computers from businesses and individuals and refurbishes them for distribution to nonprofit organizations. They also collect in-kind software from companies. In a February 27, 1995, news release from Microsoft reporting on their charitable contributions, Don Bard, President of the Lazarus Foundation is quoted as saying, "Microsoft's in-kind software support has been invaluable to our donation programs to educational institutions, nonprofit organizations, and individuals with special needs."

The cost of labor to put up and maintain a Web site is also a financial consideration. Most nonprofit Web sites in operation today are conceived, designed, and maintained by volunteer labor; some are even the after-hour projects of staff or board members. Jerome Scriptunas, Acting Board President, Big Brothers/Big Sisters of Monmouth County has a similar story of putting up a site with minimal expense. "A co-board member, Scott Barnett, Board VP of Marketing and Operations, negotiated free Web server space from his provider. Scott also had the ability to create the pages. The investment is Scott's time, and he handles that on an as available basis. There is no pressure, so it's a win situation." For the California Odyssey of the Mind, the costs were truly minimal, especially when compared with the benefits, "We have a donated site so the benefits outweigh the costs," says Steve Shearer, Association Director.

It is common for a staff member or volunteer to take the move as a personal challenge to demonstrate the value of on-line connectivity to the organization. Phillip Walker, an Information Systems Manager at the United Way of America, took on such a task, "I created my site at first to demonstrate to several people the breadth of the Web." Phillip Walker developed a site for the nonprofit community he served that was a collection of nonprofit resources that he called the "Nonprofit Resource Catalogue." The site turned into much more than a mere exercise. As Phillip explains "like many things on the Net it eventually took on a life of its own as others began to use it."

Another possibility is to have a local junior high, high school, or college computer class adopt your organization as a semester project; classes are often asked to do civic involvement projects. Why not present your organization as the volunteer project for a class as part of its civic involvement program? For example, Nonprofit Prophets, a project for using the Internet and interactive video conferencing from Pacific Bell Education First Initiative program, has set up teams of students in the San Diego, California area that identify social or environmental problems. According to Thomas March, part of the design team for the project, "the students then partner with actual nonprofit organizations to create a World Wide Web site that shares both student research as well as the information the nonprofit needs to get across."

There are some who feel that leaving Web development with only volunteers may not be to an organization's best interest. Susan Ellis, of ENERGIZE, Inc., a volunteer program development and management firm in Philadelphia points out, "Web site development is being led largely by volunteers within nonprofits who offer their personal time and expertise to put an agency on-line. This is great, but also means that key decision makers are not really vested yet in the idea."

CHAPTER 4

Communication, Outreach, and Public Awareness in Cyberspace

COMMUNICATING IN CYBERSPACE

When computers first exploded onto the scene, they were used primarily for processing information—from numbers to words. Now computers influence how we communicate and with whom we communicate. From sending e-mail messages to accessing information from a database located on the other side of the world, on-line technology offers the nonprofit a wealth of capabilities that make an organization more efficient and better informed.

For the nonprofit, strong communication conduits are essential. Amnesty International sees the Internet as a tool to connect and communicate. "Amnesty International is all about communication of its concerns on behalf of individuals in danger." Ray Mitchell, Urgent Action Coordinator of Amnesty International lists the outreach elements they employ in their World Wide Web site, "The site exists to provide information about human rights violations, to encourage Internet users to get involved in Amnesty's campaigns, and to provide them with the opportunity to act immediately." Without a doubt, the Internet allows a nonprofit to reach a broader audience than ever before.

Not only can one readily communicate with staff, members, and volunteers, but also the Internet allows the user to reach interested persons all over the world. Mitchell tells of an early experience at Amnesty International. "The first campaign featured on our Web site was the Indonesia campaign launched in late 1994. We uploaded all the documents in English, French and Spanish. We later received anecdotal evidence that the reports had been downloaded in East Timor, translated into Bahasa, Indonesia and reformatted and printed, all within the space of a week. The report was then widely circulated within East Timor."

Equally important, the Internet has numerous outreach devices that a nonprofit can employ to contact, educate, and motivate individuals. These tools include e-mail, databases, discussion groups, publications and on-line style fact sheets. It is these tools and the audiences which they serve to connect that comprise the dynamic communications component of the Internet to nonprofits.

The Internet Audience

Your organization can divide the Internet audience into two fundamental groups. First is the internal audience, one's own staff, volunteers, and members or supporters. The second audience is an external one and includes an organization's full range of contacts—potential members, professional colleagues, and government agencies, as well as the public at large.

Cyberspace helps an organization to enhance its ability to service its internal audience. For staff and volunteers, the Internet facilitates the exchange of daily or weekly updates. If an office is not networked internally, the Internet e-mail can be used for internal as well as external communication. For organizations with field or satellite offices, e-mail is a perfect means for lowering telephone bills by encouraging on-line communication instead of lengthy and expensive long distance phone calls. E-mail is also an excellent way to communicate with staff members on the road, eliminating the time zone dilemma for efficient office communication. In the area of productivity, an office that is spread out can now exchange documents as easily as messages, facilitating the collaboration and editing process of reports and proposals.

To members and supporters, cyberspace provides a window into the organization never before possible. A Web site becomes a permanent, inexpensive, and always available public awareness tool. To members and supporters, the organization is always open and available. With the click of the mouse, a supporter can learn the current state of an organization's activities, programs, or publications. With another click, he or she can look at the organization's magazine or newsletter; and with just one more click, download a copy of a specific publication. Never has communication been so immediate and interactive.

In reaching the external audience, going on-line offers many nonprofits something they have never had before—direct access to ever-expanding new markets. A nonprofit can just as easily communicate with a government agency as with a potential corporate supporter or provide material to an interested individual as it can express the organization's viewpoint to a legislator. Up until now, information was distributed primarily through limited mailing lists, the media, or word-of-mouth. The Internet allows an organization to communicate directly with millions in a matter of minutes in its own words and format. This is especially true with the media—whether print, radio, or television—which is now turning to the Internet as a resource for reference and story material.

Collaboration and cooperation have never been easier between organizations, agencies, and individuals. From facilitating the forming of coalitions to the exchanging of information and publications, the Internet allows a cross fertilization of like minds and opposing view points. The Internet removes all previous communication barriers of time, location, and access by expanding an organization's reach from a universe of hundreds to a universe of millions—quickly, efficiently, and cost effectively.

The Flexibility of Cyberspace Communication

Communicating via e-mail helps an organization save time communicating messages in three ways: in the writing, in the delivery, and in responding.

Messages are composed quickly and effortlessly because of their brevity. The conventions of Internet communication encourage brevity and clarity over length. For example, an e-mail message can include just one or two words or one or two sentences to relay its directive completely and properly. A faxed memo, on the other hand, would require a full paragraph at the very least. Unquestionably, proper spelling and grammar are a must, but the expediency of e-mail frowns on verbosity or unnecessary cosmetic additions. Moreover, the reply and forward feature of e-mail eliminates the need to repeat text from a previous message. The original text is part of the reply package. And that reply or forwarded message can just as easily be sent to one person as to many people.

Cyberspace facilitates the quick and easy delivery of the message. And one can respond merely by clicking on the respond key and composing a timely response. Never has the immediacy of communication been so available and accessible. When expediency and brevity are needed to contact a potentially large audience, cyberspace is the perfect medium; the speed with which communication occurs encourages short and timely messages.

Because words lack the emotional signals of face-to-face interaction, a collection of symbols has been adopted for Internet communication to denote voice inflections and other emotional signs. These icons, officially called *emoticons* are also known informally as "smileys" because they are built around a sideways smiley face.

:-)   Happy smiley—the user is pretty happy.

:-D   Big smiley—the user is very happy.

;-)   Winking smiley—the user made a sarcastic remark.

:-(Unhappy smiley—the user is upset or depressed about something.

There are many dictionaries available on the Web (see Exhibit 4.1) that list hundreds of smileys. A selection of such dictionaries is provided in the Online References section in Appendix A.

Expediency also leads to access. One can communicate directly to those in the know—from the Webmaster (the person who manages a Web site) to the president of a corporation. There is no executive stationary or posh e-mail addresses in cyberspace; all users are first-string players.

Communication Tools

The Internet offers the nonprofit a wealth of outreach devices to contact and communicate with its audience. These devices include e-mail, mailing lists, and newsgroups. How these tools can be put to use is discussed later in this chapter in the section titled "Advocacy on the Internet." Finally, the security and integrity of the material communicated is of growing concern and needs to be addressed.

E-mail

E-mail is mail sent over a computer network such as the Internet (see Exhibit 4.2). If the user is not at his or her computer, mail is stored and can

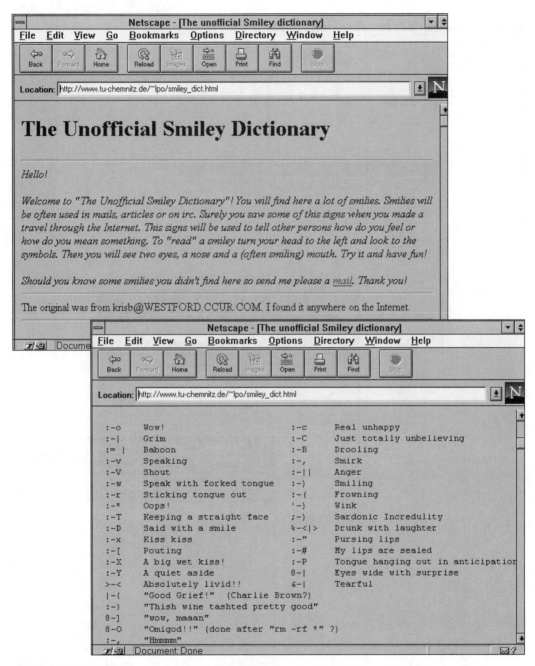

Exhibit 4.1 Emoticons from The Unofficial Smiley Dictionary. *Reprinted with permission.*

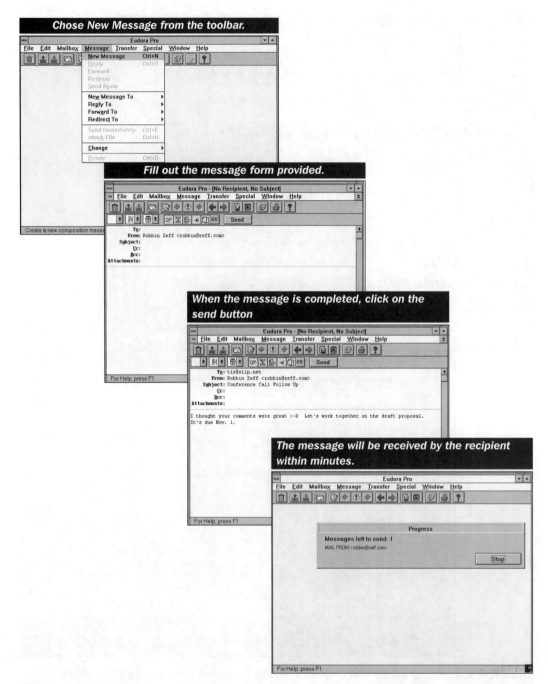

Exhibit 4.2 Sending e-mail message—Eudora Pro. *Eudora® is a registered trademark of the University of Illinois Board of Trustees, licensed to QUALCOMM Incorporated. Reprinted with permission.*

be read at any time. E-mail allows messages to be sent from one computer user to another, anywhere in the world, usually within minutes. In many ways, e-mail facilitates communication whether the receiver is in the same building or in a different city. "We're sort of a virtual organization" says Peter Ide, Treasurer of Future Generations. "With various people working out of different states and countries, the Internet is a cheaper and more versatile alternative to the telephone and fax."

When a user accesses e-mail through the computer, it is retrieved from the server to the user's machine. The server is the computer a user accesses to connect to a computer network such as the Internet. An individual may check his or her e-mail hourly or weekly, and never miss a message; it stays on the server to be accessed at any time. In this respect it is similar to the messaging service many telephone companies offer, but instead of using an answering machine, incoming messages are stored by the server to be retrieved by the user at his or her convenience.

It is difficult, if not impossible, to determine the exact number of e-mail addresses in existence worldwide because only domain names are registered. Any one domain can have multiple if not hundreds of associated e-mail addresses.

E-mail Database

Another valuable tool on the Internet is the capability for developing an e-mail database. There is no doubt that e-mail addresses will become as commonplace as phone and fax numbers, and in the very near future, e-mail databases will be as valuable to an organization in its outreach efforts as the mailing list is today.

This e-mail database can consist of addresses for both an internal and external audience. The internal audience of staff, members, volunteers, and supporters would benefit from the database because it would facilitate the fast and efficient dissemination of updates, newsletters, and correspondences. It is in the best interest of any organization to encourage its members and volunteers to get e-mail addresses.

To the external audience, encouraging both Web site visitors and information seekers to provide their e-mail addresses for future correspondence facilitates the building of a potential membership base. The use of an on-line form (Exhibit 4.3) will expedite the process by allowing easy, immediate, and interactive distribution of information. This is a very open and public way to develop an e-mail database. However, it is important to let all those

```
┌─────────────────────────────────────────────────────────────────┐
│ ─        Netscape - [Sign Our Guestbook]              ▼ ♦ │
├─────────────────────────────────────────────────────────────────┤
│ File  Edit  View  Go  Bookmarks  Options  Directory  Window  Help │
├─────────────────────────────────────────────────────────────────┤
│                                                               ♦   │
│  Please sign our Guestbook                                        │
│                                                                   │
│  We want to hear from you                                         │
│  ─────────────────────────────────────────────────────────       │
│                                                                   │
│  Name: (Last, First): [                              ]            │
│                                                                   │
│  Email: [                                            ]            │
│                                                                   │
│  Address: [                                          ]            │
│                                                                   │
│  City: [                        ] State: [   ] Zip: [     ]       │
│                                                                   │
│  How did you find us?: [Link From Another Site  ▼]               │
│                                                                   │
│  Comments:                                                        │
│  [                                                  ♦]            │
│                                                     ♦             │
├─────────────────────────────────────────────────────────────────┤
│ ⬛▦  Document: Done                                      ✉?       │
└─────────────────────────────────────────────────────────────────┘
```

Exhibit 4.3 On-line guestbook form—Netscape. *Reprinted with permission.*

who provide their e-mail addresses know the potential uses for that information; junk e-mail is currently frowned upon by the on-line community.

What are the two major benefits of an e-mail database? First, it allows the swift execution of message distribution to members and other interested persons. Second, it can be used to solicit funds, just as your organization's mailing list does today.

Mailing Lists

With over 30 million plus people actively using e-mail, one of the richest resources for information on the Internet are the users themselves. One way to directly tap this resource is through mailing lists. A *mailing list* (commonly referred to as a list or a discussion group) is a discussion carried on by a group of people through e-mail. The beauty of a mailing list is that you only have to send your message to the mailing list administrator for that message to be sent automatically to all members on the list. You receive mailing list messages just as you would any e-mail. It is your choice to either send a message, reply, or just observe.

The software that operates the mailing list is called a listserver. The three primary listservers are LISTSERV, LISTPROC and MAJORDOMO. LISTSERV is the most popular, and in fact, sometimes the brand name listserv is used synonymously with the term mailing list. LISTSERV was developed for BITNET (an academic computer network) and runs on a mainframe. LISTPROC and MAJORDOMO are UNIX based listserver software. You can tell which listserver software the list runs on by the address. To subscribe to a mailing list, one sends a message to the list administrator. Some of the popular mailing lists for the nonprofit community, especially in the area of fundraising, include:

❏ **Prspct-l**—a mailing list about prospect research and cultivation. To subscribe: send a message to *listserv@bucknell.edu.* In the message type *subscribe prspct-l* followed by your first and last name.

❏ **Fundlist**—a mailing list for fundraising professionals. To subscribe: send a message to *listproc@listproc.hcf.jhu.edu.* In the message type *subscribe fundlist* followed by your first and last name.

❏ **Fundsvcs**—a mailing list which discusses the more technical aspects of fundraising. To subscribe: send a message to *majordomo@acpub.duke.edu.* In the message type *subscribe fundsvcs* and nothing else.

❏ **Talk-amphilrev**—sponsored by the American Philanthropy Review, this mailing list addresses the broad spectrum of public sector issues. To subscribe: send a message to *majordomo@tab.com.* In the message type *subscribe talk-amphilrev* and nothing else.

❏ **Artngt-L**—the arts management discussion group. To subscribe: send a message to *listserv@bingvmb.bitnet.* In the message type subscribe *ARTMGT-L* and nothing else.

Mailing lists are wonderful resources because they allow contact and connection with people of similar interests. There are thousands of mailing lists on every topic from bike touring to folklore. The value of mailing lists in gathering information is as follows:

❏ Allows access to a group of potential experts.

❏ Allows timely answers to questions.

❐ Facilitates networking.

❐ Assists in developing a research strategy or finding related information.

Suppose you wanted to purchase new database software for your organization. You could pose the question: Which is the best nonprofit database software? Subscribers would respond with recommendations for different database software. These messages would provide you with the benefit of an organization's personal experience with a particular software.

Mailing lists are constantly active with hundreds of messages forwarded every day. All messages on a mailing are archived. This allows a user the opportunity to search mailing lists for messages about previously discussed topics. These message archives are accessed through the list-server and searched by *keyword* (the word or words that distinguish the topic).

To subscribe to a mailing list, you send a message to the listserver telling it the specific mailing list you want to join. (Exhibit 4.4). Similarly, to unsubscribe, you send a message informing the listserver that you no longer wish to be a member of the mailing list. When the listserver receives your request to subscribe or unsubscribe, a confirming e-mail is sent informing you of the action taken.

Because of the large number of mailing lists, the main challenge is to locate the one best for your interests. There are two key ways to find a mailing list: The first is to contact the listserver directly, and the second is to search the established mailing lists presented on the Web.

To get a complete roster of all associated mailing lists, you can contact the listserver directly. For example, you can send a message to the BITNET Network Information Center (BITNIC) and request their list. To do this, send an e-mail to **listserv@bitnic.bitnet** with the message list global. You will receive a directory of all mailing lists known to be part of LISTSERV. You can also target your search by modifying your message to be more specific to the topic you seek. In this case, the message would read list global/*topic of your search*. For example if you were searching for all mailing lists about fundraising you would send the message list global/ fundraising.

There are also Web sites that serve as searchable directories of mailing lists. The site **Tile.net/Lists (http://tile.net/listserv/)** has mailing lists alphabetically organized in five categories: description, name, subject, host country, and sponsoring organization. At this site, you can either survey the categories or search directly by keyword (see Exhibit 4.5).

Step 1. Send an e-mail to the list administrator in the appropriate format, stating your desire to subscribe to the list. In this case, the only required text are the words "subscribe" followed by the name of the list "ARTMGT-L."

Step 2. You receive a confirmation message from the list administrator.

Step 3. Sometimes you will be required to confirm your request.

Step 4. When you are put on the list, you will receive a welcome message explaining the purpose and protocol of the list.

Exhibit 4.4 Subscribing to a mailing list—Eudora Pro. *Eudora® is a registered trademark of the University of Illinois Board of Trustees, licensed to QUALCOMM Incorporated. Reprinted with permission.*

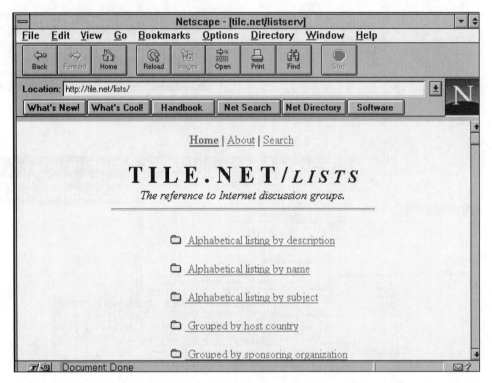

Exhibit 4.5 Searching for a mailing list—Netscape: tile.net/listserv. *Reprinted with permission.*

There are two types of mailing lists. The first is a read only service which allows only the list owner the option of posting messages; however, all subscribers will receive the message. This type is especially convenient for such things as newsletters or press releases. The second type is a discussion list. Any subscriber can post information to the list to be received by all other subscribers who may then respond. Oftentimes, there is a list moderator who ensures that all postings are relative to the purpose of the list and are not offensive to those involved.

Obviously, mailing lists have tremendous potential for nonprofits with membership. E-mail provides a quick and easy means to contact members. Additionally, the information need only be sent to one address for distribution to 100 or 10,000 people. Therefore, a large number of people, interested in the organization's activities, may be quickly and easily contacted, for minimal cost.

A primary convenience of mailing lists is the easy access to experts. Members of a certain list obviously have an interest in the particular topic.

Usually they are very well informed, educated, and willing to share their experience and ideas. The nature of e-mail allows for quick responses and easy communication.

The discussion list also provides unique opportunities for nonprofits. For example, it may be used to monitor interest in a topic. The list moderator can determine the level of response and concern exhibited by the users. Also, the organization can choose a topic that relates to a current effort such as the support of a specific legislation. The discussion list can be utilized to judge interest and concern over the issue. Most important, it keeps people involved. Be they members or random users, when individuals are subscribers to the list, they demonstrate interest in the topic and tend to stay involved in the discussion and promotion of an issue.

It is not uncommon to establish working relationships and friendships through these discussions. Many individuals begin to communicate privately on the side about a topic and other points of interest. It is a terrific way to find an expert source on a particular subject or to meet people with similar interests.

Bulletin Boards

A *bulletin board system* (also known as BBS) is a single computer or a network of computers that people dial into via modem. The difference between a bulletin board and the Internet is that with a bulletin board all users must dial into the same designated and stationary server. Some BBSs have a gateway to the Internet so that users can send e-mail via the Internet and connect to the World Wide Web, but most are free standing closed entities that are either available at no cost or for an hourly or monthly fee.

America Online and CompuServe are examples of large and elaborate bulletin boards, but many exist that are available only through one local number. You can find a listing of bulletin boards by using a Web search tool using the keyword "bulletin board" (see Chapter 5 for a full discussion on using search tools). In fact, many of today's Web sites started as bulletin boards. Another way to locate local bulletin boards is to look in local computer user magazines. For example the *Washington ComputerUser* newsletter offers a listing of local bulletin board systems in the metropolitan Washington, D.C., area that consists of three area codes (202, 703, and 301). The listing includes the name, phone number and baud rate of each BBS. The topics range from "Consumer Info Center" (202-208-7679) to Classifieds Online (703-404-0240) to "Computer Security" (301-948-5140).

Usenet Newsgroups

Usenet is an Internet application organized by topics called "newsgroups." Newsgroups, also known as discussion groups, are ongoing discussions where participants post messages called articles. A person can visit a newsgroup at any point and jump into the discussion by posting an article. A newsgroup is not live, but rather a board where messages are posted.

Newsgroups are an invaluable resource for quick answers to questions from a community of experts. A newsgroup is an interactive communication model that flows from idea to idea mirroring the dynamic nature of conversation. Newsgroups represent one of the oldest applications on the Internet. They are an open and dynamic channel for the exchange of ideas among people with similar interests. Initially newsgroups emerged on college campuses to facilitate the exchange of scholarship. Soon the concept was adopted by the Internet community in general and used as an informal vehicle to discuss everything from recipes to pet care.

To participate in a newsgroup, one needs a newsreader. Newsreaders are Internet software that assist in locating, viewing, and participating in newsgroups. Newsreaders usually come as part of a service provider software package but can also be purchased separately (see Exhibit 4.6).

In newsgroups, what is written is called an article and the article is posted on the newsgroup for all to read, similar to the protocol followed on bulletin boards. The posted message is usually written in the form of a newspaper article, although that standard is becoming less common.

The topic of the newsgroup is reflected in its naming. The name is done in a hierarchical system similar to e-mail and URL addresses. UseNet categories are shown in Exhibit 4.7.

There are innumerable newsgroups on most every subject. The primary newsgroup for nonprofits is **soc.org.nonprofit.** Newsgroup addresses move from general to specific. Soc.org.nonprofit is a soc (for social issues) newsgroup that discusses organizations specifically related to the nonprofit community.

To find a listing of newsgroups, you can use your newsreader or visit Usenet Newsgroup listing sites on the Web. Tile.net/News is a complete reference to **Usenet Newsgroups [http://tile.net/news/]** (Exhibit 4.8) that allows one to search an index of Usenet Newsgroups but is not a news server itself. One must use a newsreader to gain access to the newsgroups.

Furthermore, new subscribers have access to old postings. This is valuable to new subscribers because it provides the option of reviewing old

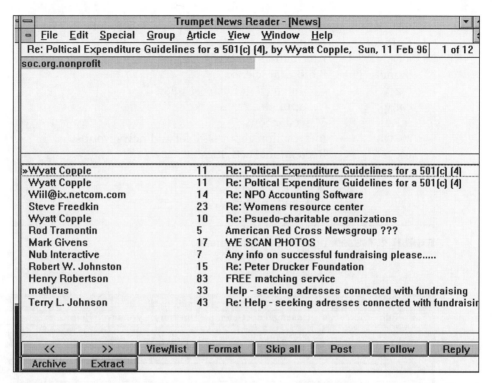

Exhibit 4.6 Usenet newsgroup—Trumpet News Reader: soc.org.nonprofit. *Reprinted with permission.*

messages for relevance and interest. However, the number of postings may be in the thousands and can become cumbersome and overwhelming. No one person, entity, company or organization controls the content of Usenet. Rather each newsgroup has a system administrator that oversees the content and netiquette (proper Internet etiquette).

FAQs

FAQ (pronounced "fack") is an acronym for frequently asked question, a standard list of questions and answers compiled by experts for use by the general on-line community. Initially designed to answer technical computer questions, FAQs are commonly used as a quick and efficient format for answering common questions. Perhaps a more appropriate definition would be "frequently answered questions." By providing answers to ques-

Category	Topic
alt	Alternative subjects
bionet	Biological sciences
biz	Commercial or business related
comp	Computers
misc	Miscellaneous
news	Information about UseNet and newsgroups
rec	Recreational activities
sci	Science
soc	Social issues
talk	Talk and conversation

Exhibit 4.7 Usenet newsgroup categories.

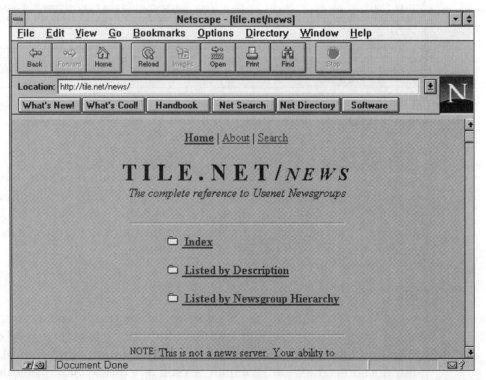

Exhibit 4.8 Searching for a newsgroup—Netscape: tile.net/news. *Reprinted with permission.*

tions before they are asked, the new user can navigate a site or learn about an organization effortlessly. In essence, experienced users have compiled lists of answers to commonly asked questions and that list is readily available on-line. The success and ease of use have made FAQs an on-line industry standard.

Web sites dedicated to technical issues often have a page devoted to FAQs. Newsgroups and discussion groups post FAQs and now many organizations with Web sites offer FAQs about their organization. It is a convenient way to explain the purpose of an organization in a manner that is standardized and readily available. For example, an organization can include its mission statement, a list of their programs, contacts, and contribution information. These points could be presented with headings such as: "Who we are," "What we do," "What we don't do," and "Our stand on *xyz* issue." (See Exhibit 4.9)

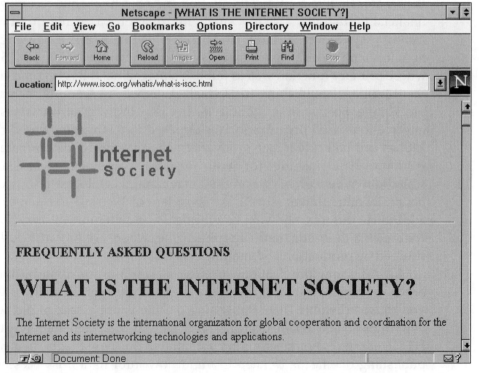

Exhibit 4.9 Frequently Asked Questions (FAQ)—Internet Society. *Reprinted with permission.*

Electronic Publishing

The Internet presents a dynamic venue for developing and disseminating information, from magazines and newsletters to press releases and reports. Electronic publishing allows a nonprofit to publish material without the often times inhibiting expense of printing and postage. "Unfortunately funds for production and mailing of a print piece are not so readily available as they once were, which sent me in search of alternative ways to keep the information flowing at less cost," says John Bancroft, Senior Editor at the Office of Arid Lands Studies at the University of Arizona. On-line distribution allows an interested party to download the publication as a file instead of receiving a hard copy via the U.S. postal service.

Just as broadcast faxing press releases to the media and action alerts to supporters was a time-saving devise for organizations, electronic publishing goes one step further in the immediacy and scope of distribution. The organization Art in the Public Interest (API) sees the Internet as a way for the organization to continue its mission and objective while recognizing its financial limitations. "We're a small, information-based nonprofit organization," says Steve Durland, Co-Director. "While API is a new organization, it is a philosophical extension of an organization we ran for 15 years, whose primary function was to publish a magazine. It has become obvious that traditional publishing for a small audience is becoming increasingly prohibitive. So this time around we decided to think of ourselves as an information-based organization (as opposed to a magazine-based organization) and take advantage of a variety of strategies to disseminate information. These include (or will include) pamphlets, workshops, a scaled-down version of our original magazine, a catalog of resources, and hopefully other things as well. We consider our Web site to be an excellent addition to this mix, allowing us a format to present more information than we are able to in our hard-copy magazine, where we are artificially constrained by production and mailing costs."

In designing publications principally for on-line distribution, one needs to change focus from paper to the computer screen as the presentation canvas (Exhibit 4.10). Publishing on-line is not a case of old wine in new bottles. Text taken from its hard copy format and merely put into HTML editing is not meeting the potential of this new media. In electronic publishing one needs to keep in mind how information is accessed, disseminated, and absorbed via the Internet. One surfs the Internet, moving quickly from site to site. Material is presented in layers: The first layer is the

Exhibit 4.10 Electronic publishing—*High Performance*: Art in the Public Interest. *Reprinted with permission.*

idea, the second layer is the concept developed, and the third layer is the entire text. In short, people tend to skim on the Web and download full text for later reading. The hyperlink feature allows one to choose how in-depth to venture on any subject.

INTERNET COMMUNICATION IN ACTION

Membership Recruitment

The Internet is a tremendous outreach vehicle for your organization to present its mission, programs and services to interested persons, potential members, and contributors. When someone surfing the Internet visits your page, they have come to you for information. This is the perfect opportunity to get that person more involved in your organization, either by having him or her participate in your e-mail database, become a member, or take some other step that will provide you with the means to contact that person at a later date. There is no better potential recruit than a satisfied customer. Because of the interactive nature of the Web, you can make it easy for the person to sign up for membership with an interactive membership form that can be filled out and immediately submitted merely by pressing the send button (See Exhibit 4.11).

Another method for Internet membership recruitment is to use the age-old organizing strategy of "have a member, get a member." On your Web site you request members or interested persons to give the e-mail addresses of 3 to 5 potentially interested people they know that the organization can then contact using the members' names as references. Since credibility is transferable, this allows an organization to open the door to potential members from the credibility awarded through friendship.

```
┌─────────────────────────────────────────────────────────────────────┐
│  ─            Netscape - [http://www.ihs1830.org/membershipns.html]   ▼ ◆│
│ File   Edit   View   Go   Bookmarks   Options   Directory   Window   Help │
│  ⇦○     ⤴     ⌂       ⊛       ▦        ⇨○     ⊟      ⌗⌗      ◉         │
│  Back  Forward Home    Reload  Images    Open    Print   Find     Stop    │
│ Location: http://www.ihs1830.org/membershipns.html                   ± │ N │
│                                                                          ▲ │
│ Membership Application: To join the Indiana Historical Society using      │
│                                                                           │
│                              ┌──────────┐                                 │
│                              │Dr.     ▲ │                                 │
│                              │Mr.       │                                 │
│                              │Mrs.      │                                 │
│                      Title:  │Ms.     ▼ │                                 │
│                              └──────────┘                                 │
│                                                                           │
│             Name: ┌──────────────────────────────────┐                    │
│          Address: ┌──────────────────────────────────────────────┐        │
│             City: ┌──────────────────────────────┐                        │
│   State/Province: ┌──────────────────────────────┐                        │
│  Zip/Postal Code: ┌──────────────────────────────┐                        │
│          Country: ┌──────────────────────────────┐                        │
│                   │VISA          ▲│                                        │
│      Credit Card: │MASTERCARD    ▼│                                      ▼ │
│ ☞/☜  Document: Done                                              ✉?       │
└─────────────────────────────────────────────────────────────────────┘
```

Exhibit 4.11 On-line membership form—Indiana Historical Society. *Reprinted with permission.*

More than anything else, the Internet is an aid in building and maintaining relationships.

Job Announcements

In addition to membership recruitment, the Internet can be used to advertise for job openings (Exhibit 4.12). This is an inexpensive method for advertising the available position. Given the expansive and diverse cyberspace community, your advertisement for potential candidates will have a wider reach than traditional advertising means. Moreover, because the job announcement is on the Web site, the interested person will have the opportunity to get a firm grounding of your organization's mission and programs, and will therefore weed out those who may not agree with your position on key issues. With the growth of Web resumes, you can even request interested persons to submit their resumes over the Web, as well as through the mail or by fax.

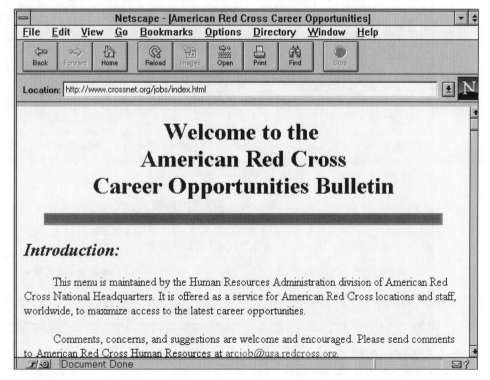

Exhibit 4.12 On-line job listings—American Red Cross. *Reprinted with permission.*

Volunteer Recruitment

The Internet is turning into fertile ground for volunteer recruitment and utilization. "It allows volunteers to work for a nonprofit without being there," says Steve Gibson, Executive Director of The Bionomics Institute. "It also builds a sense of community." In fact, the organization **Impact Online** [**http://www.impactol.org/iol/volunteer/virtual.html**], calls the on-line angels who assist in everything from typing to Web design "virtual volunteers" (Exhibit 4.13) and assists nonprofits in finding these angels.

Organizations are also placing calls for volunteer assistance right on their Web sites. On the American Red Cross Web site, each chapter is given a page. A user can locate the chapter in their area by using a zip code or clickable map search engine. Each chapter was given a page with a generic layout design that included basic information about the chapter (address,

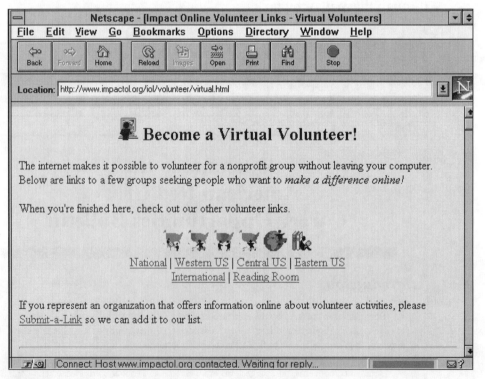

Exhibit 4.13 On-line volunteer recruiting—Impact Online Virtual Volunteers. *Reprinted with permission.*

Exhibit 4.14 On-line volunteer recruiting—Local chapters of American Red Cross. *Reprinted with permission.*

contact information, etc.). At the bottom of each chapter page, is a request for volunteer assistance in designing the Web page (Exhibit 4.14). The chapter pages are now in various stages of development. However, the American Red Cross has received over 250 volunteer responses that have resulted in wonderful chapter pages. The page for the Atlanta Chapter was the first, with the one for the Columbus Chapter following shortly thereafter (Exhibit 4.15).

In these times of diminishing resources, volunteers are playing larger roles in helping nonprofits to fulfill their missions and much of this takes place on the local level. Susan Ellis of ENERGIZE, Inc., feels strongly that volunteerism is an activity that takes place in one's own community. "I personally feel that for my field (volunteer program managers), the most important thing is to hook into local community freenets. International access and outreach may be fun, but volunteer action takes place locally."

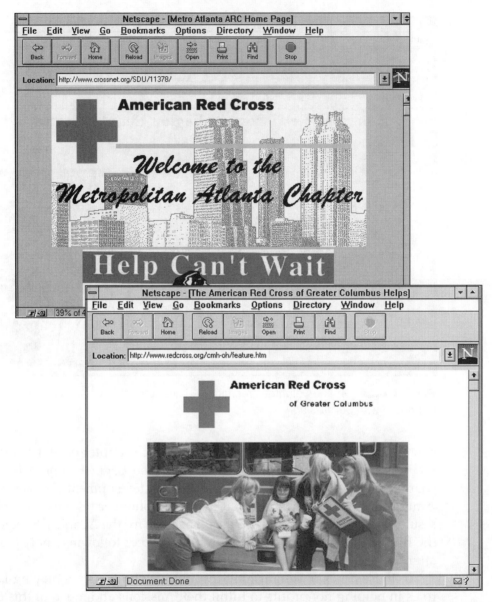

Exhibit 4.15 Volunteer designed Web pages—American Red Cross, Atlanta and Columbus chapters. *Reprinted with permission.*

ADVOCACY OVER THE INTERNET

The Internet offers an organization the ability to inform members and interested people on how to take action. For example, Congress might be reviewing legislation that an organization strongly opposes. By using the Internet, an organization could inform members through an action alert on its home page and through e-mail messages. The nonprofit could request that interested persons send e-mail messages stating their objections to their members of congress. Many members of congress have e-mail addresses, and those who do not have addresses will acquire them in the near future. E-mail responses represent an extremely expedient method for voicing citizen concern. "Cyberactivism" could have a tremendous affect on policy making by offering citizens a means to immediately voice their response to the activities of elected officials.

James Love, Director of the Taxpayer Assets Project and the Consumer Project on Technology, started using the Internet in 1991 as an organizing and advocacy tool to press for broader access to government information. His first successful organizing effort for on-line access to information on the Internet involved making Electronic Data Gathering Analysis and Retrieval (EDGAR)—a large database of corporate information—available to the public. Love next tackled a legislative proposal to put government printing office material on-line, which became law two years later. Love soon discovered that others were involved in similar efforts. Jim Warren in California launched a highly successful campaign to require that the state legislature put material on the Internet. The Internet was also being used for organizing around other types of issues. For example, Love remembers that one of his contemporaries, Ned Daily, was using the Internet to discuss old growth forests. These actions taken on the Internet were part of organizing strategies that included the traditional forms of activism: attending meetings, sending letters, making phone calls, and so on. It was the combination that proved most effective.

Love sees this form of advocacy as adding an entirely new dimension to organizing efforts. "By having access to the Internet, I was able to engage a much broader audience than I could have otherwise. Those who had a stake in it weren't professionals." Love goes on to point out the refreshing idealism people on the Internet bring to organizing around public policy issues. "People on the Internet tend to have a more idealistic view. They start out by finding what is the best public policy and then try to figure out how to make it happen. In Washington, it's the other way around. They are bringing some fresh air into public policy because they start out with an idealistic view and then start asking questions."

There are instances where advocacy on the Internet can play the lead role in defining the outcome of an issue. One such celebrated 1995 example involved a provision in a bill to re-authorize the Paperwork Reduction Act of 1980. In a new subsection of the bill, a provision was added that would abolish public access to information under the Freedom of Information Act when that information was produced by a private contractor. On inspection, it was discovered that the provision was requested by West Publishing, a leader in the publishing of federal and state court decisions, which would have directly benefited from the amendment.

A campaign against this provision was launched on the Internet on Monday, February 6, 1995. At this point, there was every indication that by Wednesday the provision would pass without opposition. But shortly after announcements about the provision were posted on the Internet, Congress began receiving telephone calls, e-mail messages, and faxes from angry constituents, citizens, and business and professional groups opposing the amendment. In just 72 hours, an advocacy campaign on the Internet resulted in the elimination of the amendment.

Internet advocacy is being conducted on a worldwide basis as well. Environmental Law Alliance Worldwide (E-LAW) is an international network of public interest environmental attorneys, scientists, and individuals. When Peru was building its constitution, Peruvian lawyers put out a call for environmental legislative strategies. The E-LAW network responded, and as a result Peru has very strong environmental legislation written into its constitution.

According to Love, advocacy on the Internet is extremely inclusive because it is hard to exclude people from Internet discussion groups. Much of what occurs on the Internet involves a mass audience, and in the realm of advocacy, bringing key players together can be most effective. For example, the discussion group (see Exhibit 4.16) that was posted by the **Consumer Project on Technology [http://www.essential.org/listproc/med-privacy/]** in September 1995 regarding the issue of medical records privacy fostered more than 95 postings in one month . The discussion group allowed for the thrashing out of complex issues and problems, something that would have never occurred if the only medium for exchange had been the formal meeting setting. Those who participated in the discussion group turned out to be the people who drafted both the house and senate bills on this topic as well as the principal critics. The debate was incredibly infor-

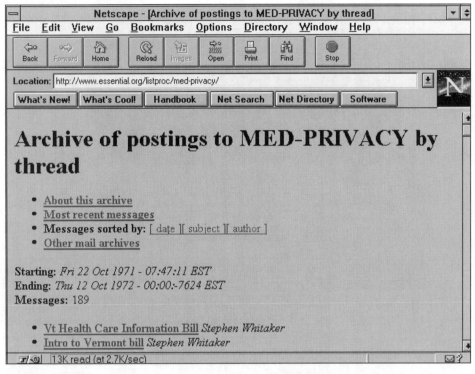

Exhibit 4.16 Newsgroup discussion archives—MED-PRIVACY. *Reprinted with permission.*

mative, especially since the exchange occurred among the key players. In fact, the print media began covering the issue based on what was happening on the Internet.

In 1995 legislation was proposed to prohibit nonprofits that spend 5 percent of their budget on advocacy work from receiving federal grants. Opposition to this bill was organized on the Internet by **Independent Sector [http://www.indepsec.org/is]** and OMB Watch and called the "Silence America" campaign. They ran mailing lists and conference areas where over a thousand individuals and groups participated. Information included updates and calls to action. As a result of these advocacy efforts, Independent Sector and OMB Watch are in the process of developing a Web site called "Let America Speak."

Generating e-mail messages and faxes is one advocacy strategy on the Internet. The **Children's Defense Fund** uses a form [**http://www.tmn.com/cdf/emailpres.html**] (Exhibit 4.17) to get concerned citizens to write to the president requesting a halt to welfare or medical reforms that would have

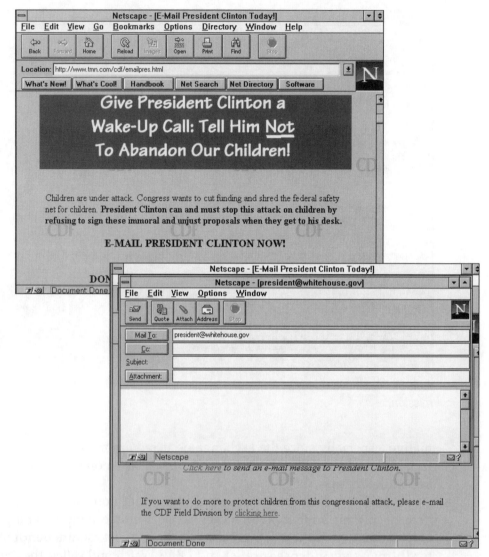

Exhibit 4.17 E-mail campaign—Children Defense Fund. *Reprinted with permission.*

a detrimental effect on funding for children's programs. Implementing discussion groups, as demonstrated with the medical privacy issue, is another organizing strategy. Other strategies include galvanizing support with such techniques as a petition or registry. **The Separation of School & State Alliance** has a **Registry of Support** on its site that lists supporters and encourages others to participate [**http://www.sepschool.org/**] (Exhibit 4.18), making this an Internet petition with unlimited reach and length.

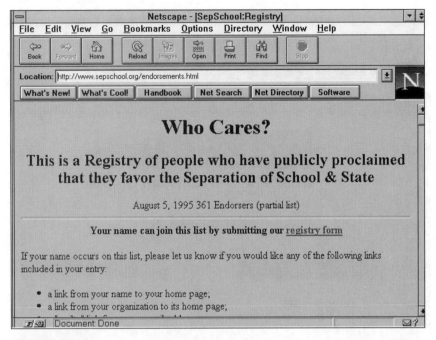

Exhibit 4.18 On-line petition—The Separation of School & State Alliance. *Reprinted with permission.*

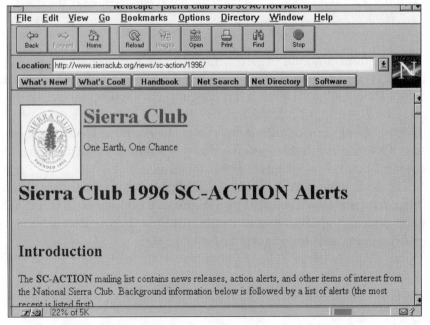

Exhibit 4.19 On-line action alerts—Sierra Club. *Reprinted with permission.*

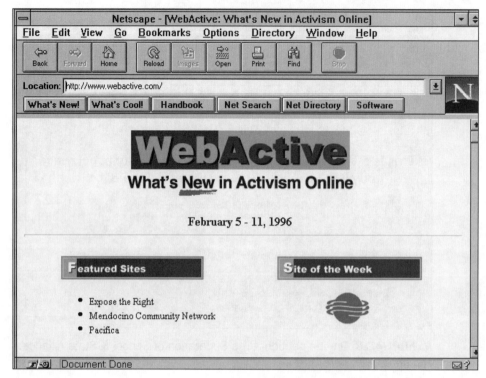

Exhibit 4.20 On-line activism by nonprofit organizations—WebActive. *Reprinted with permission.*

The environmental organization Sierra Club uses its Web site to post hot issues and suggest action steps for members and other concerned citizens. Their SC ACTION Alert page **[http://www.sierraclub.org/news/ sc-action/1996/]** and related links is the most popular feature of their site (Exhibit 4.19), as quantified by their site counter. One can join the SC ACTION mailing list to receive daily updates or visit the page to keep abreast of cutting edge environmental issues.

There is even a Web site that highlights on-line activism. **WebActive [http://www.webactive.com]** by Progressive Networks (Exhibit 4.20) provides a wealth of ideas and examples for how the Internet is being used as an organizing tool for a myriad of social issues.

CHAPTER 5

Research Tools and Tricks on the Information Superhighway

INFORMATION AS A TOOL

Gathering information on the Internet allows an organization to keep its finger on the pulse of America and the world through a few strokes on a keyboard. By monitoring on-line activity the nonprofit can determine what issues are strongly affecting either the global community or the people next door. On-line information is usually updated daily, sometime hourly, providing the immediacy required for rapid response to the pressing social concerns tackled by the nonprofit community.

CONDUCTING RESEARCH ON THE INTERNET

The Internet is an incredible resource that makes information easily and quickly accessible. Yet there is no defined organization or structure to that information. There is no definitive card catalog or index of lists to the Web, no all encompassing phone book, and no directory to serve as a road map to all available sites, even though the Web is constantly growing, changing, and evolving. There are, however, tools and applications that compensate for the lack of internal linear order in the Internet.

The Internet breaks the linear barrier of print media where information is presented in preordained packages. Research on the Internet allows one to be creative and adventurous by gliding from one piece of information to another in a free form and fluid motion. Researching in cyberspace is, in effect, wandering the stacks of the *Information Superhighway* where process leads to product. It is research where meandering and serendipity is an accepted and encouraged course of action. In conducting research on the Internet you need to develop a veritable "Internet mindset" that embraces multidimensional information exploration. The primary defining feature of the Web is its links between pages, and the concept of linked information is the defining feature of the Internet mindset.

Because no one *owns* the Internet, no one individual or group travels the Net to ensure that standards are met and information is neatly organized. A user must approach the Internet with an open mind and a patient and willing attitude. If a user cannot locate information one way, numerous other options and sources are available. The only way to learn how to conduct research on the Internet is to conduct a search that allows travel from link to link. In short, one learns by surfing the Net.

It is important to understand and recognize the Internet's limitations. Material more current than historic is available and this will undoubtedly continue to be the case. Right now, what is on the Internet is self-selected, unregulated, and unchecked.

The Internet is a tool, one of many to be used to find information. Not all information is accessible or will be accessible on the Internet. The Internet is not a singular all-encompassing research Mecca. It cannot replace all other research methods; rather, its best use is as part of an overall research strategy.

There is an old saying, "If you give a man a fish, he eats for a day. If you teach him how to fish, he eats forever." Because of the dynamic nature of the Internet, knowing how to access and exchange information opens the door for maximizing its potential. Knowing where sites are located is helpful, but sites and e-mail addresses change. In cyberspace, the saying becomes, "If you give a person a Web address, he or she will have access to that site. If you teach a person how to navigate the Internet, he or she will have access to all sites on the Information Superhighway." Understanding how to research on the Web in its relative infancy will enable an organization to best respond to the continual growth and changes that are destined to take place over time.

As discussed in the preface, a great deal of the research for this guide was gathered by surfing the Net and communicating with people via e-mail and mailing lists. All of the people contacted were extremely helpful, generous and forthcoming with information. Without a doubt, much can be gleaned from this new medium. It is a new and exciting way of doing business and research.

RESEARCH TOOLS AND TRICKS

There are many tools and tricks of the trade that assist in the Internet search process. The following section will examine them and offer suggestions on how best to maximize their effectiveness in the research process.

Two excellent books that provide step-by-step instructions on search strategies on the Internet are Paul Gilster's *Finding It On The Internet: The Essential Guide to Archie, Veronica, Gopher, WAIS, WWW (Including Mosaic), and Other Search and Browsing Tools* (John Wiley & Sons, 1994) and *Net.Search* by William Eager et al (QUE, 1995).

Search Tools

Some of the very first applications on the Internet helped to locate, organize, and present the vast amount of available information. Gopher was designed to make the information available over computer networks more accessible by providing a text menu of resource holdings. Long before browsers were developed, a user could connect to other computers via the Internet and find information by looking at a Gopher menu. To assist in searching the information listed on Gopher menus, a software application called *Veronica* was developed that searched Gopher menus using keywords. Veronica helped to locate what material was available at which location. Another application developed around the same time was *Archie*. Archie searched for files that were available for downloading by FTP. Both Archie and Veronica were developed before the Web's existence.

The Internet has a variety of means to search for Web sites available to the user. Most are free, although commercial versions are also available for more detailed searches. On the Web, a search tool is a general term used to denote a site or an application that helps to shuffle through the myriad of information accessible through the Web. A *search engine* is the software that actually conducts the search. There are Web sites that consist solely of a key-word search engine that assists in the locating of sites. Such sites include **Lycos [http://www.lycos.com]** and **WebCrawler [http://www.Webcrawler. com]**. Other sites are indices of sites that have a search engine feature to assist in locating a site listed in the index. The premiere example is the ever popular **Yahoo [http://www.yahoo.com]**. Yahoo is simply an extremely comprehensive index of sites. In 1995, Yahoo reported more than 9 million visitors (also known as *hits*) in one week, which translates into over 1 million separate visitors to the site. Many users of Yahoo are repeat customers.

Lycos and WebCrawler are two sophisticated search engines that generate broad lists of hits. EINet Galaxy searches through Internet resources using WAIS technology. In addition, SavvySearch is a "meta-search engine" that searches through search engines. All are highly efficient, easy to use, and convenient. (See Exhibit 5.1.)

In time, individual users will find the search tool or tools that most appeal to them. The search tool's URL will earn a place high on the user's *bookmark* and will probably become the most frequently visited site. These tools are the first step to a successful search for information on the World Wide Web.

For the most part, these tools are restricted to subject searches using a word or group of words relative to the topic. Many of them use the "if, then" style Boolean search method. The word or group of words is entered into a keyword field and the search engine then searches for uses of the word in site descriptions. Results appear showing the number of hits, or sites found, that make reference to the search word(s), usually with a description of the site. The name of the site most often appears in hypertext so that the user can easily link directly to the site. Keywords provide an easy and quick means of searching vast databases. Word matches are found and the file is displayed for the user—similar to a subject search in a library's card catalog. There are many options available for performing keyword searches: identical matches, case matches, whole word matches, and Boolean style.

Conveniently, if the site does not provide the information for which one is looking, a simple click on the browser's *back* button will return the user to the search results page for another try. Even if information of value is found at that site, you can still use the *back* feature to systematically examine all sites found from the keyword search.

Each search tool builds its searchable universe a little differently, and to ensure that you have conducted as comprehensive a search as possible on

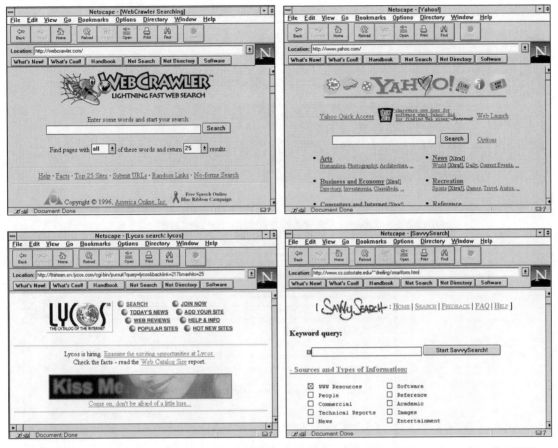

Exhibit 5.1 Popular search tools on the Web. *Reprinted with permission. Copyright © 1996 Lycos, Inc. All Rights Reserved. The Lycos™ "Catalog of the Internet". Copyright © 1994, 1995, 1996 Carnegie Mellon University. All Rights Reserved. Used by permission.*

the Internet, conduct a search on several search tools, such as Yahoo, Lycos, and WebCrawler. In fact, Yahoo provides links to other search engines at the bottom of the page.

Moreover, many larger sites contain a search tool that operates within the site (Exhibit 5.2). These are especially helpful with sites containing archived information. Again a keyword or words are typed in a field and the tool begins the search. The difference is that the search is limited only to the information available at that site instead of searching the entire Web. Remember, a site differs from a page, so even if the information does not

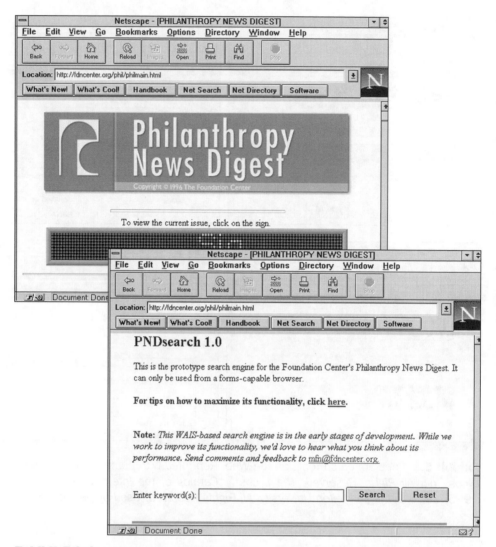

Exhibit 5.2 Search engine within a Website—*Philanthropy News Digest:* The Foundation Center. *Reprinted with permission.*

appear immediately on the home page, it may be located elsewhere within the site.

After the user enters a keyword, the search engine then searches indexes for hits that include the keyword or words. For example, you can search for foundations information using the keyword, "foundations"

(Exhibit 5.3). The search engine will then display hits that include the word foundations. This may include Web sites of foundations, articles posted on the Internet discussing foundations, and FTP sites offering downloadable files on the subject, as well as sites dedicated to information about all foundation grants and organizations with the word foundation in the title.

Often, search engines are used to find a specific Web site that is of particular interest to the user. For example, upon learning that the Foundation Center has a Web site, the new user may use a search engine to locate that specific site **[http://fdn.org]**. When hits are displayed, the site names are in blue, underlined text, which provides a clickable link directly to that site.

Creative Thinking

There is an element of alternative, creative thinking involved in Internet research. After the general search has been performed using one of the search tools, it becomes the province of the user to logically and structurally order the search strategy. Sometimes the first site visited provides the sought after information; other times, innumerable sites need to be examined before the exact item sought is found. For example, an individual wishes to find a picture of Rambo. The search tool is unable to locate any hits using the word "Rambo." Logically, the next search would use the word "Stallone." A few hits may arise, although none may be related to the portrayal of Rambo. A truly creative approach would be to take the search to a new and nonlinear level—a picture of Rambo may be found at the Hollywood Wax Museum site **[http://www.ernestallen.com/TR/CA/ HollywoodWaxMuseum/]** not at a movie or a studio site. It is certainly not the first locale to come to the mind of the searcher, but nevertheless quite effective in achieving the desired result. This type of creative and expansive thinking may be incongruous with other more traditional research methods, but is most beneficial to anyone using the Web. "It has helped us to think of new ways to categorize information," says John Longhurst, Media and Public Relations Director of the Mennonite Central Committee. "We are accustomed to using traditional categories when organizing information. But each browser can bring a unique way of categorizing information when he/she comes to the site. One person found us by looking for information on woodworking. Never in a thousand years would we think of categorizing information by that topic!"

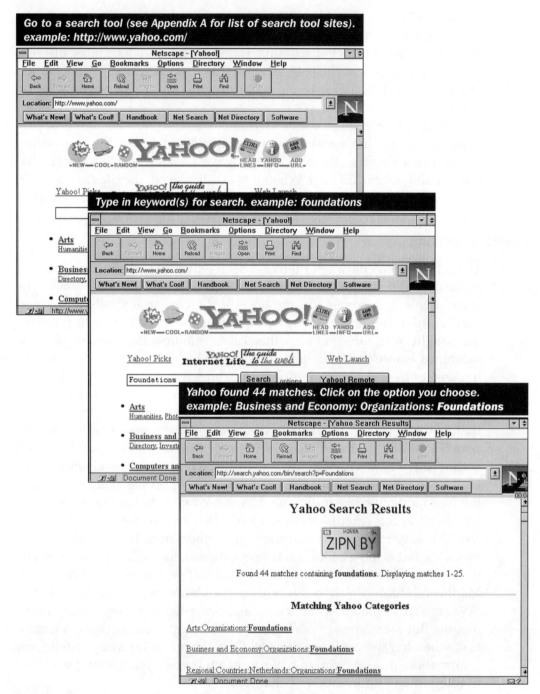

Exhibit 5.3 Conducting a search on the Internet—Yahoo. *Reprinted with permission.*

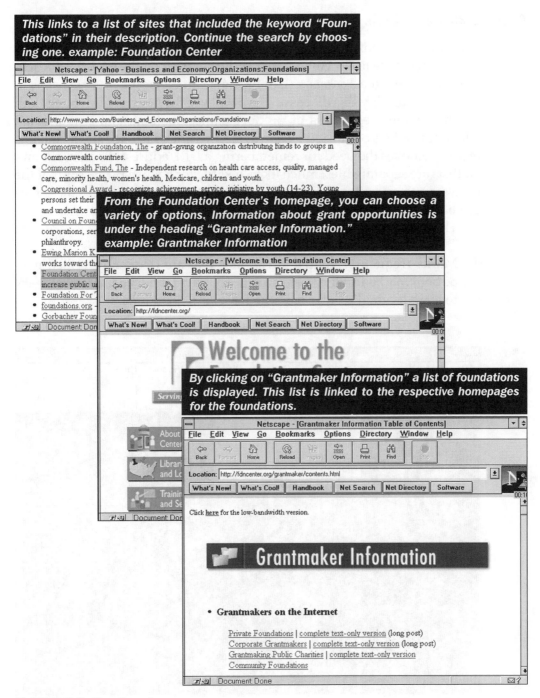

Exhibit 5.3 *(Continued)*

Bookmarks and Hotlists

One feature found on all browsers is its ability to create and maintain a readily accessible list of Web addresses. Depending on the browser, the feature can be called a *Bookmark* (Exhibit 5.4) as in Netscape or a *Hotlist* as in Mosaic. To simplify this discussion, we will use the general term bookmark for this feature, regardless of product name. Bookmarks are automated URL address lists organized by site name and linked to each site listed; this feature removes the need for remembering a URL address. Bookmarks and Hotlists are separate files, much like a text file for a word processor that the browser opens to retrieve information. Therefore, the capacity of these files can be quite extensive.

The value of bookmarks is fourfold:

1. **Marks frequently visited sites.** Sites that are frequently visited may be bookmarked so the user can quickly travel there again. A bookmark to an individual's preferred search tool is a good idea.

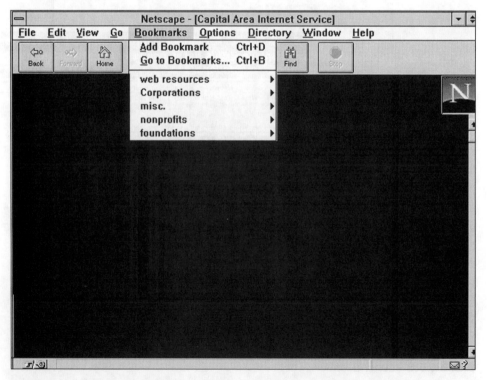

Exhibit 5.4 Netscape Bookmark. *Reprinted with permission.*

2. **Easy return to site.** When performing a search, the search results page can be captured and saved for later use, or one can bookmark interesting sites of value as one travels along. Although a site can always be revisited by using the *back* button, bookmarking allows the user to come back to the site at a much later time, even after having closed the browser. You can return to the search as often as desired without having to wait for the search to be redone. It is similar to having a card catalog for an entire subject from a library *and* the actual information source. Browsers present links in a different color and underlined text; once a link has been visited, the text changes color. Saving a search where visited sites are already identified makes one a more efficient researcher. Plus, as the search progresses, many interesting sites may be discovered that are not directly related to the search, but worth viewing at a later time.

3. **Easy transfer of lists.** Most bookmark files are easily transferable. They can be copied to disk and transferred from one computer to another. A bookmark file can be taken from your home computer and input on your office machine, or passed along to a colleague with similar interests.

4. **Customized list of related sites.** Bookmarks allow you to create a customized and personal list of Web sites. Within the large and ever-expanding world of the Web, bookmarks allow you to travel freely and easily, and only where you want to go.

Keeping the Links

The browser may be set to ensure that the color change of a traveled link does not expire. In other words, once you travel to a link, it stays the altered color of a traveled link. The Web-like structure of the Internet allows the accessibility of a site via links from many different points. As the search continues, the user may happen upon a link to a single site numerous times on many different pages. Ensuring that the links don't expire keeps users from traveling to a site they have already visited. Or, one can modify the length of time a link is altered once visited, such as a day, week or month.

E-mailing the Site

Most sites provide the e-mail address for the site Webmaster. It is becoming more common for an organization to place staff e-mail addresses and biographies on-line as well. E-mailing a site relevant to a search can often reap large rewards. Who better to know the content and complexities of an issue than those whose work revolves around it? E-mailing the site is usually invited by the operators and organizations, whose benefit is as great as the visitor's.

Retrieving the Site's Text

Text that is not downloadable from a site may be retrieved in other ways. As was previously mentioned, the site's content may also be printed. Using the "Save As" option will save the entire page into a directory of the user's choosing. However, this will include all the HTML coding as well.

As always, the "Copy Text" option works to copy the selected text to the clipboard. It then may be transferred to a word processor for viewing and manipulation. This may be done easily by highlighting the text to be selected and choosing the "Copy" option from the browser's menu.

Printing Information

Undoubtedly, one will want to capture information accessed on-line as either a text file or a hard copy. Printing site pages is also helpful, especially an index of publications or materials in an archive. A hard copy eliminates the need to constantly travel back to the site. It also allows the user to view the different places to which he or she has previously traveled. Primarily, printing allows site content to be made readily available to the user via a hard copy—similar to photocopying pages from texts. This can be very helpful in extensive research efforts. Newer browsers include the site URL, time, and date, automatically as a header when printing. This makes it easy to either reference or return to the site.

RESOURCES ON THE INTERNET

The Internet is a vast and powerful resource of still unknown potential and influence. Its magnificent size and ungoverned nature make it difficult to categorize and index. In fact, there is no complete directory of sites, no definitive index of lists because every day new Web sites emerge and established sites change their addresses or alter their focus or format.

Resources of interest to the nonprofit come in a variety of types and formats on the Internet. Nonprofits are now putting up their own home pages as public awareness and fundraising vehicles. In terms of fundraising, an organization can find a wealth of information on the Web—from foundation grants to federal and private funding sources to funding resource centers. In addition, many corporations have Web sites with a wealth of information about their philanthropic and marketing interests. Finally, one can use the Internet as a reference library to look up magazine articles, government documents, and specific research material. What makes on-line resources so valuable is the immediacy of acquisition and the contemporaneous nature of the material, often not available through other means.

This section provides an overview of on-line resources for nonprofits; it is by no means exhaustive, but is meant to provide a general overview of sites of interest to nonprofits. The resource list in Appendix A provides an annotated listing of selected sites of interest and value to nonprofits. Because of the dynamic nature of the Internet, new sites are appearing daily and therefore, Appendix A lists the sites available and accessible at the time this book went to press.

Because the Internet can be accessed in the privacy of one's own home, people are able to seek out information on topics they may be too shy, embarrassed, or timid to request in a more public and exposed format. From prostate to breast cancer, from cocaine to heroin addiction, the Internet provides a private and secure vehicle to find out about socially and/or personally sensitive subjects.

Resources and Services for Nonprofits

The Internet includes many sites for resources and services geared specifically to nonprofits.

❑ *Directories of nonprofits services.* These range from a directory consisting of links to nonprofit organizations and resources, such as the Nonprofit Resources Catalogue **[http://www.clark.net/pub/pwalker/]** to a very comprehensive downloadable guide, such as the Guide to Internet Resources for Nonprofit Public Service Organizations **[http://asa.ugl. lib.umich.edu/chdocs/nonprofits/nonprofits.html]**.

❑ *Directories of nonprofit Web sites.* Some sites are directories of nonprofit Web sites with links to those sites. These directories can be regional in scope, such as the River Project **[http://www.mtn.org/]** sponsored by the Minneapolis Telecommunications Network to more general nonprofit site listing, as found in the Teleport Directory of Nonprofits **[http//www.teleport.com/]**.

❏ *Technical assistance providers.* Many organizations that service nonprofit organizations provide their material via the Internet. There are some whose focus is on Internet assistance, such as Impact On-line **[http://www.impactol/iol]**, which provides Internet training, Web design, and virtual volunteer assistance. Others provide assistance for issues and concerns specific to the nonprofit community, such as the National Center for Nonprofit Boards **[gopher://ncnb.org:7002/]**, which offers access to their publications on board development issues through a gopher menu. The Council for Public Media **[http://www. utexas.edu/depts/output/www/cpm.html]** has a Web site that presents their mission as a resource, clearinghouse, and media training center for the nonprofit community.

❏ *Nonprofit periodicals.* Some of the key nonprofit publications are on-line, such as the *Nonprofit Times* **[http://haven.ios.com/~nptimes/ index.html]**. New publications have emerged that only exist on-line, such as the Foundation Center's *Philanthropy News Digest* **[http://www. fdncenter.org/phil/philmain.html]**.

❏ *Volunteer centers.* The Web is quickly becoming a focal point for volunteer activities with sites popping up that advertise volunteer positions locally, nationally and internationally. For example, a person in the San Francisco Bay Area of California for can find out about volunteer opportunities by looking at the Web site **Bay Area Volunteer Information Center [http://meer.net/users/taylor/]**. The site allows the user to examine a searchable database of volunteer opportunities with links to corresponding agencies seeking assistance. There are other sites that are broader in scope and that provide listings from regional, national and international volunteer centers such as the site **Volunteer Centers and Listings On-line [http://www.dnai.com/~children/volunteer.html]**.

Fundraising

A great many fundraising resources—from foundation and corporate grant-making activities to sample grant applications and sources of fundraising—can be accessed on the Internet.

❏ *Foundations.* Public, private and community foundations have Web sites where nonprofits can obtain grant guidelines, review recent grant recipients, and obtain staff and board member listings.

❏ *Fundraising resources.* From sample grant applications to brief articles on the giving activities of foundations, from prospect research databases to fundraising activity merchandise, there is a wealth of fundraising resources available on the Web.

❏ *Government funding programs.* Many federal funding agencies post information on-line about their grant programs and procedures: from the **Catalog of Federal Domestic Assistance [gopher://solar.rtd.utk. edu:70/11/Federal/CFDA]** to grants offered by government programs such as the **National Science Foundation [http://www.nsf.gov:80/ nsf/homepage.grants.htm]**.

❏ *Corporate philanthropic information.* Most Fortune 500 companies have sites on the Web that, in addition to providing a general overview of the company, its products, and services includes biographical information on top management and board members, recent press releases, new products, and charitable giving programs. *Fortune* magazine has a searchable directory of the Fortune 500 companies [**http://pathfinder. com/@@*IrbeyHPEgAAQPZc/fortune/magazine/specials/fortune500/ fortune500.html**] and one can find an alphabetical listing of links to the Fortune 500 at **Fortune 500 Industry and Service [http://ww.cs.utexas. edu/users/paris/corporate.real.html]**.

Government and Related Sites

Federal, state and local governments also provide information, documents and publications on-line. This allows nonprofit organizations to keep abreast of legislation, issues and events, as well as to gather reports and other publications. Moreover, this makes the organization located outside a metropolitan area as up-to-date and efficient as the organization housed next to city hall.

❏ *Federal government documents and legislation.* For example the **Library of Congress** has a site [**http://www.loc.gov/**]. For one interested in federal legislation, **Thomas-Legislative Information on the Internet [http://thomas.loc.gov/]** includes full texts of legislation, bill summaries, the Congressional Record, and more, cataloged by bill number, title, sponsor, year, and so on.

❏ *Federal agencies.* Agencies from the **Environmental Protection Agency [http://www.epa.gov/]** to the **U.S. Department of Commerce [http: //www.doc.gov]** have sites.

❏ *State and local governments.* Government agency and legislative information and documents are available on the state and local level as well. The site **State and Local Government on the Net [http://www. piperinfo.com/~piper/state/states.html]** provides a searchable index of all 50 states, tribal governments, and Guam. Another resource of state-specific information is **StateSearch [http://www.state.ky.us/nasire/ NASIREhome.html]**, which is a clearinghouse of state government information provided by the National Association of State Information Resource Executives.

❏ *Military.* All services of the military have a Web site: **The United States Army HomePage [http://www.army.mil/]**, NavyOnLine **[http://www. navy.mil/]**, **AirForce Link [http://www.dtic.dla.mil/airforcelink/]** and the **Marines [http://www.hqmc.usmc.mil]**.

Educational and Related Sites

There are many educational sites on the Web.

❏ *K–12.* A great deal of Internet activity is going on in the k–12 range. **EdLinks [http://www.marshall.edu/~jmullens/edlinks.html]** provides a directory of links to both commercial and nonprofit providers of educational services. In West Virginia, Bell Atlantic is providing Internet access to k–12 public schools **[http://www.bell-atl.com/wschool/]**. Educational resources have become more predominant on-line, including general curricular items as well as those directly related to computer use.

❏ *College and university level.* Universities provide a great deal of on-line traffic because they were players in the very beginning of the Internet. Most universities and colleges have Gopher and/or Web sites. There are over 744 American college and university sites on the Internet listed with Yahoo (as of January 16, 1996). These sites provide general information about schools, offer links to specific departments, connect to university databases, link to the library catalogs and collections, as well as the alumni association and more. Many of the library catalogs include periodical collections and other selected materials available for downloading.

❏ *Educational programming and training on-line.* Educational commercial services, such as the **Discovery Channel On-line [http://www.discovery.**

com/] offer their programs on-line. Resource centers, such as the **Education Center [http://www.tu-chemnitz.de/gnn/meta/edu/index.html]**, also provide curricula and projects on-line.

Commercial Services

There are many sites on the Web that provide general assistance and help to expedite office procedures for a nonprofit organization.

❑ *Overnight shipping companies.* **UPS [http://www.ups.com]** and **FedEx [http://www.fedex.com]** have Web pages with package tracking features.

❑ *Telephone directories.* The **AT&T 800 Directory [http://www.tollfree.att.net/dir800/]** is available on-line as well as many other phone directories and similar sites.

❑ *Newspapers.* Newspapers and magazines are aggressively entering the on-line market, often through commercial on-line providers that offer magazines as part of their value-added service. The benefit of accessing a magazine on-line is the ability to search text by keywords. Moreover, periodicals on-line are often updated daily, sometimes even hourly, as opposed to the printed copy, which is usually published weekly or monthly. The *Washington Post* now has its own on-line service called "Digital Ink," available for a small monthly fee. Some of the prominent daily newspapers are available on-line. The *San Jose Mercury News* **[http://www.sjmercury.com/]** offers full on-line access for $4.95 per month. The *New York Times* **[http://www.nytimesfax.com]** has a fax service available free over the Internet.

General Internet Resources

There are numerous Internet resources and tools that assist in using and maintaining a presence on the Web.

❑ *Browsers.* The software needed to access the World Wide Web is downloadable once it is connected to the Internet. The original Web browser from the University of Illinois, **Mosaic,** is available at **[http://www.ncsa.uiuc.edu/SDG/Software/Mosaic/NCSAMosaicHome.html]**. The currently most popular browser, **Netscape,** is also available and can be accessed at **[http://home.netscape.com/]**.

☐ *HTML editors.* Dozens of programs are popping up that aid in Web design. Many are available as shareware on the Internet. These include HTML Assistant and **HTML Assistant Pro [http://fox.nstn.ca/~harawitz/index.html]** that is a powerful HTML editor with a built-in spell checking feature. Some are for specific word processors, such as **Microsoft Internet Assistant [http://www.microsoft.com/msword/]**, which is an add-on application to Microsoft Word for creating Web documents.

☐ *Reference material.* There is a great deal of general reference information such as glossaries, encyclopedias, almanacs, and others available directly through the Internet. One can browse the **1995 World Factbook [http://www.odci.gov/cia/publications/pubs.html]** or look at a collection of English and foreign language dictionaries at the **On-line Reference Works** sites **[http://www.cs.cmu.edu/Web/references.html]**. Even **Roget's Thesaurus** is available on-line **[http://humanities.uchicago.edu/forms_unrest/ROGET.html]**.

☐ *Search tools.* These are among the most popular and useful resources on the Internet. Search tools aid in locating sites and information contained in databases and accessible on-line. Dozens of search tools are available, from an index of sites with a built-in search engine for locating site listings in the Index, such as **Yahoo [http://www.yahoo.com]**, to sites that are search engines that actually search the Internet looking for keyword matches, such as **Lycos [http://www.lycos.com]**. There are also search engines that search other search engines, for example, **SavvySearch [http://www.cs.colostate.edu/~dieiling/smartform.html]**.

☐ *Site announcements.* One of the major challenges in building a Web site is getting people to view the site. One way to do this is to get your site listed in as many locations as possible. There are sites that publicize and announce new sites and register those sites with search tools. **A1 Index [http://www.vir.com/~wyatt/index.html]** is an index of 280 sites that provides links to Web sites for free. **Submit It [http://www.submit-it.com/]** is a quick and easy way to submit a new site to many search tools, engines, and catalogs.

☐ *Technical assistance.* Many sites exist to assist the Internet user in gaining more effective and efficient use and understanding of the Internet. These resources include glossaries of terms **[http://www.matisse.net/files/glossary.html]** and sites that provide Web application software **[http://www.rpi.edu/Internet/Guides/decemj/internet-tools.html]**.

❐ *Internet service providers.* Gaining access to the Internet can be achieved through a commercial on-line service, a nonprofit on-line service, and directly through an Internet service provider. All of these provide access to their services through the Internet.

❐ *Information access and technology organizations.* The onslaught of the Internet has had a direct effect on fields of information access and technology. Questions concerning the communication of ideas and information among people or groups are still largely unanswered. Such a basic issue as, "Who will have access to what and how?" is still unresolved. Information access and technology organizations are rapidly emerging to tackle these issues. These organizations include the **Internet Society [http://www.isoc.org/]**, an international nongovernmental organization that supports and monitors use of the Internet, as well as the **Internet Engineering Task Forces [http://www.ietf.cnri.reston.va.us/]** that is concerned with the evolution of the Internet on an international level. There are also issue-specific organizations such as the **Electronic Freedom Foundation [http://www.eff.org/]** that promotes unrestricted access to on-line resources.

The resources available on the Internet are broad and expansive and growing at a phenomenal rate. And yet, not everything is available on the Internet, nor will it ever be. The wise net surfer will use search tools to locate new sites on new topics. Conducting research on the Internet is never a finite process.

CHAPTER 6

Cyber-Fundraising

FUNDRAISING IN CYBERSPACE

Cyber-fundraising is the fundraising technique for the next millennium. It is a new paradigm in fundraising where giving traditions need to be developed among communities just now forming. The successful fundraiser will be the one who artfully molds fundraising principles, tactics, and techniques into the very heart of this new media.

What are people in the nonprofit community saying about cyber-fundraising? Beth Kanter of Arts Wire has found that their Web site has resulted in "off-line" press such as *Internet World.* Moreover, funders have seen their site and shown interest. Stephen Karnes of the Cenikor Foundation has received some interest from potential donors because of their Web site. And Howard Lake of City University in London says, "As a fundraiser, I have benefited from the resources I have uncovered and listed on the (Web) site."

Cyber-fundraising is still in its infant, experimental stage. Its limits and true potential live in one's imagination and entrepreneurial spirit. Everything on the Internet is happening so quickly that today's infant ideas may become tomorrow's standard operating procedures. The public awareness element of maintaining a presence on the Internet grows in value as general access to the Internet expands. Without a doubt, public awareness and fundraising go hand-in-hand.

The Giving Community Revisited

Philanthropic America is aging. The average direct mail donor is now a woman in her late sixties. The baby boomer generation is proving to have a tradition of giving, but the question remains as to whether Generation X will be able to pick up the slack. Moreover, the 1990s are showing a negligible increase in charitable giving, especially from foundation and corporate philanthropic giving programs.

The profile of the on-line community today is of Generation X (ages 16 to 34). It is yet to be seen which causes will inspire this generation to give. One thing is certain, this age group is part of the cyberspace revolution and they are dialing in and logging on-line. To reach Generation X where it listens and learns will pave the way to inspiring new donations.

As use of the Internet expands in society, use demographics will spread out in age, gender, and ethnic makeup. Thus, the Internet will quickly move from being a marketing tool that reaches only specific demographic groups, to becoming one of the top means of communicating with the general public.

In 1995, Americans contributed $143.9 billion dollars to charities. According to "Giving USA" a report by American Association of Fund-Raising Counsel Trust for Philanthropy, these contributions came primarily from four communities and were divided as follows: individuals 80.8 percent, foundations 7.3 percent, bequests 6.8 percent, and corporations 5.1 percent. Close attention to these breakdowns will be key to developing a successful cyber-fundraising plan. Consequently, one can expect that the majority of contributions in cyberspace will be from individuals and will come in small dollar donations.

Cyber-fundraising will not replace other methods of fundraising. It is one more vehicle for reaching the giving community and should become a part of your organization's fundraising strategy. This chapter will look at each of the four broad giving communities (individual, foundations, corporate, and bequests) and the means by which your organization can reach them through your cyberspace fundraising efforts.

ELECTRONIC COMMERCE

The true potential of cyber-fundraising will not be reached until commerce is readily exchanged electronically and the general public becomes secure regarding the exchange of commerce on-line.

Electronic payment methods are already in practice. Telephone sales, automatic teller machines, electronic fund transfers, and even electronic filing of income tax are now commonplace. What is new in cyberspace is the direct exchange of funds in sales transactions.

The benefit of using an electronic payment method is that one maintains a fluid progression from information request, interest in making a donation, to actually making the donation. In fundraising one never wants to lose entree to that "givable moment" when a donor is ready and willing to make a contribution. Electronic payment methods minimize the potential of a distraction occurring before payment is secured.

As growth in the volume of transactions corresponds to the commercialization of the Web, the risk of interception of a financial transaction mounts. Consequently, one of the keys to moving the Web from a marketing tool to a means for exchanging commerce is the development and acceptance of secure methods of payment.

Currently, there are two basic types of systems available for the exchange of commerce. One involves direct credit card usage and the other a separate ID number tied to a credit card. Both systems are transaction based.

The first electronic commerce company to emerge was **First Virtual Holdings Inc. [http://fv.com]** of Cheyenne, Wyoming (Exhibit 6.1). Research conducted by First Virtual showed a higher comfort level with giving credit card information over the phone rather than electronically. Consequently, First Virtual designed a system where the part of the registration process that involves dispersing credit card information is done via an automated 800 number. When a person signs up with First Virtual, he or she receives a First Virtual number that is used for Internet purchases. Each transaction is verified through an e-mail confirmation notice. When something is purchased, the buyer sends the merchant a First Virtual number. The buyer is then asked to confirm the transaction through an e-mail message. The First Virtual number works like a cyberspace-specific credit card that debits an already existing credit card.

Newtwatch [http://www.cais.com/newtwatch/] (Exhibit 6.2), a political satire Web site on Speaker Newt Gingrich, was one of the first sites to use First Virtual as a means for accepting on-line contributions. Because Newtwatch is a political action committee, Federal Election Committee (FEC) regulations apply to all contributions. As a leader in the development of political Web pages, Matt Dorsey, founder and Webmaster of Newtwatch, requested and received an official FEC ruling on the acceptance of Internet political contributions.

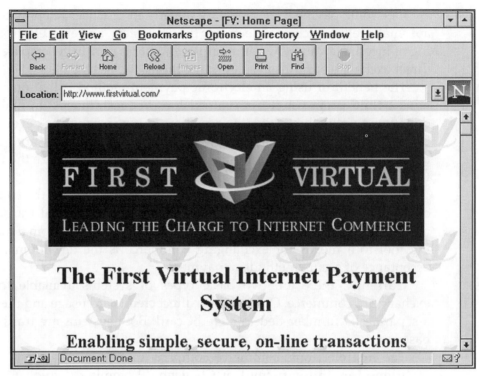

Exhibit 6.1 Electronic commerce companies—First Virtual. *Reprinted with permission.*

Most systems being developed for the exchange of electronic commerce, or more specifically electronic data interchange (EDI), are based on encryption. Encryption is a code system applied to a file to ensure the security of the transmitted information. To decode the encrypted message, the recipient needs the decoding key. In the case of a purchase, the identity of the person sending the message is available, but only the merchant's private decoding key can complete the transaction. We can expect in the near future that all buyers will have a personal digital signature to ensure authenticity.

The first type of system puts a step between the buyer and seller with encryption to ensure security. **CyberCash [http://www.cybercash.com]** (Exhibit 6.3) of Reston, Virginia, offers secured credit card transactions and will shortly provide debits through electronic card transactions. These electronic "cash" payment systems will act as trust accounts, where money is transferred into the trust account as needed and will allow for easy small dollar purchases.

Many of the leaders in the on-line industry are actively engaged in partnerships with leading credit card companies and banks to develop safe

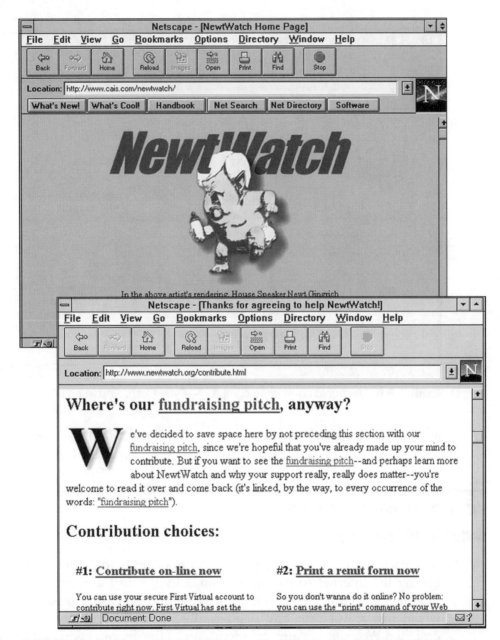

Exhibit 6.2 On-line political fundraising—NewtWatch. *Reprinted with permission.*

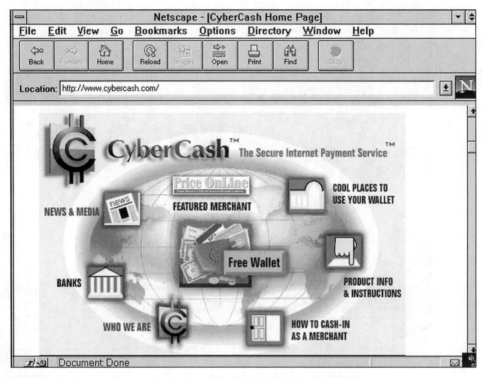

Exhibit 6.3 Electronic commerce company—CyberCash. *Reprinted with permission.*

and secure electronic payment systems. Without a doubt, electronic commerce is the key to complete the commercialization of the Internet.

INDIVIDUAL CONTRIBUTORS

Soliciting Membership

A Web site offers a nonprofit the perfect opportunity to attract persons navigating the Internet to the affairs and activities of the organization. The Internet community is extremely diverse and reaches a broad audience whose tastes, interests, and demographics are still unknown. A smartly designed Web site can attract individuals to the organization and promote membership, as well as solicit donations.

A membership form can be put directly on a Web site to facilitate easy enrollment (see Chapter 4, page 60). The form can ask the prospective member to input personal information in order to enlist in the nonprofit's activities and join as a member. When the form is completed the user can immediately be added to the organization's e-mail database and start receiving material from the organization within minutes.

Acquiring New Members

Membership organizations need a steady influx of new members to balance the natural and inevitable membership attrition process. A Web site is a great way to gain new members, because the person accessing the site did so out of a personal need or interest. Specifically, the visitor found the organization's site rather than the organization seeking out the visitor. This puts the organization in the perfect situation to engage the visitor, either through an action step such as e-mailing a member of Congress, signing the guest book at the site, or by requesting the person join the organization.

Enhancing Membership Relations

The immediacy and ease of communication in cyberspace allows an organization to provide existing members with continual and timely updates of the organization's activities and programs. The closer a member feels to an organization, the more likely that person will participate in fundraising appeals.

Soliciting Donations

Nonprofits will miss a great fundraising opportunity if a donor solicitation page is not included in an organization's Web site. The age-old saying in fundraising, "if you don't ask, you won't get" holds true in cyberspace as well.

The American Red Cross (Exhibit 6.4) uses the Internet to alert interested persons about disasters and volunteering opportunities such as donating blood or making a financial contribution. Visitors to their Web site who want to help are asked to call an 800 number. The operator asks where the caller learned of the 800 number and keeps track of the original source of contact. This direct but low-pressure solicitation approach works well. The Red Cross has found that during an average month, calls to the 800 number initiated from a visit to their Web page surpasses television commercials and other media sources. Calls generated via the Web page have resulted in additional donations totaling from $5,000 to $10,000 in a month with either small or no disasters and considerably higher during peak disaster periods. For example in September 1995, the concern generated over Hurricane Marilyn resulted in close to $30,000 in donations from visitors to the Web page.

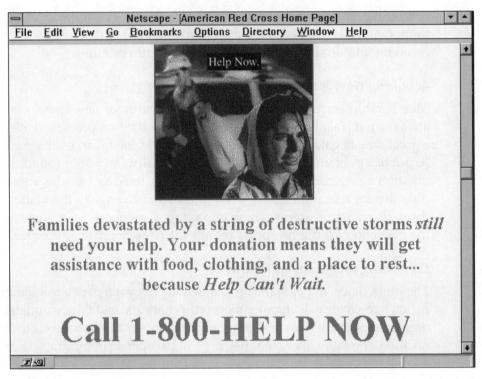

Exhibit 6.4 On-line support for 800 numbers—American Red Cross. *Reprinted with permission.*

Payment Methods

There are various payment methods being employed by nonprofit organizations for soliciting donations. The American Red Cross requests donors to call an 800 number where contributions are processed over the phone. The Ethiopian Jewry home page requests donors to mail in contributions and is receiving from 5 to 10 contributions a month via Internet interest. Majority '96, a political action committee, also requests donations be mailed but uses an interactive pledge button to automatically generate a pledge prompting e-mail message.

Special Events

Organizations are experimenting with holding virtual fundraising events in cyberspace. Impact Online launched their **Cookin' on the Net** [**http://www.cooknet.org/index.html#top**] (Exhibit 6.5) as a Web-based charity effort designed to raise money for nonprofit organizations helping to donate computer equipment and resources to disadvantaged children. Participants were asked to donate $12.00 electronically. In return, contributors received five recipes from renowned chefs in five cities: Boston, Chicago, New York, Los Angeles, and San Francisco. The event raised $1,500 in the first three weeks, although most contributions came through the mail, not electronically.

Another virtual event was held by Paranet titled **Cyberspace Challenge [http://cyberchallenge.paranet.com]** (Exhibit 6.6). The event raised $10,000 for Big Brothers and Sisters. Cyberspace Challenge was a skills-based Internet competition for children. Most of the $10,000 was donated by corporate sponsors.

The commercial on-line services are also getting into the act by using cyberspace as a medium to increase business and help charities at the same time. America Online and PC Financial Network joined forces between December 15, 1995, and January 15, 1996, to raise money for Ronald

Exhibit 6.5 Virtual fundraising events—Cookin' on the Net. *Reprinted with permission.*

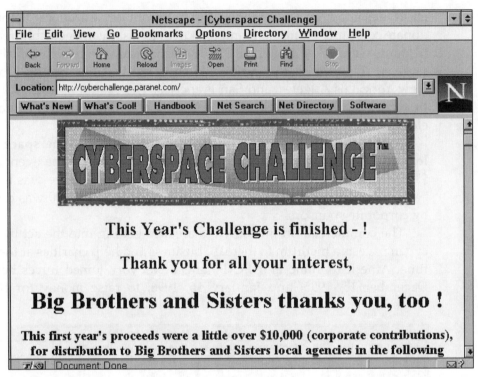

Exhibit 6.6 On-line fundraising activity—Cyberspace Challenge. *Reprinted with permission.*

McDonald Children's Charities. They jointly made donations for every on-line stock trade executed during that time period. The event raised over $84,000 and was hailed as a great success by all involved.

Advertising Virtual Events

How does one advertise virtual events? This is done by using all the outreach vehicles already at your disposal: mail, newsletters, and word of mouth as well as electronic mediums such as e-mail, newsgroups, and mailing lists on your Web site and announcements on other Web sites.

Advertising Your Event in Cyberspace

Cyberspace can also be used to advertise a fundraising event. **Philadelphia Aids Walk [http://www.cortex.net/!!tUYilCSwWtUYilCSw/aidswalk/]** built a home page for their event (Exhibit 6.7). The **Jimmy V Celebrity Gold**

Classic also has its own site [**http://jimmyv.org/golfclassic.html**] where the organization not only advertises the event, but also solicits for sponsors (Exhibit 6.8) by highlighting their sponsorship packages [**http://jimmyv. org/sponsorship.html**].

Fundraising Products

The World Wide Web is also being used as a vehicle to advertise fundraising event products to the nonprofit community. On the Web you can find dozens of fundraising ideas for your next fundraising campaign: from selling candy [**http://www.moneymp.com**] (Exhibit 6.9) to selling "make your own pizza" kits (Exhibit 6.10) [**http://webcom.com/~pets/fundr/index.html**] and from selling seminars [**http://Fox.nstn.ca/~asi/**] (Exhibit 6.11) to selling lottery-style scratch-off cards [**http://www.transformation.com/scratch/**] (Exhibit 6.12) where the amount on the card is the amount the person should donate.

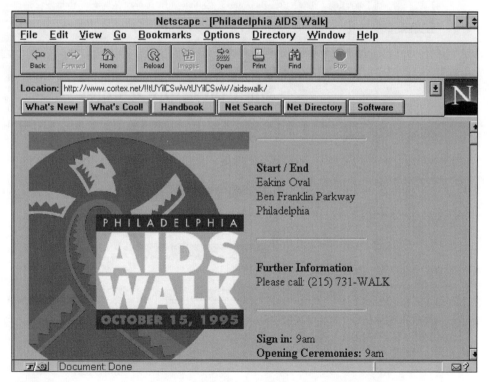

Exhibit 6.7 Promoting events on-line—Philadelphia Aids Walk. *Reprinted with permission.*

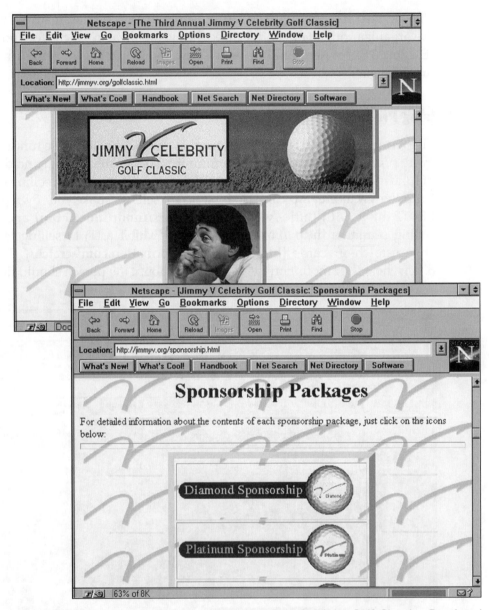

Exhibit 6.8 On-line sponsorship links—Jimmy V Celebrity Golf Classic. *Reprinted with permission.*

Exhibit 6.9 Fundraising products—Money Making Promotions. *Reprinted with permission.*

Major Donor Fundraising

The Internet is not known as the "toy" of the rich. It is not a place where the elite meet. The yacht club and the country club are still better avenues for mingling with the rich and famous. As is the case with most fundraising efforts, the majority of money to be made on the Internet will come in small dollar amounts. And yet the Internet can be a valuable tool in major donor prospect research. If you are conducting general background research, you can search newspaper and periodical databases from the *New York Times* Fax [**http://www.nytimesfax.com**] to the *San Jose Mercury News* [**http://www.sjmercury.com/**]. You can also look through **West's Legal Directory** for lawyers and law firms [**http://www.wld.com/ldsearch.htm**] (Exhibit 6.13).

Prospect research companies such as **Waltman Associates [http://www.umn.edu/nlhome/g248/bergq003/wa/]** (Exhibit 6.14) have compiled lists of Trustees of College and Universities, a Directory of Directors, and even made

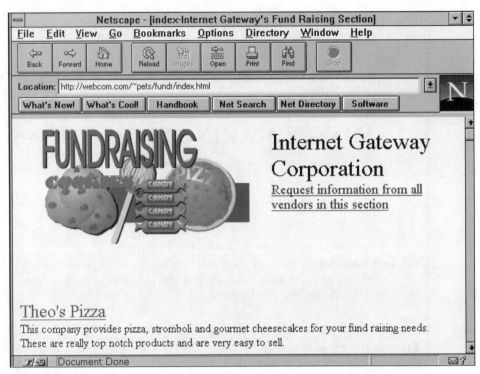

Exhibit 6.10 Fundraising products—Theo's Pizza. *Reprinted with permission.*

back issues of *Town & Country* magazine searchable for a fee. An indispensable tool for corporate research is Hoovers On-line which has a searchable directory of over 10,000 companies (Exhibit 6.15). There are also sites maintained by professional prospect researchers at public institutions such as **The Prospect Research Page [http://weber.u.washington.edu/~dlamb/research. html#corp]** (Exhibit 6.16) by David Lamb of the Development Office at the University of Washington that has links to a wide variety of valuable sites for prospect research.

There is even an Internet mailing list on prospect research called PRSPECT-L where professionals in the field exchange tips and tricks. To subscribe to this discussion group, e-mail a message to Listserv@bucknell. edu with the message subscribe prspct-l <firstname lastname>. The discussion is archived and can be accessed through a gopher menu **[gopher:// gopher.bucknell.edu:70/00/Services/listserv/prspct-l/info]** (Exhibit 6.17).

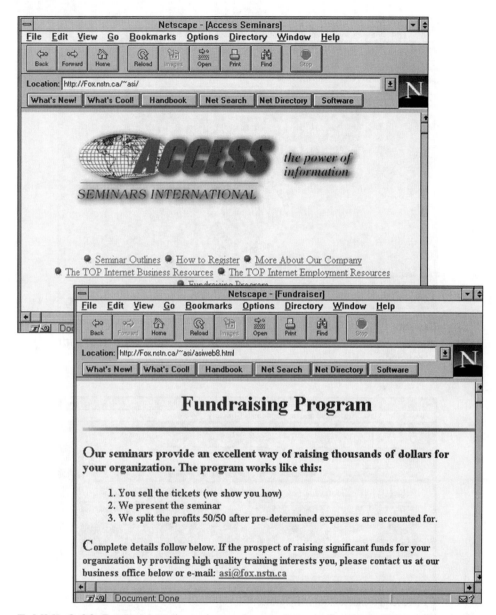

Exhibit 6.11 Fundraising through seminars—Access Seminars International. *Reprinted with permission.*

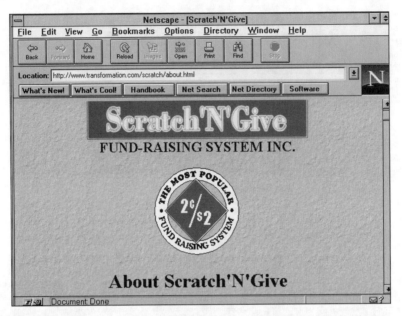

Exhibit 6.12 Fundraising promotion items for youth-centered programs—Scratch'N'Give Fund-Raising System, Inc. *Reprinted with permission.*

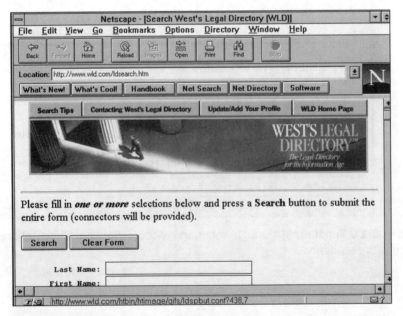

Exhibit 6.13 Prospect research: business professionals—West's Legal Directory. *Reprinted with permission.*

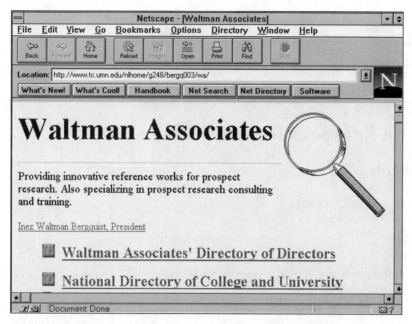

Exhibit 6.14 Prospect research: directories—Waltman Associates. *Reprinted with permission.*

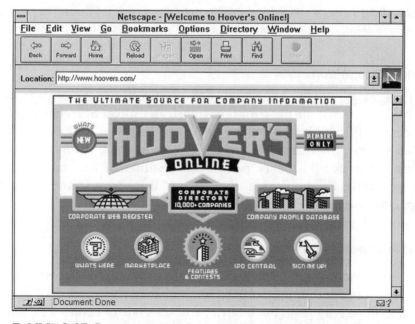

Exhibit 6.15 Prospect research: corporations—Hoover's On-line. *Reprinted with permission.*

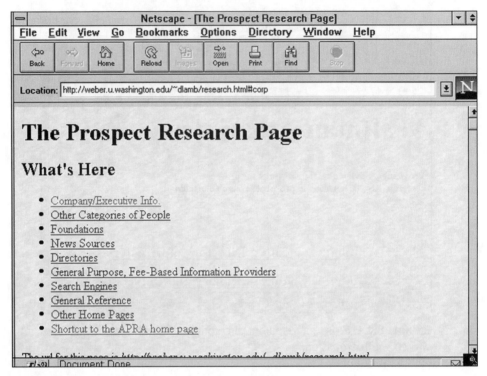

Exhibit 6.16 General information on prospect research—The Prospect Research Page. *Property of David Lamb at the University of Washington. Reprinted with permission.*

Donor Recognition

You can acknowledge and thank donors directly on your Web site. For example, on the home page for the **American Cancer Society [http://www. cancer.org/]** (Exhibit 6.18) acknowledgment is given for the support provided by the American Cancer Foundation in conjunction with Leo and Gloria Rosen for the development and maintenance of the site. Impact Online thanks its sponsors at the bottom of its home page **[http://www. impactonline.org/]** (Exhibit 6.19).

Direct Mail in Cyberspace

Like any community, the cyberspace community has developed an informal code of proper and improper behavior. For the cyberspace community, the location of activity is on the Internet and the code of conduct is called *netiquette.* A host of FAQs exist that discuss netiquette, most of which surrounds

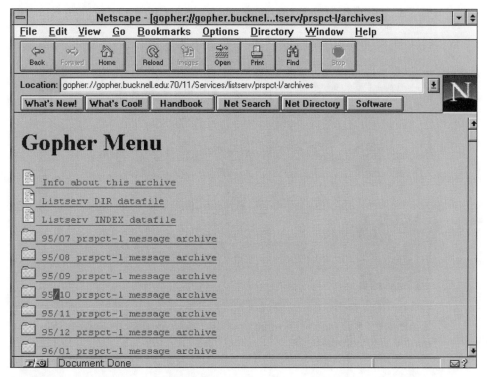

Exhibit 6.17 Prospect research listserve—PRSPCT-L. *Reprinted with permission.*

proper Usenet behavior. Netiquette becomes of central concern when one begins exploring the possibilities of direct mail via e-mail, newsgroups, mailing lists, and so on. Without a doubt, the answer to whether there will be advertising in cyberspace is no longer an "if" but a "how." And yet, utilizing the new media to facilitate direct mail techniques will require a thorough knowledge of netiquette as well as the new emerging cyberspace marketing paradigm.

The most obvious vehicle through which to do direct mail marketing is newsgroups, but that is strongly frowned upon in netiquette. One method used in direct marketing on the Internet has been given the pejorative term of *spam*. Spam is when a message is posted multiple times to a large number of newsgroups regardless of the subject of the newsgroup. The topic of the spam can be anything from an advertisement for hand cream to an alert about nuclear testing.

The term spam comes from a well known *Monty Python* sketch. In this sketch, a man is in a diner and asks the waitress what is on the menu. The

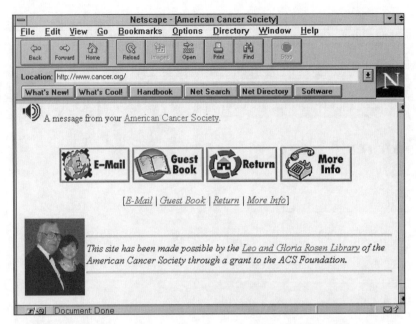

Exhibit 6.18 Donor acknowledgment—American Cancer Society. *Reprinted with permission.*

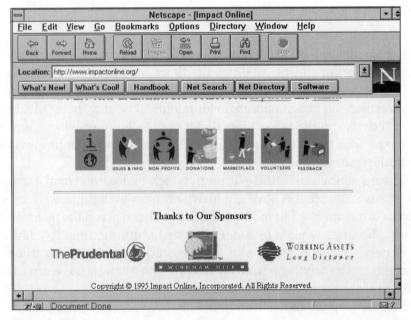

Exhibit 6.19 Sponsor list—Impact Online. *Reprinted with permission.*

waitress replies: "Well, there's egg and bacon; egg, sausage, and bacon; egg and spam; egg, bacon, and spam; egg, bacon, sausage, and spam; spam, bacon, sausage, spam, spam, spam, bacon, spam, tomato, and spam; spam, spam, spam, egg, and spam; spam, spam, spam, spam, spam, spam, baked beans, spam, spam, spam, and spam." The word spam is used in the waitress's reply repeatedly with no apparent meaning. Likewise, messages on the Internet that are out of context and considered virtual noise are considered spam.

The Internet community abhors spam; not only because it consists of inappropriate and out-of-context messages, but because it takes up space on the server. Multiple listings of the same message take up space and inspire large volumes of complaints in response to the spam. There is usually a 10 percent increase in newsgroup activity after the posting of a spam, and all this added activity can drain server space and resources.

Certain spam incidents are infamous in cyberspace. In 1994, the law firm of Canter and Siegel thought they had discovered the silver bullet for tapping the Internet as a cheap marketing medium and posted an advertisement for green card assistance to over 7,000 newsgroups. Canter and Siegel received few requests for green card assistance but the response by the Internet community was fast and swift. The server that Canter and Siegel used, Internet Direct, crashed fifteen times under the flood of thirty thousand hate mail messages and flames (argumentative messages) received in just eighteen hours. Internet Direct stopped the Canter and Siegel account.

A *flame* is an offensive or unmannerly e-mail originated in the Usenet environment. Flaming is the process whereby one user sends another an acerbic, offensive, or unmannerly e-mail. The instigation of a flame is usually an inappropriate comment or basic breach of netiquette by a veteran newsgroup user. Mistakes made by novice users rarely result in flaming. A new user is allowed much more latitude than is a long-time practitioner. Flames should be used in moderation. For those partial to flaming, there are now newsgroups dedicated to this art.

Canter and Siegel then took several steps. First they threatened to sue Internet Direct for $250,000 for loss of business. Then Canter and Siegel set up accounts on two other providers promising even more advertisements. The Internet community went wild in response. Even though Canter and Siegel received tremendous press coverage, they were blacklisted from the Internet community, with service providers choosing to drop the Canter–Siegel accounts rather than face the rampage of the Internet community.

Robert Raisch, Vice-Chairperson of the Internet Business Association and founder of The Internet Company, calls spam advertisements postage-due marketing. Raisch defines postage-due marketing as, "using the global Internet as a direct marketing vehicle to distribute messages to users with little concern for their topical appropriateness or the costs involved in their distribution." In using this type of marketing, the advertiser forces the consumer to bear part of the costs of distribution, whether the consumer is interested in the product or not. This could be likened to a telemarketer calling collect. Newsgroup participants do not want their discussion disrupted with advertisements. In response, special advertising-friendly newsgroups have been developed to deter such subject noise from cluttering up the legitimate discussion in a newsgroup.

Commercialization of the Internet is definitely here to stay. The lesson to be learned from the Canter and Siegel spam war is that advertising on the Internet is not inherently bad. Rather, advertisers need to follow proper netiquette—that is, in the appropriate locations and not through unsolicited e-mail or newsgroup advertising where the recipient is forced to read and pay for unsolicited and unwanted messages.

As with any community, cyberspace has developed internal means to punish those that break the rules. In terms of newsgroup advertising, blacklists such as the **Blacklist of Internet Advertisers [http://math-www. uni-paderborn.de/~axel/BL/blacklist.html]** have developed that document spam incidents. Moreover, when you have a burgeoning new community, the last thing your nonprofit wants is to acquire a negative image. The results of improper netiquette are that people would not visit and might even boycott your site, directories will not list your organization, and hackers might even sabotage the site (this translates into time, if not monetary expense, to repair the damage). At the extreme, the negative cyber-image translated into the general public arena tarnishes an organization's good name.

The debate on this issue is far from over. The September 29, 1995, edition of the "The Friday Report" published by Hoke Communications, reported that Marketry, Inc. a mailing list company in Bellevue, Washington was handling the product "E-Mail Internet Interest Selector" that had a list of 250,000 e-mail addresses. By November, Marketry, Inc. had dropped the product. One of the main reasons given for this was the lack of technology for allowing e-mail addresses to opt out of receiving e-mail advertisements presented to the company by the Internet community. The product was bought by **DM Group** of Aurora, Ohio [**http://www.dm1.com/**].

This begs the question, how can one successfully carry out direct mail in cyberspace? First of all, an organization needs to develop its own e-mail database and not take the apparently easy route of using an existing list-serv or newsgroup. The old saying "if it looks too good to be true, it probably is" holds true in cyberspace as well. Moreover, in developing the e-mail database, the organization should first let the user know that the organization might sell their e-mail database as a way to raise funds, and that everyone who participates in the database is aiding in the fundraising process. The user should then be given the opportunity to opt out of receiving solicitations by e-mail. With present mail list technology, this is not easily doable; however, as e-mail databases are built via Web sites, this option can be included.

Inevitably people's e-mail addresses will be as pervasive as their phone and fax numbers and as accessible to direct marketers. E-mail will be the appropriate place for solicitations—*not* a spam to unrelated or inappropriate newsgroups.

How will a virtual direct mail appeal look? E-mail tends to be short and to the point. Undoubtedly, direct mail via e-mail will follow the same style, but with the added advantage of inviting the recipient to visit the organization's Web site for a more multimedia presentation of the appeal. Moreover, when sending out e-mail solicitations, an identifying marker in the subject heading would be appropriate in order to identify the message as a solicitation.

Sale of Publications and Other Material

Nonprofits have found that selling related items can be a profitable addition to budget enrichment. The Sierra Club, one of the founders of nonprofits selling merchandise to supplement their income, has their full catalogue of books available to the Internet community [**http://www.sierraclub.org/books/**] (Exhibit 6.20). Whether one is selling publications or T-shirts, your Web site is a direct outlet for sales, and has the potential to reach a broader audience than does the mailing of catalogues alone; the Internet reaches millions worldwide. This is also an inexpensive way to continue advertising products after a new product line has been introduced.

Order forms on-line allow purchases to happen immediately by using an electronic payment method. Also, featuring products on-line one can present a full-color graphic of the item without the extravagant costs of full-color advertisement in traditional print media. For example, the Amnesty International publication page displays its full line of merchandise, from publications to T-shirts (Exhibit 6.21). The customer can choose

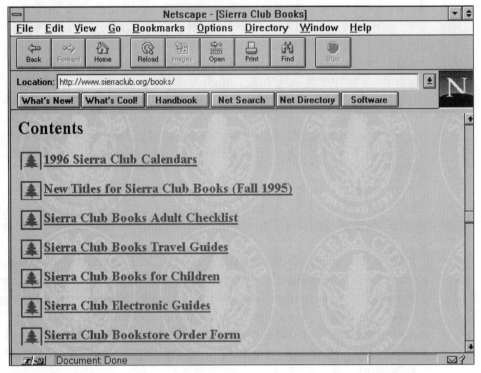

Exhibit 6.20 On-line catalogue—Sierra Club Books. *Reprinted with permission.*

to print either a page or the entire catalogue in full graphics or in a text only version.

FOUNDATION FUNDRAISING ON THE INTERNET

Foundation Prospect Research

Information on foundations can be found in three types of sites. The first are the sites of key foundation assistance and resource centers, both on a national and state-wide basis. For example, the **Foundation Center** has a Web site [**http://www.fndcenter.org/**] (Exhibit 6.22) that includes information on the grant-writing process, current and past issues of their newsletter *Philanthropy News Digest*, as well as links to foundation home pages categorized by type of foundation. The Council on Foundations' home page [**http://www.cof.org/**] (Exhibit 6.23) links to other foundation home

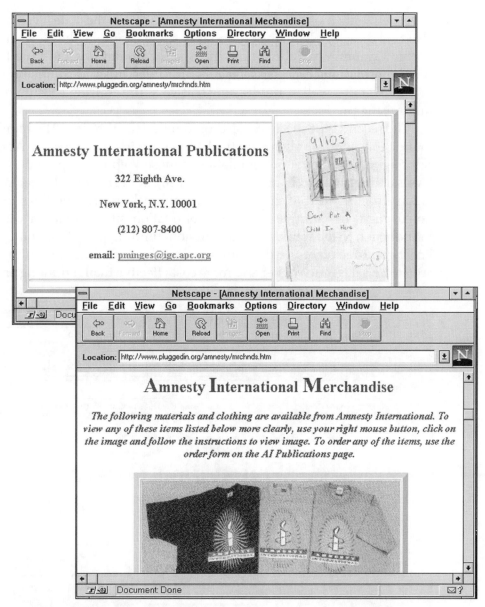

Exhibit 6.21 On-line catalogue—Amnesty International. *Reprinted with permission.*

pages, but only those that belong to the Council. On the state level, one can also find directory listings of foundations. For example, the Northern California Community Foundation, Inc.'s site **Foundations On-Line** [**http://www.foundations.org/**] (Exhibit 6.24) includes links to foundations and grantmakers, as well as fundraising software, fundraising consultants and fundraising products.

The second type of site consists of foundation Web sites. The number of foundations with a presence on the Web is growing every month. As of this printing there are over 50 foundations whose Web pages provide various levels of information (Exhibits 6.25 and 6.26). Some are merely Web presentations from the text of the organizational brochure with no links to additional pages of information. Other foundation sites provide a complete introduction to the foundation, its mission, funding priorities, grant guidelines, grant recipients, and information on the staff. Since modification of Web material is much easier and more cost effective than reprinting and dis-

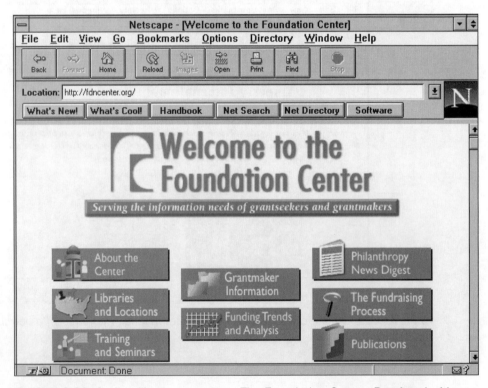

Exhibit 6.22 On-line library resources—The Foundation Center. *Reprinted with permission.*

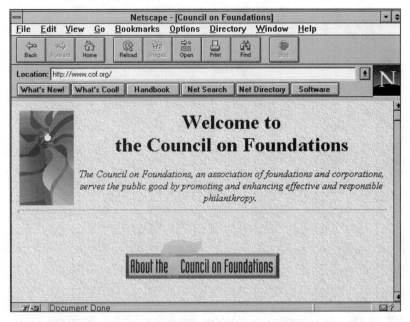

Exhibit 6.23 Links to foundations—Council on Foundations. *Reprinted with permission.*

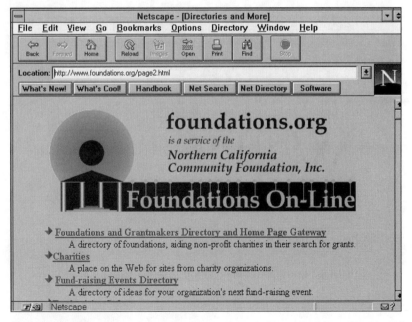

Exhibit 6.24 Links to foundations—Foundations On-Line. *Reprinted with permission.*

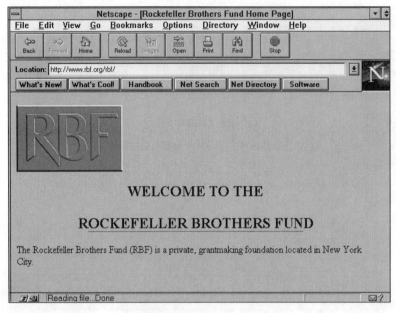

Exhibit 6.25 Giant application procedures—Rockefeller Brothers Fund. *Reprinted with permission.*

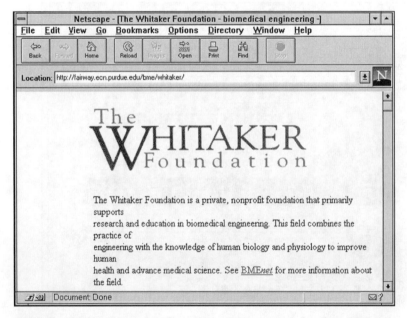

Exhibit 6.26 Information for prospective grantees—The Whitaker Foundation. *Reprinted with permission.*

seminating a brochure, material on foundations can be kept up to date more readily.

And third, commercial sites are appearing that offer access to fee-based searchable foundation databases. **Access Point Fundraising System** (Exhibit 6.27) debuted in 1996 with a keyword searchable database for foundations and another for corporate giving [**http//www.accesspt.com/ fundsys/fundsys.html**].

Applying for Grants

In the near future, one can expect more and more foundations to accept applications over the Internet. The process could take on various forms. The first step will probably be that foundations accept grant applications as transferred files, minimizing the copying and postage costs for grantees.

Another future option is to supply the grant application on an on-line form, where the grantee fills out and submits the application on-line. In this way, a uniform standard would be maintained to allow instant submission of an application.

Finally, in the future, grant writing on the Internet could follow the virtual document model where a grant application is a combination of text, graphics, and links. This interactive and multimedia grant application would provide the program officer with a broader access to the grantee's work. For example, a grantee could demonstrate success as a technical assistance provider by providing links to the organizations she or he assist. Other multimedia dimensions could consists of 15- to 30-second video or audio clips demonstrating the work of the nonprofit. This type of a virtual document also could be employed for the grant recipient's reporting requirements.

Foundations are also investigating how to assist their grantees in jumping on the Internet: What would be the best resources and assistance they could provide to facilitate this move? For example, Pfizer is in the early stages of developing a program to assist a group of current grantees to gain presence on the Internet. The program provides funding for equipment, technical assistance on Web design, and maintenance. Paula Luff, Manager of Corporate Philanthropy Programs, sees this program as providing their grantees with valuable access to a variety of tools for disseminating and gathering information. Moreover, Paula feels confident that a Web presence will help their grantees "acquire and maintain member relationships as well as expand the organization's donor base."

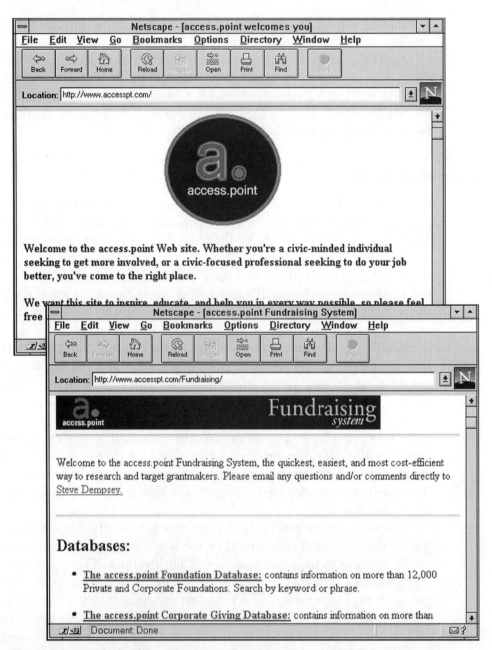

Exhibit 6.27 Fee-based database on foundation- and corporate-giving programs—access.point Fundraising System. *Reprinted with permission.*

CORPORATE FUNDRAISING

Prospect Research

The Internet holds a wealth of material for corporate prospect researching. As previously mentioned, there are Web sites by prospect research companies who offer services through their home page for a fee, and directories of prospect research resources put together by university development offices. Another equally valuable resource is to examine a company's Web site. In corporate research, one can learn about the top officers and management at a company site. Many companies include biographies of management on their Web site, some with photographs and audio tracks [**http://www.ibm. com/Finding/Welcome/**] (Exhibit 6.28).

If one is planning to approach a company for a donation, whether through the company's philanthropic giving program or in a cause-related marketing capacity through the marketing department, a good knowledge of corporate priorities is always valuable. For example, the **AMD** Web page [**http://www.amd.com/img/imagemap/shmap.conf?268,9**] (Exhibit 6.29) not only provides background about the company, the corporate mission statement, and press releases, but also discusses their target markets. Gathering this material used to require a great deal of research, now it is available all in one place. Acquiring this kind of inside material before meeting with a company is invaluable.

Corporate Partnerships—Cause-Related Marketing

One of the greatest challenges on the Web right now is getting people to look at your home page. With 100,000 plus home pages on the Web, the nonprofit needs to develop ways to lead interested persons to its page. Hyperlinks with similar nonprofits is one way, but in terms of fundraising, there is another possibility. In cause-related marketing, a company tries to link itself with a nonprofit organization in order to boost its image and sales and at the same time raise money for the organization. Cyberfundraising offers great potential for corporate and nonprofit partnerships.

The benefits of cause-related marketing to the company and nonprofit alike are now extending into cyberspace. For example, **Rhino Chasers** micro beer, a product of William & Scott Brewing Company of California, [**http://www.rhinochasers.com**] has had a relationship with the African Wildlife Foundation (AWF) for two and a half years. The company decided

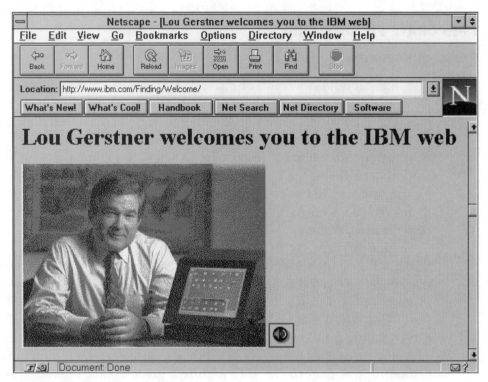

Exhibit 6.28 Corporate Web sites: executives—IBM. *Reproduced by permission from IBM. Copyright © 1996 by International Business Machines Corporation.*

to get involved in a cause-related marketing campaign because the demographics for micro beer drinkers are men and women between the ages of 25 and 35. This group is known to respond well to cause-related marketing through the good works for charity by such industry leaders as the Body Shop, Starbucks Coffee, and Ben and Jerry's Ice Cream.

The makers of Rhino Chasers decided to find a nonprofit to associate with that would tie into its name. The product name of Rhino Chasers came from a surfing term, but its association with the rhino lead to its partnership with AWF. Rhino Chasers gives a percentage of its profits to AWF. In addition, Rhino Chasers helps publicize the work of AWF by putting the AWF logo on their beer bottle labels and including AWF brochures in Rhino Chaser mailings. As Tim Pai, CFO of Rhino Chasers (Exhibit 6.30), points out, "From day one we've done our best to promote AWF." When Rhino Chasers decided to put up a Web page, they told AWF that just as they publicize AWF everywhere else, their Web page would include a link

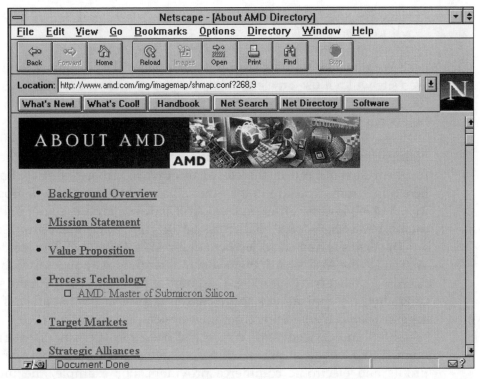

Exhibit 6.29 Corporate Web sites company profiles—AMD. *Reprinted with permission.*

to an AWF page as well—and Rhino Chasers would be happy to design the page.

Leigh Bailey, Development Associate at AWF, decided to take on the Web page assignment both in terms of content and design. Even though AWF's computer system was still DOS based, Leigh worked on the Web page at home using her PC and her personal Internet account. Leigh taught herself HTML and calculates that it took about 10 hours total to design the page, type in the text, and learn HTML. "I think people can do Web pages themselves," says Leigh.

> *In designing the pages I tried to keep it graphically simple because most computers can't pick up large images. I also tried to mimic our colors and still have colors that would look good on the Web. And finally, I tried to keep the language simple. The contents of the page include an introduction to AWF with links to pages on the rhino and the elephant. In the future we want to include highlights from our newsletter as the changing element of*

the page. Other future links include news from Africa as well as links to African and wildlife pages.

AWF plans to fundraise through their page. The first generation of the Web site will not use an electronic payment system due to concerns about the safety of electronic payment transactions at this time. Instead, Leigh points out, "We'll have our address, phone number, and e-mail."

The connection between Rhino Chasers and AWF has been beneficial to both parties. For Rhino Chasers, this association with AWF is another way for them to stand out in the crowd of other micro brews. Also, both are benefiting from exposure to the other's base: Rhino Chaser's demographics (25 to 35) is quite different from AWF's demographics (older and more established society folks). This cross-fertilization holds great promise.

The Web site had an added benefit for AWF. When Leigh presented the Web site to the AWF board, they were most enthusiastic about the job Leigh had done on her own initiative. The board is now working with the staff to upgrade the organization's entire computer system, so that all staff in the organization can go on-line from their desks.

The Rhino Chasers and AWF is just one type of partnership arrangement. Other potential partnership arrangements could be between nonprofits and electronic commerce providers. For example, the provider could advertise that every time someone signs up for or uses their service, a donation would be made to the nonprofit. If the nonprofit has a large e-mail database and membership base with demonstrable loyalty of members, associating with the nonprofit could boost the provider's market share with significant sales increases.

MEMORIALS

The Internet is still too new a fundraising technique to be the focal point in bequests, but there are a host of memorials springing up on the Internet. In fundraising, many contributions are given in honor of loved ones who have passed away. This is particularly true for health-related organizations that deal with the funding of research for specific diseases such as cancer and AIDS. Sites of this nature can facilitate memorial contributions by providing a Web site vehicle on which to make a direct donation in a loved one's honor. Also, as memorials and virtual memorial gardens spring up on the Web, a nonprofit could develop partnership links with these sites. Unlike

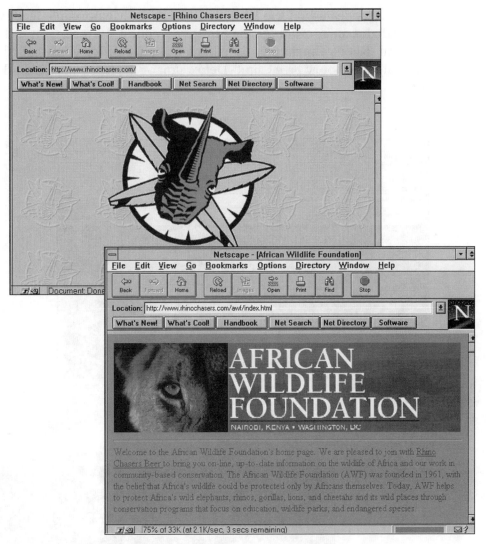

Exhibit 6.30 Cause-related marketing—Rhino Chasers Beer and African Wildlife Foundation. *Reprinted with permission.*

memorials of old where a name alone was placed on a plaque or a page in a program, a Web memorial could include pictures as well as text remembering that person's commitment to a cause or an organization's mission. For example, immediately after the death of Jerry Garcia of the rock band Grateful Dead, pages memorializing Jerry Garcia and offering a place for people

to grieve appeared on the Web. On the site **In Memoriam—Jerry Garcia**
[http://hake.com/gordon/garcia.html], a request is made on behalf of
Deborah Koons Garcia that donations in honor of Jerry be sent to either
the Haight Ashbury Free Clinic–Detox Unit or the Rex Foundation (Exhibit
6.31).

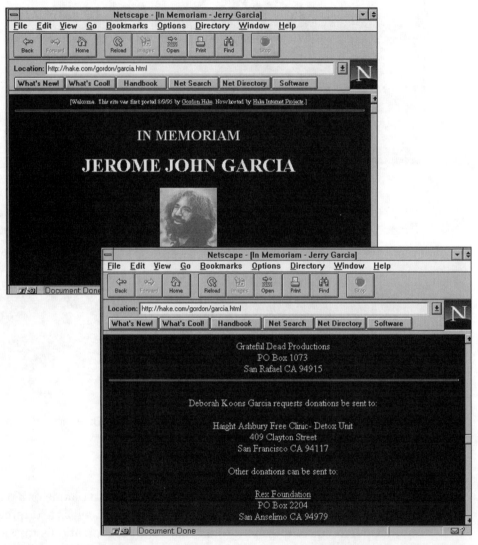

Exhibit 6.31 Donation requests in virtual memorials—In Memorian—Jerry Garcia.
Reprinted with permission.

SAVING MONEY IS RAISING MONEY

Another way of looking at raising money in cyberspace is by saving money. Cyberspace offers the nonprofit a myriad means by which to save money in postage and printing, as well as in payment for services. In other words, your organization will be able to respond to requests for information without incurring the cost of postage and without generating extra paper. A Web site is a perfect location to tell and sell your organization on a budget.

As already mentioned in other sections of this book, your Web site will help you save money in the following ways:

1. E-mailing messages to staff, volunteers, members, and interested persons as well as responding to requests for assistance.
2. Advertising and finding volunteers.
3. Posting publications and newsletters.

Without a doubt, the Web provides a wealth of opportunities for the nonprofit community to be creative as it taps the giving potential of the cyberspace community. New fundraising tactics and techniques will be developed as we blend the Web into our organization's overall marketing mix.

CHAPTER 7

Making it Happen—
Establishing Your Presence
on the World Wide Web

FORMULATING A WEB STRATEGY

Putting up a site on the World Wide Web means more than hanging a billboard on the information superhighway. It means taking charge of your site as an outreach vehicle to meet your organization's goals and objectives for entering and investing in cyberspace. The goal of this chapter is to familiarize you with Web design and provide the questions your organization needs to address and the answers to establish a presence on the World Wide Web.

There are six key elements to formulating a Web strategy:

1. Define your purpose: membership services, fundraising, outreach, publication sales, and so on.
2. Identify your audience: Who will be using your Web site and why?
3. Design the Web site: How will your site look and what will be the content?
4. Publicize your site: How will you draw an audience?
5. Determine success: Clarify from the start how you will determine if your site is successfully meeting your goals and objectives.

6. Address the issues involved in merging a Web site into your organization's operations: How will your site be truly integrated as a communication vehicle, accessed and employed by every arm of your organization? An easy reference checklist is provided in Exhibit 7.1.

Purpose

When developing a site for the Web, it is important for your organization to clearly outline your intentions for the site. By defining goals and objectives, you can determine if the site is achieving its purpose for your organization and determine if the staff time and financial investment is worthwhile for your organization in the short and long term.

What are the various functions a Web site serves?

This checklist is for brainstorming purposes; if a question is not applicable to your unique situation, skip or modify the question. This checklist should be used only as a guide.

❑ What is your purpose in putting up a Web site? Advertising? Promotion? Education? Outreach? Public awareness? Membership services? Fundraising? Merchandise sales?

❑ Who is the targeted audience?

❑ How will the site attract/find this audience? Will the site be exclusive to members?

❑ Will you use the site to attract new members?

❑ What features/techniques will you use to attract new members?

❑ Do you plan to fundraise on your site?

❑ How will you accept money? Through an electronic commerce service? Direct credit card number submission? Invoice? Request payments be submitted through the mail?

❑ Will publications be made available? Downloadable for free? For a fee?

❑ What information will be made available to visitors to your site?

❑ Who will design and develop the site?

❑ Who will maintain it?

❑ What material will be updated regularly to keep the site timely?

Exhibit 7.1 Checklist for Establishing a Web Site

❐ Provides an overall organizational profile.

❐ Informs and updates on projects and programs.

❐ Promotes your publications and other available material.

❐ Solicits new members.

❐ Services existing members.

❐ Requests donations.

❐ Functions as a clearinghouse for information.

As a premiere outreach vehicle, your site allows you to present your organization in exactly the way you want it to be known in a multimedia format. Unlike an article in the press where you are at the mercy of the reporter and the publication, on your Web site you are the designer, editor, and critic of the medium and the message.

Audience

In determining your cyberspace audience, you need first to look at your current and potential audience. Who are the people who can benefit from having access to the information, material, and/or service your organization provides? Your potential Web site audience may include the following:

❐ existing members

❐ potential members

❐ volunteers

❐ board of directors

❐ staff

❐ people affected by the issue/concern you address

❐ researchers

❐ journalists

❐ general public

Once you determine who can benefit from access and exposure to your organization, then you need to determine which part of your audience is already on the Internet. With the exponential growth of on-line access around the country and around the world, the demographics continue to expand and grow. In other words, if a part of your audience is not on the Internet today, they probably will be in the near future.

Another consideration is examining how your organization can assist its potential audience in getting on the Internet. Do you need to educate them about the values of the Internet? Should you make a partnership arrangement with an ISP so that your members get a discount on connecting to the Internet? You can assist the venture into cyberspace by informing members of your services on the Web and by partnering with software companies or Internet access providers to offer Internet services at a reduced rate to your members. The easier you make it for your constituency to get on-line, the better able you will be to use this as a communication tool.

Steve Durland, Co-Director of Art in the Public Interest knows well that one of the major downsides to the Internet is that not everyone is connected. Art in the Public Interest has chosen to put its publications online and not to publish them on paper to save costs. Steve was at a conference recently and was informing the group of his organization's work on the Web. A woman in the audience who represented an organization that is part of their constituency challenged him on the fact that too many people would not have access to their material if it was available only through their Web site. Steve responded, "If this was the only way I could afford to make the information available, it was a better alternative than not publishing at all. And if the information I published was of value to her constituents, then it was partly her responsibility to help them get access." Indeed, access is a two-way street and may prove to be one of the greatest challenges for organizations using the Web as an outreach vehicle.

Public and Private Sites

In composing your organization's menu of services, you may decide to have several purposes. In fact, a multilayered approach is quickly becoming the norm. One extension of this is that an organization may choose to establish two different sites on the Web: a public site for general use and a private one for intra-organizational matters. The public site and its elements are primarily what have been discussed throughout this book and this is what is normally meant by a Web site. However, increasingly, organizations have been taking advantage of the Internet to handle matters within.

The American Red Cross has both a public and a private presence on the Web. The public Web site of the **American Red Cross** can be reached by the URL address [**www.redcross.org**]. This site contains four main sections: what's hot, where we are, what we do, and how to help.

The American Red Cross (ARC) also has an internal corporate Web presence called "CrossNet Corpweb," which serves as a private and secure network. CrossNet Corpweb's primary role is to facilitate the internal exchange of information and ideas. The site includes discussion forums, corporate documents, policy manuals, news, interactive access into corporate databases at their national office, and more. People in the field can access this corporate Web service through ARC Online, a software bundle, and PPP Internet Access service, designed by HLC Internet that includes everything needed to get on-line. This system is completely integrated with the American Red Cross national office e-mail and provides users with the look of "one Red Cross" by giving everyone an American Red Cross e-mail address [**@usal.redcross.org**]. This secure and private service also allows its users full access to all of the common features of the Internet. The ARC Online program is an inexpensive, secure, private, and comprehensive vehicle to connect the entire 1.5 million American Red Cross army of volunteers and paid staff located in U.S. cities and countries throughout the world.

Site Design

Layout

Today, Web pages are filled with all sorts of design bells and whistles that highlight the present and future technological capabilities of the Web. However, bells and whistles do not necessarily translate into a good Web site—unless the purpose of your Web site is to showcase technology. For an organization, the factor that determines whether your site is good or not rests on its ability to fulfill the needs of its visitors. In other words, form and function over flash.

This is particularly true because most Web users have only a 14,400 modem. Knowing the equipment limitations of your audience in site design will enhance the usability of your site. For example, with a 14,400 modem, large graphics take a long time to download. This can be frustrating to a person visiting your site for the first time if they have to wait and wait for the opening graphic to appear only to be disappointed when the transfer fails. The latest Web application often is not accessible on older versions of Web browsers. In sum, know the technological capabilities and limitations of your audience when designing your site.

To begin the design process, spend some time examining the sites of other organizations on the Web. Decide what you like and what you do not like. Make a list of the features that you would want to see on your page (see Exhibits 7.2 and 7.3.). Use existing pages to give you an idea of what has been done and what can be done, both in terms of design and content. A site is intended to service its users; it is too easy for a disenchanted user to leave an organization's site, go elsewhere, and never return. Your goal is to foster repeat and loyal visitors. Judith Hengeveld of Bethany Christian Services put up a Web site to provide information about their organization and its services to anyone on the Internet. They already had a Gopher server but wanted to make the information easier to obtain and in a more presentable format. Without a doubt, the Web excels in its presentation ability.

If you want to learn more about site design and read analyses of what makes an exemplary site, visit the **David Siegel's High Five Excellence**

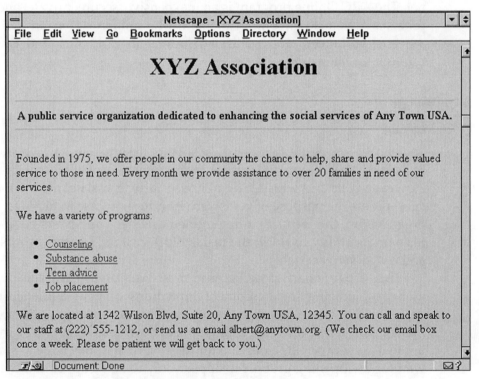

Exhibit 7.2 Simulation of a bare-bones Web page.

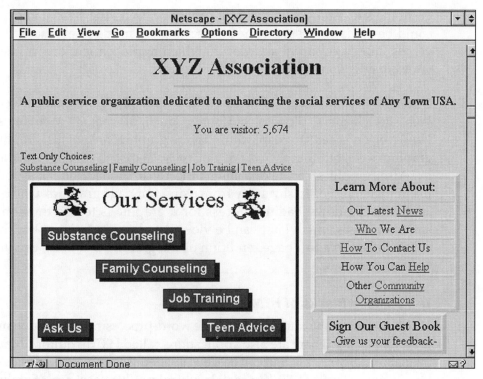

Exhibit 7.3 Simulation of an enhanced Web page.

in Site Design Web page [**http://highfive.com/**] where a new site is featured and analyzed every week. The site maintains an archive of past winners so that one can see the evolution of excellence in site design [**http://highfive.com/past_winners.html**]. There are many books available on Web design, such as two by John Wiley & Sons—*Web Page Cookbook* and *HTML Sourcebook.*

Hiring a Consultant versus Developing the Skills In-House. Should your organization hire a consultant to design your page or should you do it in-house? Learning HTML editing and designing a Web page is not difficult. As Daniel Lorenzetti wrote in his article ". . . The Big City" in the November/December 1995 (p. 9) issue of *On the Internet,* the official publication of the Internet Society, "HTML programming is not rocket science. In fact, it's easier to learn than most word processing programs . . . really." And yet, doing tasks in-house can be time consuming. Rather than learn a new computer application, many organizations hire a consultant to design and program the site. And yet, in the long run, developing the skills and expertise could be a wise investment. Your organization needs to evaluate the time versus money equation and decide which approach is more in line with your organization.

Graphics. Visual elements are essential to enhancing the look and feel of a Web site. Headers, pictures, buttons to push, all make a Web site shine. However, one needs to be mindful that the graphics are not just graphics for graphics sake, but that they serve a purpose in distributing information.

Also, graphics can take a long time to download, but this does not mean that one should shy away from using full page graphics. One trick to speed up the downloading process for a graphic is to use thumbnails—smaller images which later can be viewed as larger versions. The thumbnail is linked to a full page rendition of the graphic that users can view at their convenience.

The Building Blocks of HTML

HTML is not complicated and a simple word-processing application may be used for editing. There are also applications called HTML Editors. Many are available as Shareware and can be downloaded from the Web. HTML Assistant is one example **[FTP//ftp.cs.dal.ca/htmlasst/htmlasst.zip]** (Exhibit 7.4). It has a Windows feel, including push buttons, and allows the editor to test the site before uploading it. The best way to find shareware HTML editors is by executing a Web search with the keyword "HTML editor."

HTML was specifically designed for the Web. It is a universal, platform-independent language, which can be interpreted by any browser. Each browser may behave slightly differently, but the content is the same.

Tags. HTML is centered around *tags* (see Exhibit 7.4), which are greater than (<) and less than (>) signs. These tags are textual attributes for the browser. For example, the tag <B> tells the browser that the following text is to be bold. To end a command, a forward slash is inserted within the element </B>. The text between the two tags would then be bold.

For example, <B>Bold</B>words would appear in a browser as **Bold** words. It is recommended that tags be in capitals to allow them to be more easily identified.

Hyperlinks. *Hyperlinks* are necessary for joining the home page to other pages on the site and to other home pages. They are commands and are

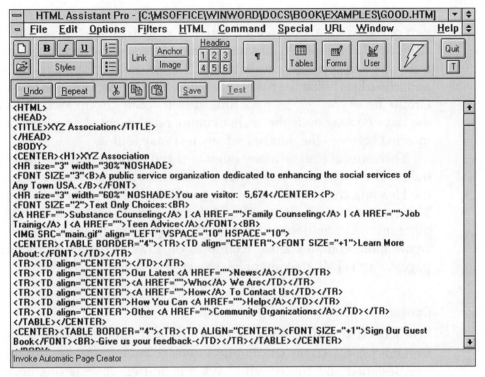

Exhibit 7.4 Exhibit 7.3 as an HTML document—HTML Assistant. *Reprinted with permission.*

surrounded by tags (see Exhibit 7.4). Hyperlinks contain the following elements:

<A HREF=" "> </A>

which can be utilized to create the hyperlink,

<A HREF="http://www.Zeff.com"> Zeff group</A>

Dissection of the command again demonstrates the straightforward nature of HTML. The "A" stands for anchor. It establishes the current location (the current Web address) as an anchor or starting point to another site. "HREF" is an attribute of the <A>. Attributes are combined with elements to specify properties of the command. In this case, the HREF attribute is telling the anchor to hyperlink to the Zeff Group home page.

The quotes contain the URL address for the Zeff Group. That is the first part of the command, and appropriately ends with the > symbol. The text "Zeff Group" is inserted and will be interpreted by the browser as a hyperlink, which the browser presents in a different color from the rest of the text and underlined. The user will then know that by clicking on the text, Zeff Group, he or she will be hyperlinked to the Zeff Group Web site. Finally, the last </A> tag ends the anchor command element. Any address may be inserted between the quotes and any text may follow.

There are, of course, many other tags and options. The <I> tag specifies italics. The <Hn> element, where *n* is a whole integer between 1 and 6, is the Heading command. It changes text size, similar to the font point size. There are numerous sites on the Web that contain HTML editing tips and other information. Books about HTML programming are also available to create more complex sites. Examples of a home page and hyperlinked pages as an HTML document are shown in Exhibit 7.4.

Content

"We looked at a lot of sites before we created ours," says Steve Durland, Co-Director of Art in the Public Interest, "and found that many were overdesigned and content shy." What is housed at your site, not merely what it looks like, will keep your audience coming back again and again. Consequently, one of the first steps in the design process is to decide what material to include in the site. Here is a list of topics to consider:

❑ Identity: Who you are—your mission statement, a listing or profiles of your staff.

❑ Programs and services: What you do—your programs, projects, meetings, seminars, conferences, and so on. What services you offer—technical assistance, counseling, information referral, and so on.

❑ Contact information: How you can be reached—address, e-mail address, phone numbers, office hours, and so on. If you have chapters or member organizations, how they can be reached.

❑ Available resources: What material you have available for free or for sale—newsletters, magazines, publications, T-shirts, posters, and so on.

❑ Current activities: What information you want to highlight—press releases, new reports, and so on.

❐ Links to related site.

❐ Help requests: What your needs are—donations of time, information, or money.

All this material will not be put on your home page. Your home page is merely the cover page menu for all the linked pages that make up your site.

You might want to begin the process by looking at your existing organizational outreach material and see what information it presents. A word of caution: Put this material aside as you write the text for your Web site. One of the mistakes the novice Web designer makes is to merely transfer material produced on paper to a cyberspace format. Different mediums require different composition and presentation styles.

Presenting Your Identity.   As previously mentioned, one of the strong points of a Web site is that it allows you to present your organization as you would like it to be presented. Moreover, you have the opportunity to provide as much information as you deem necessary in the format of your choice. This means you can have links to case statements concerning your work. Provide profiles of your staff with pictures and biographical material so that your clients get to know the staff members. You can use this as an opportunity to present your organization as a community of people with a shared sense of purpose. Many people who visit your site will be located outside the area and may not be familiar with your organization and your work. Therefore, this is your opportunity both to present your identity and strengthen your credibility.

Programs and Services.   One of the most important reasons to have a Web site is to inform the public of your programs and services. Your Web site is the perfect vehicle to get the word out about your projects, meetings, seminars, conferences, and so on. You can design a page for each of these activities that includes a summary of the program, an agenda, and photographs from previous events. Your Web site can be a brochure, flyer, and report all in one. However, as Susan Ellis of ENERGIZE, Inc. warns, "Web sites need to be different from printed forms of communication, yet most are deadly dull." The challenge is to make the site informative, visual and interactive all at the same time.

Equally important is that the material be current. Sites that have not been updated for several weeks are referred to as cobwebs. The key to a successful site is timeliness. Since the Web is accessible 24 hours a day, 7 days a week, a Web site needs to keep its information as current as possible or risk being a cobweb.

Contact Information.   Many visitors go to an organization's Web site in order to find out how to contact the group. You will need to provide the standard material of address, phone number, fax number, and e-mail address. In addition to your address, you might even include a map to your location if your office is difficult to find. The section titled Interactive Elements (p. 142) discusses how to use forms that make contacting your organization as easy as clicking a button.

If your organization has chapters or member organizations, you can have links to their Web pages. This encourages movement back and forth from their site to yours. It also shows affinity and unity. Some associations use the fact that they have links to their member organizations as a big selling point for their Web sites; this is a point greatly appreciated by the members.

Available Resources.   Your Web site is the perfect location to present the information you provide, whether it consists of reports and studies or newsletters and publications. You can have one page that lists all your resources and their availability—whether free or for a fee, whether downloadable or mail order only—and subsequent pages that feature selected resources. Lengthy documents are best in downloadable format only.

The next step is to decide what materials from the site you will provide full access to and what materials will be available for purchase only.

To encourage the purchase of your publications, you can put up abstracts of these documents with just enough information to whet the appetite, but not enough to make purchase of the documents unnecessary.

Highlighting Current Activities.   Another element of a good site is a link to a page that highlights your current activities. Included could be press releases, upcoming meetings, or the launching of a new program; this is an area where you can boast and feature your "hot" news.

Links to Related Sites.   One way to ensure that people will find your site is to establish links with other related sites. Most people surf the Internet by going from link to link. People find these links with search tools, from features on sites such as "what's new", "what's hot," or "what's cool" that link to interesting sites and from the links provided on other sites. The more links you have to other sites and other sites have to you, the more walk-through traffic your site will enjoy.

Perhaps the most important way to establish the nonprofit's on-line presence is by creating mutual links. A site dealing with clean water may have a link to a site concerned with marine life. Conversely, the marine life site would have a hyperlink to the clean water site. These links establish contacts and, in the most literal sense, networks. Users can travel throughout the Web visiting sites with similar interests. There can be numerous benefits to creating links. Many sites already exist and an organization may discover another nonprofit with similar goals. Coalitions are easily developed, and these types of links also logically organize the information on the Web by joining similar sites.

How Someone Can Help

Giving the visitor the opportunity to learn how to get involved in your organization can be the prelude to a donation of time, information, or money. A page on your site needs to address these requests boldly and aggressively. As discussed in Chapter 6, cyber-fundraising is an as yet untapped resource, and the programs now in place for the donation of time and money look extremely promising.

Each Page Has a Purpose.   In writing, just as each paragraph has a purpose, in Web design, each Web page should have a purpose. And this purpose is defined by the content.

The first page of a Web site is the home page. This is the place where first impressions are made and interest gained or lost. Regardless of the significance of information presented throughout the site, the home page is the welcome mat that invites users in and offers them fundamental instruction, information, and direction to successfully maneuver within the site.

In many ways, the purpose of the home page is to serve as a road map to all the material that lies within the site. In designing the home page remember the site's objective and the targeted audience. By viewing the home page, the user should quickly and easily be able to identify the organization, its purpose, and what's available on the site. Detailed information and excessive images should be left to linked pages. If the primary purpose of the site is to offer services, present those services with links to specific information. If soliciting members is key, concisely relate membership benefits and invite the user to take a closer look elsewhere in the site. Avoid the temptation to present all the information at once. Stick to the pre-established goals for the site and allow the home page to clearly and concisely illustrate them without overwhelming the viewer.

Interactive Elements

The Importance of Links.   As previously mentioned, one of the most popular techniques for surfing the Internet is to use links to trampoline from site to site. Links are the backbone of the Web and most sites have at least one link to a related site. The more links on your site, the more active the site becomes to the user. Just as you have links to other Web sites, encourage others to link to your site. You can do this by trading links; when you ask permission to link to a site, encourage that site to link to your site.

It is important to remember that sites come and go and one needs to check constantly to make certain that the links on your site are active. This can turn into quite a job if you have many other sites linked to your site. One alternative is to only link to the largest directory of links in your interest area. In return, you can ask the Webmaster of those sites to highlight your site in their list because of your exclusivity to those sites.

Know and Go.   A key element to any Web site is its interactivity with the user. Depending on the site's audience, the level of interactivity needs to accommodate the user's interests and purpose. For the most part, Web users trampoline quickly from site to site and frown on reading lengthy text or waiting for large graphics to download.

Ed Stern of the American Red Cross follows the three-click rule, "Information should never be more than three clicks away." The first click is from the home page to a general interest area. The second click is to a specific subject area, and the third click leads directly to the desired information. This interactivity provides the user the ability to *Know and Go—know* what is available on the site and be able to immediately *go* to that information via links.

Users enjoy any opportunity to interact with the site they are visiting. There are numerous features one can include on a site to enhance its interactiveness.

❑ *Forms.* A standardized form where the user has only to input the information and press the send button for that information to be submitted is popular on the Web. Forms allow users to provide personal information, answer questions, or offer an opinion. Forms are also a means to encourage the user to conduct an action such as signing a guest book (see Exhibit 4.3) or sending an e-mail to a member of Congress or even the President (see Exhibit 4.17) for signing on to a petition.

❏ *Counters.* One measure of the success of a site is knowing how many people visit the site (see Exhibit 7.5). A counter lets the visitor see the volume of traffic a site is receiving and registers the number of users (including the current user) who have visited the site from a specific date.

❏ *List of Visitors.* List the names of the last several users who have accessed the site. This gives the user an idea of the site's audience and makes the user feel part of the community of visitors.

In short, the site needs to look and feel appealing. Easy movement throughout the site is essential. It is important that every page includes a

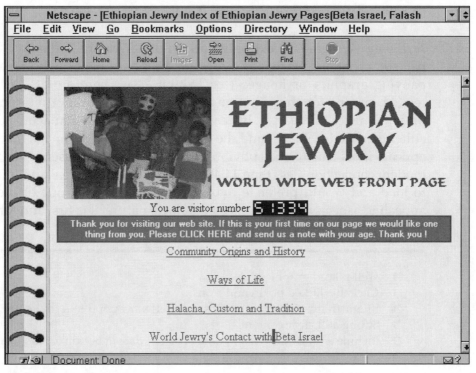

Exhibit 7.5 Counter—Ethiopian Jewry. *Reprinted with permission.*

link back to the home page. Clearly marked and defined links, often with graphical accompaniment, provide an exciting and inviting atmosphere for the user. (See Exhibits 7.6 and 7.7.)

Communicating with Users

An e-mail address for your organization must be present on the home page, even better if it appears on every page. For best results, the e-mail address should be included on a form that lets the user send a message to your organization. The form is linked directly to the mail message center so that the user can comment quickly and easily. The site's Webmaster should always be accessible via e-mail.

Guestbooks. A guestbook (see Exhibit 4.17) invites the user to sign in upon visiting a site. A guestbook may ask questions of new visitors to facilitate the gathering of user data. Valuable information may be collected during this process such as the user's name, e-mail address, street address, occupation, affiliation, and so on. The guestbook is a great technique for building an e-mail database, as was discussed at length in Chapter 4.

Text Only Versions. A text only version of a Web site refers to a linked page that contains the text of a page (or a series of pages) with no accompanying graphics or images (see Exhibit 7.3). There are at least three related reasons for this. First, many browsers still do not interpret and present images to the user. Instead, the place where the image belongs is either distorted or blank, and the time spent loading an image that never appears in its true form is obviously wasteful. Second, users with a slow modem connection (less than 14,400) often do not want to wait for images to load and would prefer to avoid them. Third, while one of the most appealing aspects of the Web is its graphical nature, it is first and foremost

---

❏ Well-placed graphics.
❏ Clickable linked boxes and icons.
❏ Interactivity: sign guestbook, send a letter, respond to a trivia quiz.
❏ Strong and clear content.
❏ Include e-mail address and date of last update at bottom of each page.

Exhibit 7.6 Positive Attributes in a Web Site.

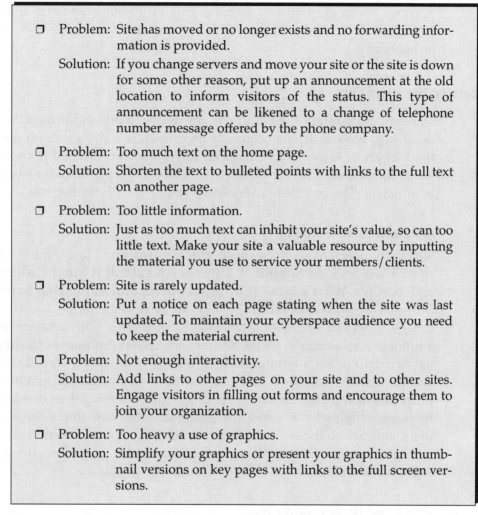

❒ Problem: Site has moved or no longer exists and no forwarding information is provided.

Solution: If you change servers and move your site or the site is down for some other reason, put up an announcement at the old location to inform visitors of the status. This type of announcement can be likened to a change of telephone number message offered by the phone company.

❒ Problem: Too much text on the home page.

Solution: Shorten the text to bulleted points with links to the full text on another page.

❒ Problem: Too little information.

Solution: Just as too much text can inhibit your site's value, so can too little text. Make your site a valuable resource by inputting the material you use to service your members / clients.

❒ Problem: Site is rarely updated.

Solution: Put a notice on each page stating when the site was last updated. To maintain your cyberspace audience you need to keep the material current.

❒ Problem: Not enough interactivity.

Solution: Add links to other pages on your site and to other sites. Engage visitors in filling out forms and encourage them to join your organization.

❒ Problem: Too heavy a use of graphics.

Solution: Simplify your graphics or present your graphics in thumbnail versions on key pages with links to the full screen versions.

Exhibit 7.7 Problems and Solutions to Web Site Weaknesses.

a resource. Many individuals prefer not to spend time waiting for the cosmetics to load up and would rather immediately begin their search for information.

Text only versions therefore can be important. Depending on the site's audience, it should be a consideration for the designer. Oftentimes, it is simply a matter of adapting the regular site into a text only version. In many cases, only certain sections of the site need to be changed for this purpose. As modem speeds increase and additional standards and commonality are reached regarding Web use, text only versions may no longer be necessary.

Getting the Word Out

Once you have established your site, the next step is to publicize it. Very little, if any, walk in traffic occurs. If no one knows you exist, no one will think or know to look for you. It's up to you to get connected to the cyberspace community. This can be done in a variety of ways. In fact, no one way is sufficient. The best Web awareness strategy is a diversified one.

Announcement Services

Site announcement services are specifically dedicated to announcing new sites. These include **Submit It [http://www.submit-it.com/]** (Exhibit 7.8) and NSCA's **What's New [http://www.nsca.uiuc.edu/SDG/Software/ Mosaic/Docs/whats-new.html]**. They all have registration forms which can be filled out and submitted. Most ask for the URL address, e-mail address, and the regular name, address, and phone number of the individual registering. Equally important is to have your site registered with the various search tools such as Lycos **[http://www.lycos.com]**, Webcrawler **[http://www.webcrawler.com]** and Yahoo **[http://www.yahoo.com]**. Search tools often highlight new and interesting sites. Because things are happening so quickly on the Internet, there is a backlog of requests and it can take several weeks for a site to be included in the index. Therefore, it is best to register immediately.

Press and On-line Coverage

Articles on the Internet are popular in the written press. Newspapers constantly highlight new and interesting Web sites. However, the benefit of these articles is subject when one is trying to stimulate hits to your site. For example, Impact Online received national press coverage for its Cookin' on the Net fund-raising campaign from such prominent newspapers as the *Los Angeles Times, Boston Globe,* and *San Francisco Chronicle*. These articles did not result in increased Web traffic. They received much more success with on-line advertising, according to Impact Online Co-Director Steve Glikman, such as an announcement on the Yahoo banner and a feature in

Exhibit 7.8 Site Announcement Services Submit It. *Reprinted with permission.*

the on-line publication *Hot Wired* [**http://www.hotwired.com**]. What this demonstrates is that the on-line world responds to on-line advertising.

Self Promotion

Equally important is to include your Web address on every and all outreach materials, from your business cards and letterhead to advertisements and publications.

Measures for Success

How do you determine the success of your site? Kimberly Adams of the Arts Foundation of Michigan judges their success by the number of hits the site receives. John Bancroft of the Office of Arid Lands Studies at the University of Arizona judges success by "both visitor feedback (which we encourage by way of forms and e-mail) and hits as measured by a hit counter." And John Longhurst of the Mennonite Central Committee measures success by the number of requests for information. Indeed, there are many means to measure success that are unique to cyberspace involvement.

Many begin their Internet experience using criteria for success pulled in from other media. How you determine if a brochure, a report, or even a campaign is successful is very different from how you determine the success or failure of a Web site. In fact, success may be a combination of factors as is the case at Macrocosm USA where Sandy Brockman determines success by a combination of the number of new memberships, the sales of their handbook, the responses to their offer to give away handbooks, and the hit counter.

Issues in Integrating Your Web Site into Your Organization

The decision to establish a presence on the World Wide Web is not only a commitment to putting up a site, but more importantly, a commitment to maintaining the site. A good site will grow continuously and become more accessible and extensive. Moreover, the Web itself is continually evolving; new sites and capabilities are constantly being introduced. Routine site maintenance is essential. In order to ensure that the site is always functioning and contemporaneous, every site needs a Webmaster. A Webmaster is the person responsible for the routine maintenance and updating of the site.

It is equally important to recognize that with the millions of people on the Internet, your site could result in a heavy load of requests for information and other staff-time demands. Your organization needs to take this into consideration so that your Internet presence is a positive organizational addition. Moreover, if requests for information, Internet generated sales, and other Internet traffic are not handled in a timely and professional manner, you will not reach the full potential that your Internet presence could achieve.

CHAPTER 8

Cyberspace Law for Nonprofits

Tova L. Zeff, Esq.

Tova L. Zeff, Esq. (t/z@sl.p.net), has her own practice in Northern California with an emphasis on business law and contracts, and is developing a practice relating to computers, software, and technology. Additionally, she provides legal advice to various nonprofit organizations, teaches at a small night law school in Oakland, CA, is a volunteer for the AIDS Legal Referral Panel, and also works for a legal publisher.

INTRODUCTION

This chapter will point out important legal issues that have arisen in relation to the Internet, especially as it relates to the issues and concerns of the nonprofit organization.

Although the Internet is not as new as one might think (see the section titled "Understanding the Internet" in Chapter 1), it is only in the past couple of years that there has been a complete explosion of interest in all things Internet. And, as always, it is only a matter of time between explosive and tremendous interest in any topic, and the subsequent regulation of the area both by the state and the federal government.

Lance Rose, in his very accessible book about Internet law entitled, *Netlaw: Your Rights in the Online World* (1995, McGraw Hill), lays low the concept that law in cyberspace should be compared to the law of the West. Rose points out that while the comparison may have made sense in the early 1990s, it no longer makes any sense at all. He further notes that online cultures have been mainly peaceable. In Chapter 4 of Rose's book titled "Dangers and Responsibilities in the Online World," he states:

> *The laws applicable to on-line affairs are not fully formed yet, of course, but this does not equate to any extension of the age of frontier justice.*

Today's earth-bound legislators and courts have most of the on-line world in their grip, even if they don't know quite what to do with it. The question is whether their control will be heavy handed, or compatible with the continuing vigorous development of on-line territories.

Essentially, this chapter will cover two points:

1. *Legal Issues for Nonprofits.* Assure that the nonprofit's actions will in no way threaten its nonprofit status. Additional regulation is on the horizon, and in the very near future Congress will be taking a look at the laws regulating nonprofits.

2. *Legal Issues for the Internet.* Make certain the nonprofit is aware of the legal issues that arise from participating in the Internet.

Whatever the laws are for activities regarding nonprofit organizations, and whether the legal issues relating to the Internet seem directly relevant, these laws do not exist in a vacuum, and the nonprofit is well advised to stay informed.

A selection of legal resources and sites on the Internet is included in Appendix A.

LEGAL ISSUES FOR NONPROFITS

In order to understand the legal issues that arise for nonprofits within the context of the Internet, one must first have at least a minimal understanding of the general legal issues for nonprofits. An excellent resource for legal issues surrounding nonprofits is *A Legal Guide to Starting and Managing A Nonprofit Organization Second Edition,* by Bruce E. Hopkins. (1993, New York: John Wiley). As discussed in Chapters 4 and 6 of this guide, fundraising and lobbying are two activities that nonprofits can make much use of on the Internet.

Fundraising

The regulation of fundraising, both at the federal and state level, is experiencing a great surge. Most governmental regulation of fundraising was initially at the state level. Many states have become very involved in the regulation of charitable solicitations by enacting charitable solicitation acts that impose laws and statutes on fundraising, and that impose registration, reporting, and other requirements on charities involved in the fundraising process. The federal government is now becoming greatly involved in the regulation of fundraising for charitable purposes, and this is being done largely through the tax laws and the various types of disclosures required of nonprofits for securing tax-exempt status from the IRS and for reporting obligations imposed on charitable organizations.

It appears that nonprofits are headed in the direction of more rather than fewer limits imposed on them by the legislators and regulators. Nonprofits are well-advised to stay informed as to the state of the regulations that affect them. They can do this by interacting with grass-roots resources; participating in activities that affect public opinion on fundraising and the regulation of fundraising in general; and finally, by engaging in self-education on the basics of the laws that regulate them. A comprehensive source of information regarding fundraising is *Fund-Raising Regulation: A State-By-State Handbook of Registration Forms, Requirements, and Procedures*, by Seth Perlman and Betsy Hills Bush (1996, New York: John Wiley).

Lobbying

Nonprofit corporations are granted their tax exempt status under Internal Revenue Service Code §501(c)(3). Under this rule, no 501(c)(3) tax exempt public charity may engage in lobbying as a *substantial* part of its total activities. Lobbying is broadly construed as any activity by the organization designed to influence the outcome of legislation at any political level. The principal laws regulating lobbying by nonprofits are the tax laws. The regulation of this area has been very active. In 1987, Congress introduced new rules in an effort to further limit lobbying by charitable organizations and other nonprofit organizations. In addition, the IRS and the Treasury Department have recently issued regulations in a renewed effort to curb lobbying both by public charities and by related organizations.

Other federal regulations impose serious constraints on lobbying by nonprofits, including restrictions under which the U.S. Postal Service will not grant second- and third-class mail privileges to otherwise qualifying nonprofits whose primary purpose is lobbying. Additionally, under the Federal Regulation of Lobbying Act, lobbying organizations and individual lobbyists are required to register with the clerks of both the House of Representatives and the Senate.

INTERNET LEGAL ISSUES

The UCLA Online Institute for Cyberspace Law and Policy has described this area of the law as the law that, "typically encompasses all cases, statutes, and constitutional provisions that impact persons and institutions when they go 'on-line' and enter cyberspace."

As this law evolves, several distinct components of cyberspace law have emerged: jurisdiction and related issues, freedom of expression, intellectual property, privacy, safety (cybercrimes), equal access concerns, and electronic commerce. It is easy to see how cyberspace law will directly affect the nonprofit once it goes on-line and enters cyberspace, regardless of the fact that nonprofits have not been specifically singled out. A brief description of each area follows.

Jurisdiction and Related Issues

Jurisdiction in cyberspace will become a key issue, given the national and international nature of the Internet. Venue and personal jurisdiction will need to be determined for acts committed in cyberspace. Venue is the particular geographical area in which a court with jurisdiction may hear and determine a case. Personal jurisdiction is the power that a court has over the defendant's person and that is required before a court can enter a personal judgment. This jurisdiction may be obtained by an act of the defendant within a jurisdiction under a law by which the defendant implies consent to the personal jurisdiction of the court. For instance, the operation of a motor vehicle on the highways of a state confers jurisdiction of the operator and owner of the vehicle on the courts of that state.

It has yet to be determined whose law applies to acts committed in cyberspace. One unresolved question is whether communications in cyberspace are controlled either by the laws of the country and state where the transmission originated, the laws where the Internet service provider is located (which could differ from the point of transmission), or the laws where the transmission is received, or by all of these laws.

Freedom of Expression

The First Amendment of the U.S. Constitution requires that:

Congress shall make no law respecting an establishment of religion, or prohibiting the free exercise thereof; or abridging the freedom of speech or of the press; or the right of the people peaceably to assemble, and to petition the Government for a redress of grievances.

According to authors Edward A. Cavazos and Gavino Morin, in their book, *Cyberspace and the Law: Your Rights and Duties in the On-Line World*, (1994, Cambridge: MIT Press), most of the messages that are conveyed in cyberspace qualify for First Amendment protection under the U.S. Constitution. Indeed, it should be true that the First Amendment assures that users of on-line systems can communicate freely with one another because it is so broadly stated.

It has been determined by the Supreme Court that the guarantee of freedom of speech and freedom of the press clause covers a broad range of communication activities that extend beyond the spoken word and include artistic expression, writing, and other activities that convey ideas. Authors Cavazos and Morin further state that most of the activities in which a person spending time in cyberspace would engage would appear to qualify as protected First Amendment activities. *Cubby, Inc. v. CompuServe, Inc.*, 776 F.Supp 135 (S.D.N.Y 1991) is the current leading case on First Amendment protection of on-line services. In *Sable Communications of California, Inc. v. FCC*, 492 U.S. 115, 109 S.Ct. 2829, 106 L.Ed. 2d 93 (1989), the Supreme Court struck down an earlier version of dial-a-porn law, and in its decision, demonstrated the necessary balancing between the First Amendment and the goal of protecting children from indecent materials.

The First Amendment protects citizens from the federal government, and the Fourteenth Amendment extends this protection to cover acts of state and local governments. The U.S. Constitution does not prohibit acts by private citizens that might abridge the right of free speech. Instead, the First Amendment prohibits government officials and agents, and no one else, from violating the right of free speech.

On February 8, 1996, President Clinton signed into law the 1996 Telecommunications Act, a sweeping telecommunications reform bill. The signing of this bill put to rest a long legislative fight over the contents of the bill itself, but ignited an important battle over the issue of free speech on the Internet. The new law revamps the 1934 Communications Act, and allows local and long-distance phone companies and cable companies into each others' businesses, deregulates cable rates and allows media companies to expand their holdings more easily. Also included in the new law is the Communications Decency Act, which imposes civil and criminal penalties for knowingly making indecent material available to children over computer networks.

Shortly after the bill was signed, the American Civil Liberties Union, the Electronic Frontier Foundation (EFF), and many other organizations and individual plaintiffs, most of them on-line content producers, filed suit in the United States District Court for the Eastern District of Pennsylvania to block the censorship provisions of the 1996 Telecommunications Act by seeking an immediate temporary injunction blocking these provisions, saying they were unconstitutional and would cause irreparable harm to First Amendment free speech rights if allowed to take effect. This lawsuit represents the most serious test to date of the federal government's ability to control the rapidly expanding boundaries of cyberspace. At issue is the determination of exactly what type of medium the Internet should be considered; whether cyberspace should be treated as a broadcast medium such as television, and therefore subject to regulation by the Federal Communications Commission, or whether cyberspace should enjoy broader First Amendment protections.

Under the clause at issue, the Communications Decency Act of 1996, a person convicted of making available indecent material to a minor faces $100,000 in fines and up to five years in prison. The penalty for transmitting or receiving abortion-related information, is $250,000 in fines and five years in prison.

According to a press release issued by EFF on February 7, 1996, the complaint in the lawsuit contains three basic arguments for declaring the Communications Decency Act of 1996 unconstitutional.

1. *Unconstitutional Expansion of Federal Authority.* It is inappropriate for the Federal Communications Commission or any other federal agency to dictate standards for content in a medium where there is no independent constitutional justification for federal regulation, as there has been in the broadcast arena and in certain narrow areas of voice telephone service. Like newspapers and bookstores, the Internet is fully protected by the First Amendment.

2. *Vagueness and Overbreadth.* The terms the act relies on—"indecency" and "patently offensive"—have never been positively defined by the Supreme Court or by Congress, and so create uncertainty as to the scope of the restrictions, necessarily resulting in a "chilling effect" on protected speech. Moreover, these terms criminalize broad classes of speech that are understood to be protected by the First Amendment, including material that has serious scientific, literary, artistic, political, and cultural value.

3. *Failure to Use the "Least Restrictive Means" to Regulate Speech.* Even if there were Constitutional authority for this legislation and even if its terms were neither overly broad nor vague, the censorship prescriptions built into this legislation cannot survive the Supreme Court's "least restrictive means" test. That is, if otherwise-legal government regulation of speech content does not minimize its restriction of lawful speech, it fails to qualify as the "least restrictive means" of implementing the government's goal. Our Bill of Rights requires that such regulations be struck down. In addition to these traditional First Amendment challenges, the lawsuit also challenges a provision that may infringe on speech concerning abortion when that speech takes place on-line. In the case of the Internet, the censorship provisions of the Telecommunications Reform Act are not the least restrictive means, since filtering, rating and labeling technologies and services are already available. There already are software tools to help parents shield their children from inappropriate material and these tools are vastly more flexible and effective than this ill-considered legislation. Unlike the censorship provisions, these tools prevent harm to children before it happens.

Government attorneys were given one week to file a written argument in response to the ACLU lawsuit. After a subsequent hearing, the United States District Court Judge issued a temporary restraining order against enforcement of certain provisions of the Communications Decency Act (CDA). The Justice Department agreed not to enforce any of the challenged portions of the CDA until after the decision in the injunction trial, set to take place in April 1996 in front of a three-judge panel in Philadelphia. Closing arguments in the injunction trial will be presented in May 1996. The three-judge panel will likely issue its decision within one month after the injunction trial, and appeals of the decision will go directly to the United States Supreme Court.

There are certain types of speech that can be restricted by the government, because it has been determined that the harm caused by these particular types of "speech" outweigh the value of allowing the speaker to go unpunished. These categories include: clear and present danger (where a communication is used to advocate illegal, dangerous, or violent activity), fighting words (where a communication is so offensive and abusive that it is likely to cause or incite immediate physical retaliation by the recipient of the communication), defamation (where a person's reputation is harmed by false and damaging statements, slander if spoken and libel if written), obscenity and child pornography (material deemed legally obscene and child pornography receive no First Amendment protection at all), and false or deceptive advertising (false and deceptive advertisements can be regulated because of the potential harm to the public through such misrepresentations).

Intellectual Property

The extent to which traditional intellectual property concepts apply in cyberspace is a subject of continuing debate among legal scholars and practitioners. Patent law, trademark, and trade secret laws are relevant to cyberspace, but it is copyright law that continues to receive the most attention. This may be true because so much of the material found on-line and in networks is copyrightable, from text files, to image files, and software.

There appears to be a casual attitude among Internet users toward copying because the ease of copying makes it easy to forget that copyrighted material on the Internet is protected by the same copyright law as in the rest of the world. Authors Cavazos and Morin note that "with the vast powers of digital connectivity, instantaneous duplication and distribution of someone else's work is easier today than ever before. . . . Never before has an individual been able to distribute his or her own work more readily to such a wide audience."

In the area of copyright law, several basic questions arise:

❏ What is copyrightable?
❏ What protections are given to copyright holders?
❏ What constitutes infringement of copyright?
❏ What are the liabilities for such infringement?
❏ What is considered fair use of copyrighted material?

U.S. copyright laws protect the expression of ideas, but not the underlying ideas. Copyright protection extends to: (1) original works of authorship, that are (2) fixed in a tangible medium of expression. 17 U.S.C. §102(a). Copyright issues are abundant in cyberspace, largely because almost everything communicated on a network, an on-line service, or a BBS is subject to copyright protection.

Virtually all on-line communication is an expression that has been fixed in a tangible medium, as defined by copyright law. Authors of e-mail automatically hold a copyright in their words, even if the copyright notice has not been attached to the e-mail declaring ownership, unless the person posting a message to a newsgroup relinquishes all claims to that posting. Digital image files are protected by a copyright held by the creator of the image, unless the author has specifically waived ownership rights in the image. As a result of the recommendations of the CONTU Commission, in 1980 Congress expressly amended the 1976 Copyright Act to provide that software be treated as a "literary work." *Apple Computer, Inc. v. Formula Int'l, Inc.*, 725 F.2d 521 (9th Cir. 1984).

Copyright protection may be obtained for: literary works; musical works, including any accompanying words; dramatic works, including any accompanying music; pantomimes and choreographic works; pictorial, graphic and sculptural works; motion pictures and other audiovisual works; sound recordings; and architectural works.

Copyright protection does not extend to any idea, procedure, process, system, method of operation, concept, principle, or discovery, regardless of the form in which it is described, explained, illustrated, or embodied in such work. 17 U.S.C. §102(b). In *Feist Publications, Inc. v. Rural Telephone Co.* 449 U.S. 340, 111 S.Ct. 1282, 113 L.Ed. 2d 358 (1991), the Supreme Court held that there can be no copyright in facts, or fact databases, unless there is original selection, coordination, or arrangement of the facts.

The owner of a copyright is granted the exclusive right to do and authorize any of the following (subject to the first sale doctrine): to reproduce the copyrighted work in copies or phonorecords, to prepare derivative works based upon the copyrighted work, to distribute copies or phonorecords of the copyrighted work to the public by sale or other transfer of ownership, or by rental, lease, or lending; in the case of literary, musical, dramatic, and choreographic works, pantomimes, and pictorial, graphic, or sculptural works, including images of a motion picture and other audiovisual work, to display the copyrighted work publicly. 17 U.S.C. §106.

In October, 1995, bills were introduced in the House and the Senate to amend 17 U.S.C. §106 to add the exclusive right of electronic "transmission" to the list of copyright owners' rights of distribution. "Transmission" would be defined as a reproduction "by any device or process whereby a copy or phonorecord of the work is fixed beyond the place from which it was sent." S. 1284, 104th Cong., 1st Sess (1995); H.R. 2441, 104th Cong., 1st Sess. (1995).

A "multimedia work" refers to a work that incorporates more than one form of media, and can include film, video, text, audio, photographs, graphics, and animation, and is typically stored in digital form. Multimedia works will generally be characterized as "derivative works" under the Copyright Act because they are based on preexisting works. 17 U.S.C. §101. The copyright protection of a derivative work or compilation will extend only to the material contributed by the author of such work and will not grant rights in the preexisting works included in the new work. 17 U.S.C. §103. With multimedia works, it becomes important to obtain permission for use of each aspect of the work that has been obtained. Typically, the rights to each prior work included in a multimedia work are owned by different authors and additionally, since each of the rights included in copyright ownership may be separately licensed, several entities may hold exclusive licenses to different forms of the same work. Issues of clearance with multimedia works can therefore be very complex and must be properly addressed.

Authors may transfer away a portion of their rights in a work by licensing their copyright. Licensing must be set forth in a licensing agreement in writing, and authors cannot license away more than they actually own. The most common form of a legal licensing arrangement found in cyberspace may be software that is marketed as shareware. This has become increasingly popular as a marketing and distributing tool for independent software authors and small publishers. Users of shareware have the right to make a copy of the software program for a trial use, and if they want to continue using the program, the shareware licensing agreement will require the user to register the program with the author, usually by sending in a registration fee.

Authors may also explicitly state that they want their work to enter the public domain. In this instance, there are no restrictions at all on the distribution, duplication, or any other manipulation of the work. It should be noted that the lack of a copyright notice on any type of work, including software, does not mean that a piece of software is in the public domain.

A copyright is considered "infringed" when someone other than the copyright owner exercises any one of the copyright owner's exclusive rights. In order to prevail in a copyright infringement action, the owner must prove: (1) ownership of a valid copyright, and (2) infringement of the copyright by the defendant. The Federal District Court in *Grand Upright Music v. Warner Brothers*, 780 F.Supp. 182 (S.D.N.Y. 1991) held that the use of a small, digitized sample of a pop song within a hiphop song can constitute copyright infringement.

Once a plaintiff has successfully demonstrated that an infringement has taken place, several types of damages may be awarded. "Actual" damages are used to compensate the copyright owner for the harm caused by the infringement and requires the plaintiff to prove the specific damages caused by the wrongful use of his or her work. If a work was registered prior to the infringement, then a plaintiff need not show actual damage to recover. Statutory damages are set out in the Copyright Act and alleviate the burden of demonstrating actual damages. These damages can include statutory damages of up to $100,000 per infringement for "willful" action, as well as payment of attorney's fees of the copyright owner.

Fair use is a complete defense to copyright infringement. 17 U.S.C. §107. This defense applies where a work is used "for purposes such as criticism, comment, news reporting, teaching . . . scholarship or research." *Id.* When evaluating whether the fair use defense is available, courts must consider the following: (1) the purpose and character of the use, including whether such use is of a commercial nature or is for nonprofit educational purposes; (2) the nature of the work; (3) the amount and substantiality of the portion used in relation to the copyrighted work as a whole; and (4) the effect of the use upon the potential market for or value of the copyrighted work. *Id.* When an alleged copyright infringer asserts the fair use defense, the judge or jury will consider each of the four above-mentioned concerns and weigh them against the right of the author or creator of the work. It should be noted that using someone else's work for commercial purposes is less likely to be considered fair use than using the work for nonprofit or academic purposes.

Another issue that falls under the heading of intellectual property is domain names (see Chapter 2 for a full discussion on domain names). Networks Solutions, Inc. (NSI), a private, nongovernment organization, is responsible for assigning second-level domain names for InterNic. These domain names are registered by NSI on a first-come, first-served basis, and effective October 1, 1995, NSI began charging $100 for each new domain registration and $50 per year to maintain domain names in all but the "mil" and "int" domains. In July 1995, NSI issued a policy statement which would limit the potential abuses of domain name registration and resolve conflicts where more than one party claimed rights to a given domain name. The Policy Statement was then revised effective November 23, 1995, in part to delete the word "resolution" from the title of the Policy Statement.

In an attempt to discourage the acquisition of domain names obtained merely to block future registrants, applicants for domain names must certify they have the intention to use the domain name on a regular basis on the Internet, and that the proposed name "does not interfere or infringe the right of any third party in any jurisdiction with respect to trademark, service mark, trade name, company name, or any other intellectual property right . . ."

The NSI reserves the right to force a domain name registrant to give up any domain name that is not regularly used during any 3-month period. Additionally, the policy statement provides NSI with the right to withdraw a name from use or registration if it is presented with an order from an arbitration panel chosen by the parties or from a United States court that a domain name rightfully belongs to another party.

Privacy

There is an implied right of privacy in the U.S. Constitution, and in some states, including Alaska, California, Hawaii, Illinois, and Washington, there is an express privacy right. Privacy rights may arise in the context of the workplace and in the home, particularly in the area of privacy of e-mail messages, as well as in tortious acts, including public disclosure of private facts, misappropriation, wrongful intrusion, and trade secrets.

One particular area that has received much attention is the privacy rights in an e-mail communication. In this context, the privacy rights of e-mail users may be pitted against workplace surveillance, but the users' privacy rights will always be balanced against the right of employers to their businesses. A critical issue when employees complain that their privacy rights have been violated is whether the employee actually has an "expectation of privacy" in e-mail sent at the workplace. Companies are well advised to formulate and communicate a clear policy regarding their e-mail systems that informs employees that the e-mail system is for business use and that e-mail messages may be subject to review. Though not officially published, two potentially important cases in California have refused to recognize e-mail privacy rights: *Bourke v. Nissan Motor Corp.*, No. B068705 (Cal.App. 2d Dist., Div. 5, 1993), and *Shoars v. Epson America, Inc.*, No. B073234 (Cal.App. 2d Dist., Div. 2, 1993). A recent case in the District Court of Pennsylvania held that an at-will employee had no privacy interest in transmitting messages on his employer's e-mail system. *Smyth v. Pillsbury Co.*, 914 F.Supp. 97 (E.D. Pa. 1996).

There is also the consideration of privacy rights in users of e-mail communications in the nonworkplace environment, including the privacy rights of users that coexist with the rights and responsibilities of system providers. At least one case has held that e-mail sent from or received on a home computer will be considered private. In *United States v. Maxwell* (U.S.

Air Force Crim. App. 1995) 42 M.J. 568, the U.S. Air Force Court of Criminal Appeals upheld the defendant's court martial conviction, but also held that the Electronic Communications Privacy Act applies to e-mail transmissions. The Court found that defendant had an objective expectation of privacy in e-mail messages stored in America Online's computers, which he alone could retrieve via his personal password, as well as in e-mail transmitted to other America Online subscribers who had their own individually assigned passwords.

There has been much debate on the use of "encryption" for e-mail transmissions as a form of Internet security. Encryption is the process of converting data into an incomprehensible code through the use of algorithms to increase the security of e-mail messages sent over the Internet.

Additionally, people have the right not to be "injured" when they enter cyberspace, and these rights tend to arise initially in the context of privacy and criminal issues. Included among these privacy rights is the right not to be libeled or defamed by other on-line users, the right not to have on-line materials stolen or damaged by others, and the right not to have your computer damaged by intentionally placed harmful files that have been downloaded (e.g., viruses).

Safety—Cybercrime

The legal issues that arise in this context concern computer fraud and abuse, credit card abuse, federal wiretapping. With criminal issues being raised, Fourth Amendment protections against "unreasonable searches and seizures" come into play, and in particular, the search and seizure rules applicable to electronic communications services or publishers. Other legal issues dealing with criminal acts include the areas of cyberstalking, cybertheft, hacking, and obscenity and child pornography.

Criminal laws can be divided into two categories: substantive and procedural laws. The substantive laws define and make illegal certain illegal activities. Computer-specific laws are included in this category: the Federal Computer Fraud and Abuse Act, the Counterfeit Access Device Act, and many state computer crime laws. Other criminal laws, although not specific to "computer crime," also apply in this context, including laws against gambling, wire fraud laws, laws against stealing credit card codes, and laws against obscenity.

The procedural rules put limits on the activities of law enforcement officials. These laws are found in the U.S. Constitution and other statutes, both federal and state, and case law. These laws and rules include the Electronic

Communications Privacy Act, federal and state rules and statutes which spell out search and seizure and warrant requirements, the requirements for an arrest and for seizing and retaining evidence obtained in a search.

Equal Access

The issue of equal access is probably the newest legal issue in cyberspace. This issue brings up the nature and the extent of the right to retrieve information from the Internet, as well as the problems inherent in providing equal access to cyberspace for public school children, and others.

Electronic Commerce

Electronic commerce is emerging as another legal issue in cyberspace as more and more business is being conducted on the Internet. Commercial transactions in cyberspace necessitate an examination of electronic contracts under common law contract principles and the Uniform Commercial Code. The Uniform Commercial Code (U.C.C.) is one of the Uniform Laws drafted by the National Conference of Commissioners on Uniform State Laws governing commercial transactions. The U.C.C. has been adopted by all states, except Louisiana.

Almost every business transaction that takes place in cyberspace involves a question of contract law. This is true because contracts form the basis of most business transactions, and are used to create a form of security in commercial transactions so that consumers have something to rely on other than the good faith of the parties with whom they deal commercially.

The January 1996 issue of *Upside,* a publication concerned with the investment and financial side of computer-related high tech industries, with a focus on on-line issues, contained an article by Howard Anderson entitled, "Showdown over E-cash." In this article, Anderson states that "the old-line banking industry and new technology powerhouses will be fighting like cats and dogs over the control of electronic cash. Potentially one of the biggest Internet-related markets, e-cash will be driven by transactions, and dominated by the companies that can deliver the needed speed, convenience and security." Anderson further states that, "the hidden agenda of the internet is transactions. The superstructure of transactions will be a new form of money—electronic cash, or e-cash."

There are very high stakes involved with the possibilities of transferring money, and even property, through cyberspace. Financial laws regarding the use of credit cards for purchases and charitable contributions on-line, and other forms of electronic banking are in the development stages. It goes without saying, however, that financial institutions are most interested in developing the procedures and the laws to allow people to conduct transactions on-line.

IN WHAT DIRECTION IS INTERNET LAW HEADING?

In an insightful law review article, Professor Trotter Hardy of the College of William and Mary School of Law, set forth his theories as to how the law should be applied to the Internet (Hardy, Trotter, "The Proper Legal Regime for 'Cyberspace'." 55 *University of Pittsburgh Law Review* 993 (1994). Professor Hardy posed a two-part question: "Does the existence of wide-spread computer-assisted communication—cyberspace—really raise novel legal issues? Or does it raise the same issues that lawyers have had to grapple with for decades, only in a different medium?"

In this well-reasoned article, Professor Hardy offers several conclusions about these questions. He concludes that "popular concern over the legal questions of cyberspace arises in some instances when, in fact, there is no 'new' issue worth discussing. A more important conclusion, however, is that many of the circumstances of cyberspace do indeed give rise to new legal questions." When a new legal issue arises in cyberspace, Hardy suggests that a prompt and specific legislation or regulation may be called for to bring immediate clarity to that problem. But statutory regulation is only one of many possible responses to new legal questions. Professor Hardy suggests that case law will be another response to new issues, and there are other mechanisms through which individuals may regulate their conduct, including contracts, private associations, and by custom.

CONCLUSION

In conclusion, it is recommended that nonprofit organizations continue paying attention to the laws that do exist, and to the legal issues described within this chapter. In other words, nonprofits are well-advised to stay informed and keep informed as to the growing and changing status of the law.

Internet Resources
for the Nonprofit

The following is a list of information on the Internet of particular interest and relevancy to the nonprofit community. It is divided into seven main categories: Resources and Services for Nonprofits, Fundraising, Government and Related Sites, Educational and Related Sites, Commercial Service, General Internet Resources, and Web Sites Featured in Guide. The entrees are presented in alphabetical order by site name, and include the site URL and a brief description.

Most of the sites are on the World Wide Web. Some, however, are FTP, Gopher sites, or Usenet newsgroups. All of the sites were active and accessible as of this printing. However, the Internet is dynamic and oftentimes sites change locations. If a URL will not work, attempt a search with search tools using the site's or organization's name. If that is unsuccessful, try a search by subject focusing on topics or language mentioned in the annotation.

A-1 Resources and services for nonprofits

❒ Directories

❒ Technical assistance

❒ Periodicals and newsletters

❒ Volunteer information

A-2 Fundraising

❒ Foundations and grantmaking organizations

Foundations

Government funding programs

In-kind

❒ Resources

❒ Corporate

Indices

Fortune 500 Companies

A-3 Government and related sites

❒ Directories

❒ Federal government and related sites

❒ State and local government and related sites

❒ Legal resources

❒ Armed Forces

A-4 Educational and related sites

A-5 Commercial services

A-6 General Internet resources

❒ Browsers

❒ HTML editors

❒ Information access and technology organizations

❒ Internet Service Providers

❒ Reference material

❒ Search tools

❒ Site announcements

❒ Technical assistance

A-7 Web sites featured in guide

RESOURCES AND SERVICES FOR NONPROFITS

Directories

Communications Policy Project-Cyber pages: Resources on the Internet
Web Address: http://cdinet.com/Benton/Cyber/links.html
E-mail Address: benton-webmaster@cdinet.com
Description: This Web site is designed to be an indication of the emerging National Information Infrastructure and includes a selection of nonprofit sites on the Internet.
Site Includes: directory.

Guide to Internet Resources for Nonprofit Public Service Organizations
Web Address: http://www.sils.umich.edu/~nesbeitt/nonprofits/nonprofits.html
E-mail Address: public-services@umich.edu
Description: A very comprehensive downloadable guide to Internet resources for nonprofits.
Site Includes: directory.

Impact Online
Web Address: http://www.impactonline.org/
E-mail Address: info@impactonline.org
Description: Organization dedicated to helping people connect and get involved with nonprofits through on-line technology. Provides Internet access to non-profits.
Site Includes: volunteer links, profiles of nonprofit organizations, technology course for nonprofits.

Internet Nonprofit Center
Web Address: http://www.human.com/inc/
E-mail Address: clandesm@panix.com
Description: Web site provides information to donors and volunteers about non-profits.
Site Includes: library and directory of and for nonprofits.

Internet Resources For Not-For-Profits In Housing, Health and Human Services
Web Address: http://www.duke.edu/~ptavern/housing.html
E-mail Address: munn@interaccess.com
Description: Directory of resources available on the Web dealing with housing, health and human services.
Site Includes: document.

Latino Web Nonprofit Organizations
Web Address: http://www.catalog.com/favision/non.htm

E-mail Address: not available
Description: Directory of Latino, Hispanic and other nonprofit related sites.
Site Includes: directory.

Netherlands Business School - Management of Public and Nonprofit Organizations
Web Address: http://www.nijenrode.nl/nbr/public/
E-mail Address: duparaq@nijenrode.nl
Description: Directory of select nonprofit organizations.
Site Includes: directory.

Nonprofit Information Center
Web Address: http://www.silcom.com/~paladin/nonprofits.html
E-mail Address: Paladin@PaladinGroup.com
Description: Hyperlinks to nonprofit resources on the Internet.
Site Includes: directory.

Nonprofit Resources Catalogue
Web Address: http://www.clark.net/pub/pwalker/
E-mail Address: pwalker@clark.net
Description: Sponsored and developed by Phillip A. Walker, it is a comprehensive guide to on-line nonprofit activity and resources.
Site Includes: directory.

Political Activism Resources
Web Address: http://www.kimsoft.com/kimpol.htm
E-mail Address: info@kimsoft.com
Description: Detailed and diverse list of political activist resources available on-line.
Site Includes: directory.

Putnam Barber's Resources for Nonprofits
Web Address: http://www.eskimo.com/~pbarber/
E-mail Address: pbarber@eskimo.com
Description: Contains news and hyperlinks of resources for nonprofits.
Site Includes: directory.

River Project
Web Address: http://www.mtn.org/
E-mail Address: mtn@mtn.org
Description: Internet node sponsored by the Minneapolis Telecommunications Network which also helps nonprofits get on-line.
Site Includes: directory.

Select Nonprofit Organizations on the Internet
Web Address: http://www.ai.mit.edu/people/ellens/non.html
E-mail Address: ellens@ai.mit.edu

Description: A list of nonprofit organizations on the Internet.
Site Includes: directory.

Teleport Directory of Nonprofits
Web Address: http://www.teleport.com/~sparking/directory.shtml
E-mail Address: not available
Description: Alphabetical directory of nonprofits.
Site Includes: directory.

Technical Assistance

Aspen Institute
Web Address: http://www.aspeninst.org/Index.html
E-mail Address: wdwright@aspeninst.org
Description: Public policy organization concerned with the issue of leadership in today's world whose programs include seminars and trainings for businesses, governments and nonprofits worldwide.
Site Includes: current events and programs.

Communications as Engagement
Web Address: http://www.cdinet.com/Mill/
E-mail Address: not available
Description: The Millennium Report to the Rockefeller Foundation on communications strategies for community revitalization. This is a collection of documents regarding the economics of the Internet, information goods, and related issues.
Site Includes: project information, the Report, and resource listing.

Contact Center Network
Web Address: http://www.contact.org/contact.htm
E-mail Address: info@contact.org
Description: Community based regional centers established to aid individuals and organizations with personal, social and environmental problems.
Site Includes: program and services information.

Council for Public Media
Web Address: http://www.utexas.edu/depts/output/www/cpm.html
E-mail Address: cmbg@mail.utexas.edu
Description: Organization which serves as a resource, clearinghouse and training center about all forms of news media for nonprofits.
Site Includes: program information.

Handsnet on the Web
Web Address: http://www.igc.apc.org/handsnet/
E-mail Address: hninfo@handsnet.org

Description: National nonprofit network promoting collaboration, information sharing and advocacy on a broad range of public interest issues among individuals and organizations. Also operates commercial on-line service for nonprofit community.

Site Includes: news and program information.

Human Factor

Web Address: http://www.human.com/

E-mail Address: humans@human.com

Description: Business dedicated to helping individuals use the Internet. Also provides free pages to nonprofits doing worthwhile work.

Site Includes: program information and links.

Human Services Institute

Web Address: http://www.infi.net/~sillsh/

E-mail Address: sillsh@infi.net

Description: Organization dedicated to helping communities, nonprofits, government related agencies, religious congregations and coalitions through research, consulting and training services.

Site Includes: project information and links.

Independent Sector

Web Address: http://www.indepsec.org/

E-mail Address: not available

Description: A national nonprofit coalition of corporate, foundation and voluntary organization members with national interest and impact in philanthropic and voluntary issues.

Site Includes: program information.

Minority On-line Information Service

Web Address: http://web.fie.com/web/mol/

E-mail Address: molis-m@fedic.fie.com

Description: Web site offers information about Minority Institutions, Federal Opportunities for minorities, Historically Black Colleges and Universities, scholarship and Fellowship information as well as other minority related information.

Site Includes: directory of information.

National Center for Nonprofit Boards (NCNB)

Gopher address: gopher://ncnb.org:7002/

E-mail Address: ncnb@ncnb.org

Description: National organization dedicated to improving the effectiveness of nonprofits through the development of programs and services for their boards of directors.

Site Includes: FAQ's, publications, and program and membership information.

Organic Online: Nonprofit Organizations
Web Address: http://www.organic.com/Home/Info/non.profits.html
E-mail Address: www@organic.com
Description: Company which provides consulting, Web site development and other on-line services for nonprofits.
Site Includes: company services and information.

Public Service Curriculum Exchange
Web Address: http://cases.pubaf.washington.edu/0c:/center.html/
E-mail Address: cascade@cases.pubaf.washington.edu
Description: Web site serves as a network to transfer information between public policy and management faculty throughout the United States.
Site Includes: program information.

RAIN (Regional Alliance for Information Networking)
Web Address: http://usnonprofit-1@coyote.rain.org
E-mail Address: www@rain.org
Description: An Internet education and access project focused on developing local information resources.
Site Includes: program information and resources.

soc.org.nonprofit FAQ
Web Address: http://www.eskimo.com/~pbarber/npo-faq.html
Description: The Frequently Asked Questions (faqs) file for the newsgroup soc. org.nonprofit. The faq is divided into 20 topical sections.
Site Includes: fundraising and marketing information, Internet and general resources.

Technology Resource Consortium (TRC)
Web Address: http://www.igc.apc.org/trc/
E-mail Address: itrc@igc.apc.org
Description: An association of nonprofit technology assistance organizations that provide education about and access to information technology to private and public nonprofit organizations.
Site Includes: program and services information.

Teleport Nonprofit Center
Web Address: http://www.teleport.com/community/nonprofits.shtml
E-mail Address: www@teleport.com
Description: Web site with services for nonprofit organizations on Teleport. Helps nonprofits get on-line.
Site Includes: program information and resources.

Periodicals

The NonProfit Times
Web Address: http://haven.ios.com/~nptimes/index.html
Description: Monthly publication for nonprofit management.
Site Includes: periodical.

Volunteer Information Organizations

Bay Area Volunteer Information Center
Web Address: http://meer.net/users/taylor/
E-mail Address: taylor@meer.net
Description: Organization which provides information about volunteer opportunities in the San Francisco Bay area in California.
Site Includes: searchable database of volunteer opportunities and links to area nonprofits.

Voluntary Action Center
Web Address: http://ftp.std.com/NE/uway.html
E-mail Address: okeeffe@cmo.ultranet.com
Description: Organization which provides information about volunteer opportunities with the United Way in Massachusetts.
Site Includes: program information and listing.

Volunteer Center
Web Address: http://www.netrep.com/local/org/vvc/vvc.html
E-mail Address: not available
Description: Clearinghouse of volunteers for nonprofits in the Tri-Valley area of California.
Site Includes: organization and program information.

Volunteer Center of Dallas
Web Address: http://www.pic.net/vc/
E-mail Address: vc@it.netcom.com
Description: Organization that recruits and refers volunteers to more than 700 nonprofit agencies in Dallas County, Texas.
Site Includes: list of current volunteer opportunities, specialized volunteer programs, and list of local social service agencies and their needs.

Volunteer Center of Portland
Web Address: http://www.aracnet.com/~vcoregon/
E-mail Address: vcoregon@aracnet.com
Description: Organization which provides information about volunteer opportunities in the Portland, Oregon area.
Site Includes: organization information and resources.

Volunteer Centers and Listings Online

Web Address: http://www.dnai.com/~children/volunteer.html

E-mail Address: children@dnai.com

Description: Web site which lists international, national and regional volunteers centers and other related listings.

Site Includes: listing.

Volunteer Opportunities for 1994—Greater Mankato, Minnesota Area

Web Address: http://www.mankato.mn.us/reg9/volunteers/volunteers.html

E-mail Address: not available

Description: Provided by the Council for Local Organizations, this is a listing of volunteer opportunities in the Greater Mankato area in Minnesota.

Site Includes: listing.

FUNDRAISING

Foundations and Grantmaking Organizations

Foundations

The Aaron Copland Fund for Music

Web Address: http://www.ingress.com/amc/grants.htm

E-mail Address: center@amc.net

Description: Foundation supports organizations which encourage and improve public knowledge and appreciation of serious contemporary American music.

Site Includes: grant information, application guidelines and criteria.

Andrew W. Mellon Foundation

Web Address: http://www.mellon.org/

E-mail Address: unavailable

Description: The site houses general information about the work and operations of the foundation.

Site Includes: links to their annual reports, program descriptions and general foundation information.

AT&T Foundation

Web Address: http://www.att.com/foundation

E-mail Address: webmaster@att.com

Description: Diversified funding program. Grants to communities, families, schools, science and technology, the arts and more.

Site Includes: description of programs and initiatives, information for grantseekers, foundation guidelines, listing of officers and staff.

Ben & Jerry's Foundation
Web Address: http://www.benjerry.com/scoop/partnershops.html
E-mail Address: joe@benjerry.com
Description: Foundation promotes collaborative efforts between Ben and Jerry's and nonprofits for the development of "PartnerShops" or donated franchises. The PartnerShops provide economic, employment and job training opportunities for the nonprofits and their communities.
Site Includes: listing of PartnerShops.

The Benton Foundation's Communications Policy Project
Web Address: http://www.cdinet.com/benton/Cyberlinks.html
E-mail Address: benton@benton.org
Description: Project orientated toward researching the impact of the National Information Infrastructure on noncommercial entities.
Site Includes: discussion forum, publications, and project information.

Carnegie Corporation of New York
Web Address: http://www.ezweb.com/carnegie/
E-mail Address: not available
Description: Foundation dedicated to the education and development of children and youth, prevention of deadly conflicts, development of human resources in developing countries and special projects.
Site Includes: proposal information, grant restrictions and policies, and more.

Charles A. Dana Foundation
Web Address: http://www.dana.org/
E-mail Address: danainfo@damany.dana.org
Description: Foundation with grant making programs in health and education, and operating programs in awards in health and education as well as public affairs.
Site Includes: grant and awards information, directors and staff list, news and events, and publications.

Charles E. Culpeper Foundation
ftp://ftp.dartmouth.edu/pub/LLTI-IALL/Funding/Culpeper_Foundation_5_3_94.txt
E-mail Address: not available
Description: Foundation supports educational programs targeted toward liberal arts and sciences in private institutions of higher education. One area of particular interest is foreign language teaching programs using new technologies.
Site Includes: application information.

Commonwealth Fund
Web Address: http://cmwf.org/
E-mail Address: mlr@cmwf.org

Description: New York City-based national foundation which engages in research on health and social policy issues.

Site Includes: links to recent fund work, programs, publications and grant guidelines.

David and Lucile Packard Foundation
Web Address: http://www.packfound.org/packhome.htm
E-mail Address: unavailable
Description: Web site of Packard Foundation.
Site Includes: links to information about the foundation, application procedures, and annual report.

Eastman Product Grant Program
Web Address: http://www.kodak.com/aboutKodak/bu/mptvi/tradtion/programs/student/granh17b.shtml
E-mail Address: webmaster@kodak.com
Description: Kodak provides cash and product grants to selected motion picture film school programs.
Site Includes: listing of area representatives and phone numbers.

Edward Lowe Foundation
Web Address: http://www.lowe.org/
E-mail Address: unavailable
Description: The site houses information about the foundation as well as their "smallbiz Net," an information toolbox for entrepreneurs and small business owners.
Site Includes: links to grant information, publications and smallbiz Net.

Ewing Marion Kauffman Foundation
Web Address: http://www.emkf.org/
E-mail Address: infoemkf@emkf.org
Description: A resource site for this foundation which works toward "the vision of self-sufficient people in healthy communities." The Kauffman Foundation's key funding areas are youth development and entrepreneurial leadership.
Site Includes: links to their program areas of interest and grant guidelines.

Flinn Foundation
Web Address: http://aspin.asu.edu/flinn/index.html
E-mail Address: flinn@enet.net
Description: Foundation that awards grants only to nonprofit organizations based in Arizona. The foundation's mission is to improve the quality of life in Arizona by supporting charitable projects in health care and medical research, education, and the arts.
Site Includes: links to grants awarded in health care, education and arts, and grant request procedures.

George Lucas Educational Foundation
Web Address: http://glef.org/
E-mail Address: edutopia@glef.org
Description: The Lucas Foundation promotes innovative efforts to improve education through a variety of communications media so students are prepared to live and work in an increasingly complex world.
Site Includes: program information, foundation history, and contact information.

Global Fund for Women
Web Address: http://www.igc.apc.org/gfw/
E-mail Address: gfw@igc.apc.org
Description: An international grantmaking organization dedicated to strengthening and linking organizations and programs for women all over the world.
Site Includes: program and organizational information, grantmaking guidelines.

Gunk Foundation
Web Address: http://www1.mhv.net/~gunk/welcome.html
E-mail Address: unavailable
Description: Information on the foundation's public arts grants and critical press publishing projects.
Site Includes: links to project areas.

The Hartford Foundation for Public Giving
Web Address: http://shakti.trincoll.edu/arts/HFPG.html
E-mail Address: not available
Description: Community foundation dedicated to serving Connecticut's Capitol Region.
Site Includes: grant and application information.

Heinz Endowments
Web Address: http://www.heinz.org/menu.html
E-mail Address: feedback@heinz.org
Description: Web site highlighting the work of the endowment.
Site Includes: links to information about the endowment, application procedures and program areas of support.

Henry J. Kaiser Family Foundation
Web Address: http://open.igc.org/kff/
E-mail Address: not available
Description: Foundation funds in four areas: health policy, reproductive health, HIV policy, and health and development in South Africa. Foundation is also interested in health policy and innovation in California.
Site Includes: grant and application information accessible via fax on demand.

Hewlett-Packard (HP) Philanthropy

Web Address: http://www.corp.hp.com/Publish/UG/index.html

E-mail Address: not available

Description: Foundation supports higher education and nonprofits through equipment and funding grants in the areas of math and science, health and human services, culture and the arts, as well as areas where employees are located.

Site Includes: description of grant programs and criteria, and application information.

Irvine Health Foundation

Web Address: http://www.ihf.org/mission_frame.html

E-mail Address: unavailable

Description: Web site for foundation whose goal is to improve the health of the residents of Orange County, California.

Site Includes: links to program areas of support.

James S. McDonnell Foundation

Web Address: http://jsmf.org/

E-mail Address: c6819sf@wuvmd.wustl.edu

Description: Information about the foundation which has three main funding areas: biomedical and behavioral sciences, research and innovation in education and global understanding.

Site Includes: links to grant guidelines and statement from the president of the foundation.

John Simon Guggenheim Memorial Foundation

Web Address: http://www.gf.org/index.html

E-mail Address: fellowships@gf.org

Description: Foundation provides fellowships to professionals in all fields except for the performing arts. Fellowships are divided in two geographic areas: U.S./Canada and Latin America/Caribbean.

Site Includes: program information, grant and application information.

MacArthur Foundation

Gopher Address: gopher://gopher.macfdn.org:3016/

E-mail Address: 4answers@macfdn.org

Description: Dedicated to helping groups and individuals to improve the human condition. The Foundation makes grants through Foundation-wide initiatives.

Site Includes: foundation, program, and application information.

Marin Community Foundation

Web Address: http://midas.org/mcf/mcf.html

E-mail Address: MCF@marin.org

Description: A community foundation dedicated to improving the human condition and the enhancement of the community.
Site Includes: grant and program information.

Markle Foundation
ftp://ftp.dartmouth.edu/pub/LLTI-IALL/Funding/Markle_Foundation_5_3_94.txt
E-mail Address: not available
Description: Foundation provides grants for research, development and demonstration projects. It does not fund endowments, scholarships or operating budgets.
Site Includes: application information.

Mitsubishi Electric America Foundation
Web Address: http://www.hri.com/MEA/meafhome.html
E-mail Address: webmaster@meitca.com
Description: Foundation supports national programs of impact with priority going to organizations and projects for youth with disabilities.
Site Includes: listing of previous grants, staff and officers.

Mundt Foundation and Archives
Web Address: http://www.dsu.edu/departments/library/found.html
E-mail Address: smith@columbia.dsu.edu
Description: Foundation established for the archives and memorabilia of Senator Mundt. It supports programs relating to Agriculture, Free Enterprise, Humanities, History and Education.
Site Includes: foundation information.

Nieman Foundation
Web Address: http://www.Nieman.harvard.edu/nieman.html
E-mail Address: cknell@ccm.harvard.edu
Description: Foundation provides fellowships of one academic year to working journalists of accomplishment.
Site Includes: program and recipient information.

Open Society Institute
Web Address: http://www.soros.org/
E-mail Address: agalietti@sorosny.org
Description: Information on the work of the Open Society Institute.
Site Includes: links to information on the Institute, George Soros, the activities of the Institute, programs and application procedures.

Ottinger Foundation
Web Address: http://www.igc.apc.org/ottinger/
E-mail Address: ottinger@igc.apc.org
Description: Web site for private family foundation that supports organizations promoting democratic participation, economic justice, environmental preservation and energy conservation.

Site Includes: links to foundation grants awarded as well as information about application procedures.

Pauline Oliveros Foundation Inc.
Web Address: http://www.tmn.com/0h/Artswire/www/pof/pof.html
E-mail Address: oliveriosfd@aol.com
Description: Foundation dedicated to the development of the arts for the benefit of society. It provides grants in the areas of music, literature, performance art and creative collaborations.
Site Includes: foundation and program information.

Robert Wood Johnson Foundation
Gopher Address: gopher://gopher.rwjf.org:4500/
E-mail Address: mail@rwjf.org
Description: Foundation established to help the nation address the problem of escalating health care costs.
Site Includes: 1994 Annual Report, grant topics, grant application and information.

Rockefeller Brothers Fund
Web Address: http://www.igc.apc.org/rbf/
E-mail Address: jhortin-rbf@mcimail.com
Description: Foundation dedicated to the theme of "one world" with focus on two components: sustainable resource use and world security.
Site Includes: fund, grant and application information and publications list.

Rotary Foundation
ftp://ftp.rilibs.datastorm.com/GENERAL/RIO084.TXT
E-mail Address: 75457.3602@compuserve.com
Description: Dedicated to the furthering of world relations, the Rotary Foundation provides grants for worldwide projects and sponsors international ambassadorships for university students, as well as exchanges for business and professionals.
Site Includes: program and grant information.

Russell Sage Foundation
Web Address: http://www.epn.org/sage.html#ourwork
E-mail Address: info@rsage.org
Description: Web site of foundation located in New York City that pursues four areas of funding: decline in demand for low-skill workers in advanced economies; U.S. immigration; curricula design for disadvantaged students; improving relations between racial and ethnic groups in schools, workplaces and neighborhood settings.
Site Includes: links to program information and grant application procedures.

Sega Foundation
Web Address: http://www.segaoa.com/inside/foundation/index.html

E-mail Address: not available

Description: Foundation funds national youth programs including Take Our Daughters to Work, Sega Mission Control and the National Geographic Kids Network.

Site Includes: description of programs, upcoming events, grant applications and list of grant recipients.

Sloan Foundation
Web Address: http://www.sloan.org/
E-mail Address: banister@uiuc.edu
Description: Foundation primarily oriented towards science and technology, including education, research and national issues.
Site Includes: program and information about the foundation.

Spencer Foundation
ftp://ftp.dartmouth.edu/pub/LLTI-IALL/Funding/Spencer_Foundation_5_3_94.txt
E-mail Address: not available
Description: The foundation provides grants for research projects concerned with the development of new knowledge about education.
Site Includes: proposal information.

Stern Family Fund
Web Address: http://www.essential.org/stern/
E-mail Address: sternfnd@essential.org
Description: An on-line resource center for the foundation.
Site Includes: links to program information and grant application procedures and grant recipients.

Sun Microsystems Foundation
Web Address: http://www.sun.com/cgi-bin/show?corporateoverview/CorporateAffairs/grants.html
E-mail Address: webmaster@sun.com
Description: The Sun Microsystems Foundation invests in communities that are often characterized by low income, high unemployment, and disturbing school drop-out rates.
Site Includes: funding criteria, application and funding cycle information, and more.

Surdna Foundation
Web Address: http://www.igc.apc.org/surdna/
E-mail Address: request@surdna.org
Description: Web site for this private grantmaking foundation located in New York City.
Site Includes: links to information about the foundation, their approach to grantmaking, their program areas and guidelines for application and grant restrictions.

Toshiba America Foundation (TAF)
Web Address: http://www.toshiba.com/tai/ta_taifn.htm
E-mail Address: not available
Description: Foundation supports science and mathematics programs and projects at the middle and senior high school levels, and community based initiatives throughout the U.S.
Site Includes: program area descriptions.

Twentieth Century Fund
Web Address: http://epn.org/tcf.html
E-mail Address: unavailable
Description: Web site for this nonpartisan foundation that produces books, reports and other publications with an eye toward finding fresh approaches to the major issues of the day.
Site Includes: links to their publications, current projects and calendar of events.

W. Alton Jones Foundation
Web Address: http://wajones.org/wajones/
E-mail Address: unavailable
Description: An information resource for this private grantmaking foundation which funds projects dealing with global environmental protection and the prevention of nuclear war or other massive release of radioactive material.
Site Includes: links to application procedures, program initiatives and list of grant recipients, trustees, officers and staff.

Wellspring Foundation
Web Address: http://www.isp.net/Wellspring/index.html
E-mail Address: sales@isp.net
Description: Web site that presents the work and interests of this New York City foundation. Their program areas of support are education, southeast Asia, documentary film production and environmental conservation.
Site Includes: links to grant guidelines and recent grant recipients.

Whitaker Foundation
Web Address: http://fairway.ecn.purdue.edu/bme/whitaker/
E-mail Address: not available
Description: Foundation dedicated to research and training in biomedical engineering.
Site Includes: program, grant, fellowship, award, and application information.

Wilburforce Foundation
Web Address: http://www.envirolink.org/orgs/wilburforce/
E-mail Address: unavailable

Description: Web site of this private philanthropic foundation located in Seattle, Washington that awards grants to organizations in the Pacific Northwest and Canada. They fund projects focused on the environment and human population.

The Winston Foundation for World Peace
Gopher Address: gopher://people.human.com:70/00/inc/alpha/winston
E-mail Address: winstonfoun@igc.apc.org
Description: Foundation dedicated to the permanent prevention of nuclear war through public education efforts and the strengthening of non-governmental organizations worldwide.
Site Includes: foundation and application information.

Wray Trust
Web Address: http://www.io.com/wraytrust/
E-mail Address: wnd_todd@txinfinet.com
Description: General information about the Wray Trust, a small family foundation which focuses on environmental projects in Texas.
Site Includes: links to grant information.

Z. Smith Reynolds Foundation
Web Address: http://zsr.org/
E-mail Address: webmaster@zsr.org
Description: Web site of this North Carolina foundation.
Site Includes: links to information about the foundation and grant application procedures.

Government Funding Programs

Catalog of Federal Domestic Assistance
Gopher Address: gopher://solar.rtd.utk.edu:70/11/Federal/CFDA
E-mail Address: not available
Description: A directory of Federal programs, projects, service and activities which provide assistance or benefits to the American Public. It contains financial and nonfinancial assistance programs administered by departments and establishments of the Federal government.
Site Includes: searchable directory.

Federal Information Exchange
Web Address: http://web.fie.com
E-mail Address: webmaster@fedix.fie.com
Description: A searchable database of government agency grant opportunities.
Site Includes: searchable database.

FIPSE—Fund for the Improvement of Postsecondary Education
Web Address: http://www.ed.gov/prog_info/FIPSE
E-mail Address: FIPSE@edu.gov

Description: The program supports innovative postsecondary educational projects as well as "special focus competitions."
Site Includes: information about FIPSE and guidelines and application materials.

Money Matters
Web Address: http://www.ed.gov/money.html
E-mail Address: webmaster@inet.ed.gov
Description: The U.S. Department of Education provides grants for student financial assistants, schools, and educational programs.
Site Includes: program and grant information.

NASA Education Division
Web Address: http://www.gsfc.nasa.gov/NASA_homepage.html
E-mail Address: comments@www.hq.nasa.gov
Description: Information on NASA's public initiatives and public relation activities. Site is primarily science oriented.
Site Includes: material on programs and grants.

National Institute of Health (NIH) Grants
Gopher Address: gopher://gopher.nih.gov/11/res
E-mail Address: gopher@gopher.nih.gov
Description: NIH gopher site.
Site Includes: guide for grants and contracts, past grant recipients and more.

National Science Foundation
Web Address: http://www.nsf.gov:80/nsf/homepage/grants.htm
E-mail Address: info@nsf.gov
Description: Science and technology oriented funding for education and research.
Site Includes: program areas and deadlines, and a grant proposal guide, grant policy manual, and grant proposal forms.

National Telecommunications and Information Administration
Gopher Address: gopher://gopher.ntia.doc.gov/
E-mail Address: not available
Description: The National Telecommunications and Information Administration offers assistance with grants, training information and research to the general public in the telecommunications area.
Site Includes: program and grant information.

In-Kind

The Computer Recycling Project
Web Address: http://www.wco.com/~dale/crp.html
E-mail Address: DALE@wco.com
Description: Nonprofit established to collect and donate surplus computers to nonprofits, educational programs, NGO's and low income individuals in the

Northern California area. The project provides information about other computer recycling organizations throughout the U.S.

Site Includes: project and donation information and list of computer recycling organizations.

Resources

Ada's Project Fellowship/Grant/Awards Directory
Web Address: http://www.cs.yale.edu/HTML/YALE/CS/HyPlans/tap/tap.html
E-mail Address: tap-comments@cs.yale.edu
Description: Clearinghouse of information and resources relating to women in computing.
Site Includes: information on conferences, projects, discussion groups and organizations, fellowships and grants, notable women in Computer Science, and other electronically accessible information sites.

Annenberg/CPB
Web Address: http://www.cpb.org/annenberg
E-mail Address: ahatcher@cpb.org
Description: Joint project of the Annenberg foundation and the Corporation for Public Broadcasting, information about projects, videos and reports on education.
Site Includes: information about projects.

ArtsNet
Web Address: http://artsnet.heinz.cmu.edu/
E-mail Address: not available
Description: Project of the Master of Arts program and Heinz School of Public Policy and Management which provides services and information related to arts management and cultural resources.
Site Includes: development resources (funding), career services, discussion forums, and management resources.

Association of Professional Researchers for Advancement
Web Address: http://weber.u.washington.edu/~dlamb/apra/APRA.html
E-mail Address: apra@adminsys.com
Description: Association dedicated to fostering professional development and promotion of standards for development research and information professionals worldwide.
Site Includes: organization and prospecting information.

Charities USA
Web Address: http://www.charitiesusa.com/
E-mail Address: request-for-info@charitiesusa.com

Description: National membership of charitable organizations.
Site Includes: news and links to member charities.

College Money Matters
Web Address: http://www.infi.net/collegemoney/
E-mail Address: signet@infi.net
Description: Sponsored by Signet Bank, offers information about educational
    expenses.
Site Includes: information about financing a college education.

Community Consulting Consortium LTD.
Web Address: http://www.ccconsult.com/
E-mail Address: grants@ccconsult.com
Description: Company which offers assistance with grant proposal writing, strate-
    gic planning and freelance writing for educators, nonprofits, small business
    and individuals.
Site Includes: list of services and contact information.

Council on Foundations
Web Address: http://www.cof.org/
E-mail Address: webmaster@cof.org
Description: The Council on Foundations, an association of foundations and corpo-
    rations, serves the public good by promoting and enhancing effective and
    responsible philanthropy.
Site Includes: information on foundations, publications, and news.

Donors Forum of Chicago
Web Address: http://www.uic.edu:80/~mhurst/donors/
E-mail Address: HN4065@Handsnet.org
Description: A membership association of Chicago-area grantmaking institutions.
Site Includes: donors forum library, educational and program opportunities.

Foundation Center
Web Address: http://fdncenter.org/
E-mail Address: mfn@fdncenter.org
Description: Library for nonprofits.
Site Includes: publications, training information, libraries, and grantmaker infor-
    mation.

Foundations On-line
Web Address: http://www.foundations.org/
E-mail Address: callahanje@aol.com
Description: A directory of charitable grantmakers.
Site Includes: foundations and grantmakers directory, and links to home pages,
    charities, fundraising software and more.

Funding Opportunities for Educators
Web Address: http://www.neirl.org/funding.html
E-mail Address: jeff@neirl.org
Description: The Regional Laboratory for Educational Improvement of the North-east and Islands provides information about programs for educators and educational agencies.
Site Includes: program information and funding opportunities.

Funding Sources for Violence Prevention
Gopher Address: gopher://cyfer.esusda.gov:70/11/violence/fundsource
E-mail Address: not available
Description: List of foundations and federal agencies with funding programs addressing violence and youth.
Site Includes: funding sources, foundations, and publications.

Giving discussion list (GIVING)
Discussion Address: giving@envirolink.org (to post)
Description: To subscribe, e-mail to listproc@envirolink and type *subscribe giving* in message body. Discussion of philanthropy and volunteer issues.
Group Includes: list for donors and volunteers, postings and information on the subject.

Grant Agency Deadlines
Gopher Address: gopher://ukcc.uky.edu/1menu%20UKR200%21191/DEADLINE.INFO
E-mail Address: not available
Description: Listing of grant deadlines for both governmental and non-governmental agencies. Divided into four categories: Arts/Humanities/International, Education/Human and Community Development, Health/Mental Health, Science/Engineering.
Site Includes: links to grant agency information, deadlines, and contacts.

Grant Discussion List (GRANTS-L)
Discussion Address: grants-l@gsuvm1.bitnet
Description: Group site intended to promote funding for international education and research. To subscribe, e-mail to listserv@gsuvm1.bitnet and type *subscribe grants-l* in message body.
Group Includes: postings and information on international travel grants and funding opportunities.

Grant-Writing
Gopher Address: gopher://info.irex.org:70/11/grant.writing
E-mail Address: not available

Description: Suggestions for applicants to Social Science Research Council Competitions.

Site Includes: document.

GrantsNet

Web Address: http://www.os.dhhs.gov/progorg/grantsnet/index.html

E-mail Address: SuzanneNeill, gnet@os.dhhs.gov

Description: Web site for information about Health and Human services and other selected federal grant programs.

Site Includes: subscription information, resource and funding information.

Hoover's Online

Web Address: http://www.hoovers.com/

E-mail Address: jspede@hoovers.com

Description: Directory of corporate information.

Site Includes: directories of company information.

The Illinois Researcher Information Service (IRIS)

Web Address: http://www.grainger.uiuc.edu/iris/default.htm

E-mail Address: a-trehub@uiuc.edu

Description: Division of University of Illinois Library provides a listing of publications of funding agencies.

Site Includes: funding opportunities database.

International Foundation for Gender Education

Web Address: http://www.transgender.org/tg/ifge/index.html

E-mail Address: ifge@world.std.com

Description: Educational and charitable organization addressing gender issues.

Site Includes: information about transgender issues, listing of transgender groups worldwide.

Internet Prospector

Web Address: http://PLAINS.UWYO.EDU/~prospect/

E-mail Address: Bunney@uwyo.edu

Description: Prospect newsletter.

Site Includes: newsletter.

Internet Resources for Grantwriters

Web Address: http://www.umich.edu/~trinket/Resources_for_Grant.html

E-mail Address: trinket@umich.edu

Description: Links and organization descriptions of Internet resources for grantwriters.

Site Includes: 22 links.

Joseph and Matthew Payton Philanthropic Studies Library
Web Address: http://www-Lib.iupui.edu/philanthropy/payton.html
E-mail Address: zerping@ucs.indiana.edu
Description: Library of the Indiana University Center of Philanthropy.
Site Includes: resources and information.

Nonprofit Resource Center: Grant Links
Web Address: http://www.teleport.com/~sparking/grants.shtml
E-mail Address: info@teleport.com
Description: Directory of grantmaking organizations and resources.
Site Includes: directory.

Online Research Funding Information
Web Address: http://www.uic.edu/depts/ovcr/non-prof.html
E-mail Address: hemmings@uic.edu
Description: Directory of on-line sources of funding and information sponsored by
    the University of Illinois at Chicago.
Site Includes: on-line funding search tools, federal departments and agencies, and
    listing of nonprofit foundations, corporations and associations.

Philanthropy Journal of North Carolina
Web Address: http://www.nando.net/philant/nov/novphil6.html
E-mail Address: not available
Description: Journal of philanthropic activity in state.
Site Includes: document.

Planned Giving Discussion List (GIFT-PL)
Discussion Address: gift-pl@vm1.spcs.umn.edu (to post)
Description: To subscribe, e-mail to listserv@vm1.spcs.umn.edu and type *subscribe
    gift-pl* in message body. Discussion of planned giving issues.
Group Includes: postings and information on planned giving.

Potential Sources of Support for Graduate Students: Compiled in Fall 1993
Web Address: http://bunny.cs.uiuc.edu:80/funding/generalInfo/gradStudents.txt
E-mail Address: not available
Description: A comprehensive list of scholarship opportunities for graduate students.
Site Includes: list of opportunities.

The Prospect Research Page
Web Address: http://weber.u.washington.edu/~dlamb/research.html
E-mail Address: dlamb@u.washington.edu
Description: Contains hyperlinks to valuable research tools, and resources on the
    Internet. Includes company and executive information, foundations, search
    engines, commercial information providers and more.
Site Includes: directory.

Prospex Incorporated
Web Address: http://prospex.com/
E-mail Address: info@prospex.com
Description: Prospect research firm
Site Includes: company services and free information on corporate, foundation, private-company, and major donor prospects.

Research Funding Opportunities and Administration (TRAM)
Web Address: http://tram.rice.edu/TRAM/
E-mail Address: sdc@rice.edu
Description: A service initially developed by the Texas Research Administrators Group (TRAM). It contains searchable research funding sources available from one location.
Site Includes: set of grant application forms collected from various sources, standard agreements for subcontracts, non-disclosures, licenses, searchable database and links.

Rice University Grants Gopher
Gopher Address: gopher://chico.rice.edu:70/11/Subject/Grants
E-mail Address: riceinfo@rice.edu
Description: Directory of grant and funding information.
Site Includes: links to resources.

Sources of Funding in the Newly Independent States
Web Address: http://solar.rtd.utk.edu/friends/funding/world.learning.funding.html
E-mail Address: not available
Description: List of alternative funding sources for the newly independent states of the former Soviet Union.

Virtual Prospect Research
Web Address: http://www.butler.edu/~mmurphy/index.html
E-mail Address: MMurphy@Butler.edu
Description: Prospect Research is the first step in the process of increasing the philanthropic resources of an institution. Company identifies the shared values between an organization and its prospective donors through the collection, organization, and presentation of significant information for development purposes.
Site Includes: directory of prospect and related links.

Waltman Associates
Web Address: http://www.umn.edu/nlhome/g248/bergq003/wa/
E-mail Address: berg003@gold.tc.umn.edu
Description: Company which provides prospect research information and services.
Site Includes: Waltman Associates' Directory of Directors, National Directory of College and University Trustees, *Town & Country* Magazine Personal Name Index, Family Trees, and Biographical Profiles.

Corporate

Indices

Fortune
Web Address: http://pathfinder.com/@@*IrbeyHPEgAAQPZc/fortune/magazine/
specials/fortune500/fortune500.html
Description: Fortune magazine's site.
Site Includes: searchable directory of the Fortune 500.

Fortune 500: Industry and Service
Web Address: http://www.cs.utexas.edu/users/paris/corporate.real.html
Description: Directory of Fortune 500 companies.
Site Includes: alphabetical listing of links to the Fortune 500.

Fortune 500 Companies (List incomplete. Not all companies have Web sites.)

3Com
Web Address:
http://www.3com.com

Ameritech
Web Address:
http://www.ameritech.com

3M
Web Address:
http://www.mmm.com

AMP
Web Address:
http://www.amp.com

Addison-Wesley Publishing Group
Web Address:
http://aw.com

AMR Corporation
Web Address:
http://www.amrcorp.com

Adobe Systems
Web Address:
http://www.adobe.com

AMS
Web Address:
http://www.amsinc.com

AMD
Web Address:
http://www.amd.com

Anderson Consulting
Web Address:
http://www.ac.com

Amdahl
Web Address:
http://www.amdahl.com

Apple
Web Address:
http://www.apple.com

American Stock Exchange
Web Address:
http://www.amex.com

AT&T
Web Address:
http://www.att.com

Bank of America
Web Address:
http://www.bofa.com

Bay Networks
Web Address:
http://www.wellfleet.com

Bell Atlantic
Web Address:
http://www.ba.com

Bell Canada
Web Address:
http://www.bell.ca

Bell South
Web Address:
http://www.bst.bls.com

Bellcore
Web Address:
http://www.bellcore.com

Boeing
Web Address:
http://www.boeing.com

Borland
Web Address:
http://www.borland.com

British Telecom
Web Address:
http://www.bt.net

Cabletron Systems, Inc.
Web Address:
http://www.ctron.com

Cadence
Web Address:
http://www.cadence.com

Canadian Airlines International
Web Address:
http://www.cdnair.ca

CBS
Web Address:
http://www.cbs.com

Cisco Systems
Web Address:
http://www.cisco.com

Citicorp
Web Address:
http://www.tti.com

Coca-Cola
Web Address:
http://www.cocacola.com

Compaq
Web Address:
http://www.compaq.com/homepage.
graphic.html

Compuserve
Web Address:
http://www.compuserve.com

Computer Associates
Web Address:
http://www.cai.com

Convex
Web Address:
http://www.convex.com

Cray
Web Address:
http://www.cray.com

Crestar
Web Address:
http://www.crestar.com

Data General
Web Address:
http://www.dg.com

Dell
Web Address:
http://www.dell.com

Deloitte Touche
Web Address:
http://www.dttus.com

Digital
Web Address:
http://www.dec.com

Dow Chemical
Web Address:
http://www.dow.com

Dow Jones
Web Address:
http://bis.dowjones.com

Du Pont
Web Address:
http://www.dupont.com

Dunn and Bradstreet Corporation
Web Address:
http://www.dnb.com

EDS
Web Address:
http://www.eds.com

Ericsson
Web Address:
http://www.ericsson.com

Ernst and Young
Web Address:
http://www.ey.com

Fannie Mae
Web Address:
http://www.fanniemae.com

FedEx
Web Address:
http://www.fedex.com

First Union
Web Address:
http://www.firstunion.com

Ford
Web Address:
http://www.ford.com

Fujitsu America
Web Address:
http://www.fujitsu.com/sub-directory.
html

GE
Web Address:
http://www.ge.com

General Instruments
Web Address:
http://www.gi.com

General Magic
Web Address:
http://www.genmagic.com

Global Village
Web Address:
http://www.globalvillage.com

Goodyear
Web Address:
http://www.goodyear.com

Groupe Bull
Web Address:
http://www.bull.com

Gruntal
Web Address:
http://www.gruntal.com

GTE
Web Address:
http://info.gte.com

Harris
Web Address:
http://www.harris.com

HBO & Company
Web Address:
http://www.hboc.com

HBO Home Video
Web Address:
http://hbohomevideo.com

Hewlett Packard
Web Address:
http://www.hp.com

IBM
Web Address:
http://www.ibm.com

Informix
Web Address:
http://www.informix.com

Intel
Web Address:
http://www.intel.com

Intergraph
Web Address:
http://www.intergraph.com

ITT Hartford
Web Address:
http://www.itthartford.com

JC Penney
Web Address:
http://www.jcpenney.com

Kodak
Web Address:
http://www.kodak.com

Lilly
Web Address:
http://www.lilly.com

Lockheed Martin
Web Address:
http://www.mmc.com

Lotus
Web Address:
http://www.lotus.com

Mastercard
Web Address:
http://www.mastercard.com

MCI
Web Address:
http://www.mci.com

Microsoft
Web Address:
http://www.microsoft.com

Mips
Web Address:
http://www.mips.com

Mobile
Web Address:
http://www.mobile.com

Molex
Web Address:
http://www.molex.com

Monsanto
Web Address:
http://www.monsanto.com

Motorola
Web Address:
http://www.mot.com

Nations Bank
Web Address:
http://www.nationsbank.com

NCD
Web Address:
http://www.ncd.com

NetManage
Web Address:
http://www.netmanage.com

New York Times
Web Address:
http://nytimesfax.com

Next
Web Address:
http://www.next.com

Nintendo
Web Address:
http://www.nintendo.com

Nokia
Web Address:
http://www.nokia.com

Nortel
Web Address:
http://www.nortel.com

Novell
Web Address:
http://www.novell.com

Oracle
Web Address:
http://www.oracle.com

Pacific Bell
Web Address:
http://www.pacbell.com

Paramount
Web Address:
http://www.paramount.com

Price Waterhouse
Web Address:
http://www.pw.com

Qualcomm Inc.
Web Address:
http://www.qualcomm.com

Quantum
Web Address:
http://www.quantum.com

Reebok
Web Address:
http://planetreebok.com

Rockwell
Web Address:
http://www.rockwell.com

SAS
Web Address:
http://www.sas.com

Schlumberger
Web Address:
http://www.slb.com

SCO
Web Address:
http://www.sco.com

Seagate
Web Address:
http://www.seagate.com

Sega
Web Address:
http://www.segaoa.com

Shell
Web Address:
http://www.shellus.com

Siemens
Web Address:
http://www.pdb.sni.de

Silicon Graphics
Web Address:
http://www.sgi.com

Southwest
Web Address:
http://www.iflyswa.com

Southwestern Bell Telephone
Web Address:
http://www.sbc.com

Sprint
Web Address:
http://www.sprintlink.net

Sun Microsystems
Web Address:
http://www.sun.com

Sybase
Web Address:
http://www.sybase.com

Symantec
Web Address:
http://www.symantec.com

Taligent
Web Address:
http://www.taligent.com

Tandem
Web Address:
http://www.tandem.com

Tatung
Web Address:
http://www.tatung.com

TCI
Web Address:
http://www.tcinc.com

Tektronix
Web Address:
http://www.tek.com

Texaco
Web Address:
http://www.texaco.com

Thinking Machines
Web Address:
http://www.think.com/"><img src=
"think.gif"></a><p>

Unisys
Web Address:
http://www.unisys.com

United Technologies
Web Address:
http://www.utc.com

UPS
Web Address:
http://www.ups.com

US West
Web Address:
http://www.uswest.com

Viacom
Web Address:
http://here.viacom.com

Wal-Mart
Web Address:
http://sam.wal-mart.com

Walt Disney
Web Address:
http://www.disney.com

Wells Fargo
Web Address:
http://www.wellsfargo.com

Whirlpool
Web Address:
http://www.whirlpool.com

WordPerfect
Web Address:
http://www.wordperfect.com

Xerox
Web Address:
http://www.xerox.com

GOVERNMENT AND RELATED SITES

Directories

Catalog of Federal Domestic Assistance
Gopher Address: gopher://solar.rtd.utk.edu:70/11/Federal/CFDA
E-mail Address: not available
Description: A directory of Federal programs, projects, services and activities which
provide assistance or benefits to the American Public. It contains financial and
nonfinancial assistance programs administered by departments and establish-
ments of the Federal government.
Site Includes: searchable directory.

Constitutions, Statutes, and Codes
Web Address: http://www.law.cornell.edu/statutes.html
E-mail Address: lii@lii.law.cornell.edu
Description: Catalog of constitutions, statutes, and codes operated by the Legal
Information Institute at Cornell University.
Site Includes: site offers both federal and state constitutions, statutes and related
legislative information, as well as current legislation pending in the House
and Senate.

Decisions of the US Supreme Court
Web Address: http://www.law.cornell.edu/supct/supct.table.html
E-mail Address: lii@lii.law.cornell.edu
Description: A searchable index of decisions since 1990, and key decisions before
then. A service of Cornell Law School.
Site Includes: searchable index.

Demography and Population Studies
Web Address: http://coombs.anu.edu.au/ResFacilities/DemographyPage.html
E-mail Address: Diana Crow@anu.edu.au
Description: Page from the World Wide Web Virtual Library containing 150 links to
demographic information facilities world-wide.
Site Includes: directory.

Electronic Activist
Web Address: http://www.berkshire.net/~ifas/activist/
E-mail Address: ifas@berkshire.net
Description: A directory of e-mail addresses of Members of Congress, state govern-
ment officials, and media organizations.
Site Includes: directory.

Federal Information Exchange, Inc.
Web Address: http://www.fie.com/www/us_gov.htm

E-mail Address: www_request@fedix.fie.gov

Description: Contains links to multiple agency site servers, single agency site servers, and consortium servers for the U.S. Government and its activities.

Site Includes: directory.

FedWorld

Web Address: http://www.fedworld.gov/

E-mail Address: helpdesk@fedworld.gov

Description: Directory of U.S. Government information developed by the National Technical Information Service (NTIS).

Site Includes: directory.

Government and Law Clearinghouse

Web Address: http://www.lib.umich.edu/chouse/tree/govlaw.html

E-mail Address: clearinghouse@argus-inc.com

Description: A directory of links related to government and law including: citizen's rights, elections, regulations, environment, criminology, grants, resources and more.

Site Includes: directory.

Government Information

Web Address: http://library.microsoft.com/govt.htm

E-mail Address: not available

Description: Links to government resources available on the Web, including: armed forces, CIA World Factbook, demography and population studies, U.S. Supreme Court decisions and more.

Site Includes: directory.

Information Infrastructure Task Force (IITF)

Web Address: http://iitf.doc.gov/

E-mail Address: nii@ntia.doc.gov

Description: Official site of the U.S. Government task force responsible for the National Information Infrastructure (NII).

Site Includes: News and reports from working groups, the NII Advisory Council, and a calendar of events.

Legi-Slate Service

Web Address: http://gopher.legislate.com/

E-mail Address: legislate@gopher.legislate.com

Description: Database of Congressional and regulatory information.

Site Includes: database.

Thomas-Legislative Information on the Internet

Web Address: http://thomas.loc.gov/

E-mail Address: Thomas@loc.gov

Description: Searchable database of full texts of legislation, bill summaries, the Congressional Record and more. Catalogued by bill number, title, sponsor, year, etc.
Site Includes: searchable database.

US Federal Government Resources
Web Address: http://www.trincoll.edu/pols/us/usgov.html
E-mail Address: padmas@trincoll.edu
Description: Directory of links to federal government resources.
Site Includes: directory.

US Government Information
Web Address: http://govtdoc.law.csuohio.edu/usgov.html
E-mail Address: mgooch@inca.law.csuohio.edu
Description: Contains links to the branches of government, agencies, government references, and a hot items list. Sponsored by the Cleveland State University College of Law.
Site Includes: directory.

US Government Web Pages
Web Address: http://www.igc.apc.org/igc/www.gov.html
E-mail Address: not available
Description: Directory of U.S. Government sites on-line. Includes all branches of government, agencies, departments, services, and more.
Site Includes: directory.

US National Information Infrastructure Virtual Library
Web Address: http://nii.nist.gov/
E-mail Address: carolyn.garnes@nist.gov
Description: Provides information about the future of the National Information Infrastructure.
Site Includes: organization information.

Federal Government and Related Sites

Center for Disease Control (CDC)
Web Address: http://www.cdc.gov/
E-mail Address: netinfo@cdc1.cdc.gov
Description: Official site of the Center for Disease Control.
Site Includes: information on: diseases, health risks, prevention guidelines and strategies, travelers' health, publications, products, and subscription services, scientific data, surveillance, and health statistics, funding opportunities (contracts, cooperative agreements and grants, RFPs), and more.

CYFERNet—Children Youth and Family Education and Research Network
Gopher Address: gopher://cyfer.esusda.gov:70/00/about_gopher
E-mail Address: gopher@boombox.micro.umn.edu
Description: Provides information and resources concerning child, youth, and family issues. Maintained by USDA's Office of Research, Education and Extension and the National Agricultural Library's Youth Development Information Center.
Site Includes: links to other national information resources that support federal initiatives in child, youth and family programming.

Economic Bulletin Board
Web Address: http://www.stat-usa.gov/BEN/Services/ebbhome.html or gopher. lib.umich.edu
E-mail Address: not available
Description: An essential site for economic statistics from the Department of Commerce. The site via the Department of Commerce is fee-based but is free from the Michigan Gopher.
Site Includes: Over 5,000 files available on such topics as: advance retail and wholesale trade, business cycle indications, consumer price index, housing starts and building permits, national income and product accounts, and note and treasury bill auction results.

EDGAR Online
Web Address: http://www.edgar-online.com/
E-mail Address: edgar-online@pequot.com
Description: EDGAR (Electronic Data Gathering Analysis and Retrieval), the SEC data base provides up-to-date corporate information.
Site Includes: SEC filings, registration, new features, and more.

Environmental Protection Agency
Web Address: http://www.epa.gov/
E-mail Address: info@epa.gov
Description: Access to the EPA server.
Site Includes: news, initiatives, studies and reports, grants, publications, and more.

Federal Bureau of Investigation
Web Address: http://www.fbi.gov/
E-mail Address: not available
Description: Official site of the FBI.
Site Includes: FBI Fact Sheet, investigations, reports, publications, and more.

Federal Communications Commission
Web Address: http://www.fcc.gov/
E-mail Address: fccinfo@fcc.gov
Description: Official site of the Federal Communications Commission.

Site Includes: News, announcements, and daily events, including FCC's Daily Digest, the Commission's agendas, current rulemaking, auctions, and speeches. Includes links to FCC's eight bureaus.

Federal Emergency Management Agency
Web Address: http://www.fema.gov/homepage.html
E-mail Address: eipa@fema.gov
Description: The Federal Emergency Management Agency's official site on the Web.
Site Includes: searchable index, program and organization information, and more.

Library of Congress
Web Address: http://www.loc.gov/
E-mail Address: lcweb@loc.gov
Description: Information and materials from the collection at the Library of Congress.
Site Includes: searchable database.

National Coordination Office for High Performance Computing and Communications
Web Address: http://www.hpcc.gov/
E-mail Address: nco@hpcc.gov
Description: Information on the multiagency federal program developing the technology for the National Information Infrastructure with links to participating agencies.
Site Includes: publications, grants, committee, and organization information.

National Science Foundation
Web Address: http://www.nsf.gov/
E-mail Address: webmaster@nsf.gov
Description: Promotes the progress of grants and engineering.
Site Includes: staff, publications, news and grants information.

National Telecommunications and Information Administration
Web Address: http://www.ntia.doc.gov/
E-mail Address: webmaster@ntia.doc.gov
Description: Promotes and represents U.S. businesses in the telecommunications and information arena.
Site Includes: sections on the National Information Infrastructure and the Global Information Infrastructure, grants and assistance, and research and technology.

United Nations Development Programme (UNDP)
Web Address: http://www.undp.org/
E-mail Address: webmaster@undp.org

Description: Official UNDP site.
Site Includes: press releases, program information, and links to other UN sites.

US Census
Web Address: http://www.census.gov/
E-mail Address: WebMaster@Census.GOV
Description: U.S. census statistics.
Site Includes: population clocks, data maps, genealogy tips, population and housing, and more.

US Department of Commerce
Web Address: http://www.doc.gov/
E-mail Address: stat-usa@doc.gov
Description: Official site of the U.S. Department of Commerce.
Site Includes: statistics, Commerce Information Locator Service (CILS), agency listing, and publications.

US Department of Education
Web Address: http://www.ed.gov/
E-mail Address: not available
Description: Official site of the U.S. Department of Education.
Site Includes: news, guides, programs, grant information and more.

US Department of Health and Human Services
Web Address: http://www.os.dhhs.gov/
E-mail Address: tthompso@os.dhhs.gov
Description: The U.S. Department of Health and Human Services' Web site.
Site Includes: department's agencies on the Internet, public affairs, news, and Grantsnet
[(*Web Address:* http://www.os.dhhs.gov/progorg/grantsnet/index.html) *see Foundations and Grantmaking Organizations*].

US Department of Justice
Web Address: http://www.usdoj.gov/
E-mail Address: web@usdoj.gov
Description: Site of the U.S. Department of Justice.
Site Includes: access to the five organizations within the Justice Department, as well as pertinent issues, investigations, publications and activities.

US Food and Drug Administration
Web Address: http://www.fda.gov/fdahomepage.html
E-mail Address: info@bangate.fda.gov
Description: Official site of the U.S. Food and Drug Association.
Site Includes: FDA news, food, drug, and medical updates.

White House
Web Address: http://www.whitehouse.gov
E-mail Address: feedback@www.whitehouse.gov
Description: The Executive Branch of the U.S. Government.
Site Includes: tours, the first family, publications and what's new are all available.

State and Local Government and Related Sites

Government Online
Web Address: http://www.gol.org/
E-mail Address: webmaster@gol.org
Description: Information service promoting state and local government agencies' relationship with the technology industry.
Site Includes: information and directory.

State and Local Government on the Net
Web Address: http://www.piperinfo.com/~piper/state/states.html
E-mail Address: piper@piper.info.com
Description: A searchable index of all 50 states, Tribal governments, and Guam.
Site Includes: directory includes federal resources related to state and local government, national organizations serving state and local governments, and more.

StateSearch
Web Address: http://www.state.ky.us/nasire/NASIREhome.html
E-mail Address: darnold@ukcc.uky.edu
Description: Clearinghouse of state government information provided by the National Association of State Information Resource Executives.
Site Includes: searchable database.

Legal Resources

Counsel Connect
Web Address: http://www.counsel.com/
E-mail Address: jlondinn@counsel.com
Description: Resource for attorneys for Internet-related and legal information. Affiliated with Court TV Law Center.
Site Includes: organized in a newsletter format with links to articles, lists of attorneys, seminars, etc.

Cyberspace Law Center
Web Address: http://www.cybersquirrel.com/clc/clcindex.html
E-mail Address: stacy@cybersquirrel.com
Description: resources of exceptionally wide variety relating to cyberspace law.

Site Includes: directories, resources, periodical materials, organizations, links to other law sites, newsgroups.

FindLaw
Web Address: http://www.findlaw.com/
E-mail Address: info@findlaw.com
Description: Resource for all aspects of law and the Internet.
Site Includes: search engine for listings, directories, articles, etc.

Legal and Ethical Internet Resources
Web Address: http://www.nau.edu/legal.html
E-mail Address: jdc@nuxi.ucc.nau.edu
Description: Links to resources available on the Internet dealing with legal and ethical Internet issues such as copyright and intellectual property.
Site Includes: list of links.

UCLA Online Institute for Cyberspace Law and Policy
Web Address: http://www.gse.ucla.edu/iclp/hp.html
E-mail Address: none available
Description: Institute based at UCLA to provide innovative opportunities for the on-line community to share resources and new directions in cyberspace law.
Site Includes: articles and links to legal resources.

Armed Forces

AirForce Link
Web Address: http://www.dtic.dla.mil/airforcelink/
E-mail Address: not available
Description: The Air Force's home page.
Site Includes: information about Air Force activities.

Marines
Web Address: http://www.hqmc.usmc.mil
E-mail Address: usmc@hqinotes.hqmc.usmc.mil
Description: The official U.S. Marines Web site.
Site Includes: FAQ's, history, mission, links to related sites and more.

NavyOnLine
Web Address: http://www.navy.mil/
E-mail Address: webmaster@ncts.navy.mil
Description: The official Navy Web site.
Site Includes: Searchable index of all Navy departments and agencies.

The United States Army HomePage
Web Address: http://www.army.mil/
E-mail Address: webmaster@pentagon-1dms2.army.mil
Description: The official home page of the U.S. Army.
Site Includes: links to Soldier Magazine, the Department of Defense, Army Chief of Staff, recruiting and veteran information, and more.

EDUCATIONAL AND RELATED SITES

Bell Atlantic-WV World School Project
Web Address: http://www.bell-atl.com/wschool/
E-mail Address: world.school@bell-atl.com
Description: Program designed to provide Internet access to K-12 public schools in West Virginia.
Site Includes: program information.

Consortium for School Networking—CoSN
Web Address: http://cosn.org/
E-mail Address: cosnwebmaster@cosn.org
Description: National voice for advocating access to the emerging National Information Infrastructure in schools.
Site Includes: technology resource planning guide, newsletter, funding information, and links for legislative action.

Daily Report Card
Web Address: http://www.utopia.com/mailings/reportcard/
E-mail Address: info@utopia.com
Description: A summary digest of news in K-12 education. Recently cut back to thrice-weekly.
Site Includes: publication.

Discovery Channel Online
Web Address: http://www.discovery.com/
E-mail Address: not available
Description: Programs and interactive stories from the Discovery Channel.
Site Includes: programs, educational opportunities, and more.

EdLinks
Web Address: http://www.marshall.edu/~jmullens/edlinks.html
E-mail Address: jmullens@marshall.edu
Description: A directory of educational links on the Web, both commercial and non-profit.
Site Includes: directory.

Educom
Web Address: http://educom.edu/
E-mail Address: inquiry@educom.edu
Description: Membership organization promoting information technology in higher education.
Site Includes: news, conferences, programs, and more.

EdWeb
Web Address: http://K12.cnidr.org:90/
E-mail Address: acarvin@k12.cnidr.org
Description: Resource for information on the role of information technology in education.
Site Includes: links to educational activities and resources.

InfoList for All Teachers
Web Address: http://www.electriciti.com/~rlakin/
E-mail Address: rlakin@cello.gina.calstate.edu
Description: Digest of information on education.
Site Includes: digest.

Quest-NASA's K-12 Internet Initiative
Web Address: http://quest.arc.nasa.gov/index.html
E-mail Address:
Description: Program promotes the use of the Internet in schools. Sponsored by the NASA Information Infrastructure Technology Applications (IITA) project and the High Performance Computing and Communication (HPCC) program.
Site Includes: program information.

Urban Education Web
Web Address: http://eric-web.tc.columbia.edu/
E-mail Address:
Description: Organization promotes activities in support of urban education initiatives.
Site Includes: project, activity, and program information, as well as the ERIC database, a national clearinghouse of educational information.

COMMERCIAL SERVICES

AT&T—Toll-Free 800 Directory
Web Address: http://www.tollfree.att.net/dir800/
Description: AT&T's directory of toll free numbers.
Site Includes: directory.

Commercial Sites Index
Web Address: http://www.directory.net
Description: Directory of commercial services, products, and information on the Internet.
Site Includes: directory.

The Electronic Telegraph
Web Address: http://www.telegraph.co.uk/
Description: On-line London based newspaper.
Site Includes: newspaper.

FedEx
Web Address: http://www.fedex.com
Description: Allows visitors to download package tracking software and learn about company operations.
Site Includes: delivery options, tracking information, and a searchable database.

The New York Times Fax
Web Address: http://www.nytimesfax.com
Description: New York Times' fax service available free over the Internet.
Site Includes: Times digest.

Pathfinder
Web Address: http://www.pathfinder.com
Description: Time-Warner's site. Access to all of the company's publications.
Site Includes: news and publications.

San Jose Mercury News
Web Address: http://www.sjmercury.com/
Description: Full access costs $4.95 per month. Headlines and short clips are free.
Site Includes: newspaper.

UPS
Web Address: http://www.ups.com
Description: Offers services and company information.
Site Includes: downloadable software and package tracking.

Wiley Publishing
Web Address: http://www.wiley.com/
Description: Company develops, publishes, and sells products in print and electronic media for the educational, professional, scientific, technical, and consumer markets worldwide.
Site Includes: company and product information.

GENERAL INTERNET RESOURCES

Browsers

NSCA Mosaic
Web Address: http://www.ncsa.uiuc.edu/SDG/Software/Mosaic/NCSAMosaic Home.html
Description: The original Web browser from the University of Illinois. Mac and Windows versions available.
Site Includes: downloadable browser.

Netscape Navigator
Web Address: http://home.netscape.com/
Description: Netscape Navigator is the most popular browser on the Web. Mac and Windows versions available. Browser downloadable from homepage by pressing the *Netscape Now* button. Available for free for educational and non-profit users.
Site Includes: downloadable browser.

EINEt's MacWeb
Web Address: ftp://ftp.einet.net/einet/mac/macweb/macweb.latest.sea.hqx
Description: Web browser specifically for the Mac. Available for downloading at no cost.
Site Includes: downloadable browser.

HTML Text Editors

HoTMetal and HoTMetal Pro
Web Address: http://www.sq.com/products/hotmetal/hmp-org.htm
Description: Editor includes list of currently valid HTML tags for easy formatting into a multi-media Web document.
Site Includes: downloadable application.

HTML Assistant and HTML Assistant Pro
Web Address: http://fox.nstn.ca/~harawitz/index.html
Description: A powerful HTML editor which can automatically create tables and forms and includes a spell checker.
Site Includes: downloadable application.

HTML Author
Web Address: http://www.salford.ac.uk/iti/gsc/htmlauth/summary.html

Description: HTML editor, used in conjunction with Word 6.0, takes advantage of WYSIWYG (What You See Is What You Get) technology to format standard word processing text for the Web.
Site Includes: downloadable application.

Microsoft Internet Assistant
Web Address: http://www.microsoft.com/msword/
Description: Add on application to Microsoft Word for creating Web documents.
Site Includes: downloadable application.

WebMagic and WebMagic Pro
Web Address: http://www.sgi.com/Products/WebFORCE/WebForceSoft.html
Description: HTML Editor for creating Web documents that automatically formats plain text into HTML.
Site Includes: downloadable application.

Information Access and Technology Organizations

Annenberg Washington Program
Web Address: http://www.annenberg.nwu.edu/
E-mail Address: awp@nwu.edu
Description: Program concerned with "assessing the impact of communications technologies and public policies."
Site Includes: publication and program information.

Center on Information Technology Accommodation (CITA)
Web Address: http://www.gsa.gov/coca/cocamain.htm
E-mail Address: paul.fontaine@gsa.gov
Description: Clearinghouse promoting public access to information resources.
Site Includes: legislation and policies, resources, and program information.

Computer Professionals for Social Responsibility
Web Address: http://www.cpsr.org/home.html
E-mail Address: webmaster@cpsr.org
Description: A public interest association concerned with the impact of technology on society.
Site Includes: organization, membership, and program information.

Electronic Pathways
Web Address: http://hanksville.phast.umass.edu:80/defs/independent/ElecPath/elecpath.html
E-mail Address: elpath@stripe.colorado.edu
Description: National alliance promoting electronic access for Native Americans.
Site Includes: organization and program information.

The Freedom Forum
Web Address: http://www.freedomforum.org/
E-mail Address: news@freedomforum.org
Description: An international organization promoting free press, free speech and free spirit.
Site Includes: news, magazine, organization and program information, and more.

The Internet Engineering Task Force (IETF)
Web Address: http://www.ietf.cnri.reston.va.us/
E-mail Address: ietf-web@cnri.reston.va.us
Description: International membership organization concerned with the evolution of the Internet.
Site Includes: organization information and activities.

Internet Society
Web Address: http://www.isoc.org/
E-mail Address: amr@isoc.org
Description: International non-governmental organization supporting Internet use.
Site Includes: news, papers and presentations, conferences, Internet standards, organization information, and more.

Internet Town Hall
Web Address: http://www.town.hall.org/
E-mail Address: webmaster@town.hall.org
Description: Directory of information regarding international Internet developments.
Site Includes: directory.

InterNIC
Web Address: http://is.internic.net/
E-mail Address: domreg@internic.net
Description: The official organization in the United States which registers new sites and domain names.
Site Includes: directory and database services, registration services, NIC support services.

The Morino Institute
Web Address: http://www.cais.com/morino/htdocs/pand.htm
E-mail Address: feedback@morino.org
Description: Nonprofit organization which publishes the Directory of Public Access Networks to promote information sharing among specific geographic communities.
Site Includes: directory.

National Information Infrastructure Testbed
Web Address: http://www.niit.org/

E-mail Address: niit_info.niit.org

Description: A technology industry led consortium promoting the growth of the National Information Infrastructure.

Site Includes: news, membership, and organization information.

Telecom Information Resources on the Internet

Web Address: http://www.spp.umich.edu/telecom-info.html

E-mail Address: jmm@umich.edu

Description: Document containing information on technical, economic, public policy, and social elements of telecommunications.

Site Includes: searchable database.

The World Wide Web Consortium-W3C

Web Address: http://www.w3.org/pub/WWW/

E-mail Address: info@mail.w3.org

Description: International consortium promoting Web use and growth.

Site Includes: newsletters, FAQ's, meeting and organization information.

Internet Service Providers

Directories

GTLUG Internet Service Provider Index Index

Web Address: http://www.gtlug.org/isp/

E-mail Address: simmons@gtlug.org

Description: Links to ISPs.

Site Includes: Different methods to locate an ISP in your area: by area code or U.S. clickable map.

The List

Web Address: http://thelist.com

E-mail Address: thelist@colossus.net

Description: A listing of 1,584 Internet Service Providers listed by state, province and area code, and by country and country code.

Site Includes: listing.

"The NEtAccess Worldwide List

Web Address: http://www.best.be/iap.html

E-mail Address: lips@best.be

Description: Links to ISPs around the world. Links organized by country.

Site Includes: ISP links and information.

Sample Internet Service Providers

Online Communication Services

Web Address: http://www.netcom.com/

E-mail Address: info@netcom.com
Description: Nationwide provider of direct Internet access.
Site Includes: subscription information, rates, products and services.

PSINet
Web Address: http://www.psi.net/
E-mail Address: webmaster@psi.com
Description: National Internet service provider for businesses and individuals.
Site Includes: products and services, and company information.

The Well
Web Address: http://www.well.com/
E-mail Address: web@well.com
Description: The Whole Earth 'Lectronic Link (Well) is an on-line interactive, Cyber-
space community based in San Francisco. It also provides Internet access.
Site Includes: searchable database, community, conference, and membership infor-
mation.

Nonprofit On-line Services

HandsNet
Web Address: http://www.handsnet.org/handsnet
E-mail Address: hninfo@handsnet.org
Description: Nonprofit on-line service which links approximately 5,000 public
interest and human service organizations in the United States
Site Includes: public policy alerts and analyses, notices of legal and administrative
actions, abstracts of key studies and reports, Federal Register notices, funding
information, and daily updates of crucial human services news.

The Institute for Global Communications (IGC)
Web Address: http://www.igc.apc.org/
E-mail Address: webweaver@igc.apc.org
Description: IGC provides on-line communication services to the progressive com-
munity through: PeaceNet, EcoNet, ConflictNet, LaborNet, and WomensNet.
Site Includes: program links and membership directory.

Commercial On-line Services with Special Nonprofit Features

America Online
Web Address: http://www.aol.com
E-mail Address: postmaster@aol.com
Description: Commercial on-line service with over 5 million subscribers.
Site Includes: news services, shopping, chat rooms as well as a downloadable soft-
ware to connect to America Online. America Online is the hosts access.point
Civic Involvement System. Available to both Mac and Windows users.

CompuServe
Web Address: http://www.compuserve.com/index2.html
E-mail Address: info@compuserve.com
Description: Commercial on-line service with over 4 million subscribers worldwide.
Site Includes: Business and financial services, chat rooms, News services, rooms as well as a downloadable software to connect to CompuServe. CompuServe is the home of the NonProfit Forum™—for access contact 75162.3366@compuserve.com. Available to both Mac and Windows users.

eWorld
Web Address: http://www.eworld.com
E-mail Address:
Description: This is the Web address of Apple's on-line service. Most Macs come with eWorld software installed. eWorld has a well polished look but with its small membership base results in light traffic in most message areas.
Site Includes: Wide range of information services. Available to Mac users only.

Microsoft Network (MSN)
Web Address: http://www.msn.com
E-mail Address:
Description: MSN was originally marketed as a full commercial on-line service, but has been transformed into a new type of ISP. It not only provides Internet access, but also has Web sites that are available to the public at large.
Site Includes: Gateway to the Internet. Available to Windows users only at this time.

Prodigy
Web Address: http://www.prodigy.com
E-mail Address:
Description:
Site Includes: Available to both Mac and Windows users.

Internet Service Providers that Offer Free Web Space to Nonprofits

Achievement International World Wide Web Design Center
Web Address: http://www.achiever.com/design/freehmpg.html
Description: Offers free home pages to people and organizations.
Site Includes: Home pages and application.

Vive Web Connections
Web Address: http://www.vive.com/connect/
E-mail Address: webmaster@vive.com
Description: Business site offering free Web space to nonprofits, schools, and community centers.
Site Includes: organization information and links to member sites.

Reference Material

The Alex Catalog
Web Address: http://www.lib.ncsu.edu/stacks/alex-index.html
E-mail Address: alex@rsl.ox.ac.uk
Description: Catalog of books and other works on the Internet.
Site Includes: catalog.

ARTFL Project: ROGET Form
Web Address: http://humanities.uchicago.edu/forms_unrest/ROGET.html
E-mail Address: mark@gide.uchicago.edu
Description: Roget's Thesaurus version 1.02 on-line.
Site Includes: thesaurus.

Bill's Library
Web Address: http://www.io.org/~jgcom/library.htm
E-mail Address: jgcom@io.org
Description: Well organized library of hyperlinks to valuable resources.
Site Includes: The Magazine Rack, Stop By the Poet's Corner, My Favourite Writers and Works, The Public Library, The Law Library.

CIA Publications and Handbooks
Web Address: http://www.odci.gov/cia/publications/pubs.html
E-mail Address: not available
Description: Publications of the Central Intelligence Agency.
Site Includes: 1995 World Factbook, 1995 Factbook on Intelligence, CIA Maps & Publications and more.

City.Net
Web Address: http://www.city.net
E-mail Address: altis@city.net
Description: A comprehensive international guide to communities around the world.
Site Includes: directory and guide.

Computer Journals/Magazines Online
Web Address: http://www.library.cmu.edu/bySubject/CS+ECE/lib/journals.html
E-mail Address: missy@cs.cmu.edu
Description: Alphabetized collection of on-line journals and magazines covering computer related topics
Site Includes: directory.

Global Encyclopedia
Web Address: http://204.32.221.16/
E-mail Address: not available

Description: A free encyclopedia which takes submissions from anyone. It is rapidly growing, and easy to use, but the articles are not necessarily written by experts in the field.
Site Includes: encyclopedia.

Helwig's Smiley Dictionary
Web Address: http://www.cg.tuwien.ac.at/~helwig/smiley.html
E-mail Address: unavailable
Description: A large and diverse dictionary of emoticons.
Site Includes: examples of emoticons with definitions.

The IBIC Guide to Book-Related Resources on the Internet
Web Address: http://sunsite.unc.edu/ibic/IBIC-homepage.html#Guide
E-mail Address: ibic@sunsite.unc.edu
Description: Directory of information relating to books.
Site Includes: directory and some texts.

Internet Public Library
Web Address: http://ipl.sils.umich.edu/
E-mail Address: ipl@umich.edu
Description: Provides services and information to promote efficient and effective Internet use.
Site Includes: links to various reference information and texts.

Library Information Servers via WWW
Web Address: http://sunsite.berkeley.edu/Libweb/
E-mail Address: tdowling@ohiolink.edu
Description: International directory of libraries on the Web, organized by country.
Site Includes: directory.

The On-line Books Page
Web Address: http://www.cs.cmu.edu/Web/books.html
E-mail Address: spok+books@cs.cmu.edu
Description: Index of over 1600 on-line books.
Site Includes: directory.

Online Computer Library Center, Inc.
Web Address: http://www.oclc.org/
E-mail Address: not available
Description: A not-for-profit computer library service and research organization.
Site Includes: on-line reference systems, electronic journals.

Online Reference Works
Web Address: http://www.cs.cmu.edu/Web/references.html
E-mail Address: spok@cs.cmu.edu

Description: A small collection of on-line reference works.

Site Includes: English dictionaries, foreign language dictionaries, thesauruses, maps, area and zip code information, and more.

Saint Joseph's Public Library

Web Address: http://sjcpl.lib.in.us/homepage/PublicLibraries/ PublicLibraryServers.html

E-mail Address: donald.napoli@gomail.sjcpl.lib.in.us

Description: List of public libraries with Internet services.

Site Includes: Gopher, Telnet, and World Wide Web, as well as a search tool.

The Smiley Dictionary

Web Address: http://olympe.polytechnique.fr/~violet/Smileys/

E-mail Address: unavailable

Description: A dictionary of emoticons divided into four parts: classic smileys, funny smileys, people smileys and more.

Site Includes: examples of emoticons with definitions.

The Unofficial Smiley Dictionary

Web Address: http://info.ox.ac.uk/~keb10376/smilies.html

E-mail Address: unavailable

Description: A dictionary of emoticons.

Site Includes: examples of emoticons with definitions.

WWW Virtual Library

Web Address: http://www.w3.org/hypertext/DataSources/bySubject/Overview.html

E-mail Address: www-request@mail.w3.org

Description: A subject index of numerous reference oriented Web sites cataloged and indexed like a library.

Site Includes: directory.

Search Tools

Galaxy

Web Address: http://galaxy.einet.net

Description: A powerful search engine which provides comprehensive site descriptions.

Site Includes: search tool.

InfoSeek Guide

Web Address: http://www.infoseek.com

Description: Allows for broad based searches of the entire Internet or specific searches of a single element: FAQ's, FTP sites, Newsgroups, or Web sites.

Site Includes: search tool.

List of Web Robots
Web Address: http://info.webcrawler.com/mak/projects/robots/active.html
E-mail Address: m.koster@webcrawler.com
Description: List of Web robots, spiders, and engines.
Site Includes: directory.

Lycos
Web Address: http://www.lycos.com
Description: Described as "The Catalog of the Internet" it returns a significant number of hits, but the descriptions are usually text taken from the beginning of the document and are difficult to sort through.
Site Includes: search tool.

Magellan
Web Address: http://www.mckinley.com/
Description: Reviews, rates and categorizes Web sites.
Site Includes: directory.

Mecklerweb
Web Address: http://www.mecklerweb.com/imall
Description: Lists services and products sold via the Internet.
Site Includes: directory.

Net Search
Web Address: http://home.netscape.com/home/internet-search.html
Description: The search tool accessed when clicking on the toolbar of the Netscape browser. Performs a select search with descriptions which are usually text taken from the beginning of the document.
Site Includes: search tool.

SavvySearch
Web Address: http://www.cs.colostate.edu/~dreiling/smartform.html
Description: A "meta-search engine" that searches the major Internet search engine.
Site Includes: search engine.

Starting Point
Web Address: http://www.stpt.com
Description: Performs Meta-Searches which allow the user to perform a keyword search of many databases from single starting point.
Site Includes: search tool.

The Virtual Tourist
Web Address: http://wings.buffalo.edu/world/
Description: The Virtual Tourist is a geographic directory of WWW servers in the world. Allows users to zero in on a specific region, anywhere in the world, to

locate on-line Internet resources including: cities and towns, hospitals, corporations, educational institutions, Internet Service Providers, and more.
Site Includes: directory.

WebCrawler
Web Address: http://www.webcrawler.com
Description: America Online's search tool for the Web provides a list of hits based on a keyword search.
Site Includes: search tool.

Yahoo
Web Address: http://www.yahoo.com
Description: A popular keyword search tool, which also provides 14 subject directories for more general, and often interesting, searches.
Site Includes: search tool.

Site Announcements

A1's Searchable Directory of Fee WWW Web Page Promotion Sites
Web Address: http://www.a1co.com/home.html
Description: Index of 636 sites which will promote or link a Web site for free, including: search tools and subject directories.
Site Includes: directory and new site application.

NCSA What's New
Web Address: http://www.ncsa.uiuc.edu/SDG/Software/Mosaic/Docs/whats-new.html
Description: Listing of new or changed Web sites.
Site Includes: directory and new site application.

Netscape's What's New
Web Address: http://home.netscape.com/home/whats-new.html
Description: Dedicated only to unique or well designed new sites.
Site Includes: directory.

Submit It
Web Address: http://www.submit-it.com/
Description: Easy and quick way to submit a new site to many search tools, engines and catalogs.
Site Includes: submission form.

URL-minder
Web Address: http://www.netmind.com/URL-minder/URL-minder.html
Description: Sends users an e-mail message when a site with which they have registered changes.
Site Includes: information and submission form.

Technical Assistance

Computer-Mediated Communication Studies Center (CMC)
Web Address: http://www.december.com/cmc/study/center.html
E-mail Address: john@december.com
Description: A clearinghouse of information on computer-mediated communication.
Site Includes: CMC magazine, activities, and resource listing.

Free On-line Dictionary of Computing
Web Address: http://wombat.doc.ic.ac.uk/
E-mail Address: dbh@doc.ic.ac.uk
Description: Searchable index of computing terms. Includes hyperlinks in the definitions for easy travelling to help with a word in the definition which is also unknown.
Site Includes: dictionary.

Glossary of Internet Terms
Web Address: http://www.matisse.net/files/glossary.html
E-mail Address: admin@matisse.net
Description: Alphabetized, searchable glossary of Internet terms.
Site Includes: glossary.

Internet Resources
Web Address: http://www.brandonu.ca/~ennsnr/Resources/Welcome.html
E-mail Address: ennsnr@brandon.ca
Description: Directory of Internet resources.
Site Includes: links to lists of Internet guides, Internet resource lists, ftp archives, USENET newsgroup, mailing lists, Interest course descriptions and more.

Newbie Newsgroup
Group Address: news.newusers.questions
Description: Newsgroup for new users.
Group Includes: questions and answers for new users.

The Telecommunications Glossary
Web Address: http://www.wiltel.com/glossary/glossary.html
E-mail Address: info@wiltel.com
Description: Glossary of telecommunications terms.
Site Includes: glossary.

Web Style Manual
Web Address: http://info.med.yale.edu/caim/StyleManual_Top.HTML
E-mail Address: lynch@biomed.med.yale.edu

Description: Manual describing design technique for Web pages created by the Center for Advanced Instructional Media.
Site Includes: manual.

Yanoff's Internet Services List
Web Address: http://slacvx.slac.stanford.edu:80/misc/internet-services.html
E-mail Address: not available
Description: A subject list of Internet resources, from Agriculture to Math to Women.
Site Includes: directory.

WEB SITES FEATURED IN GUIDE

Abwenzi African Studies
Web Address: http://www.infosphere.com:80/abwenzi/
E-mail Address: abwenzi@infosphere.com
Description: Nonprofit corporation promoting friendships between Americans and Africans.
Site Includes: program and activity information.

American Academy of Pediatrics-(AAP)
Web Address: http://www.aap.org
E-mail Address: webmaster@aap.org
Description: National association of pediatricians.
Site Includes: news, organization, program, and membership information.

Amnesty International
Web Address: http://www.amnesty.org
E-mail Address: rmitchellai@gn.apc.org
Description: Amnesty International is a worldwide human rights watchdog organization.
Site Includes: activity, program, and organization information.

Art in the Public Interest
Web Address: http://artswire.org/Community/highperf/APIhome.html
E-mail Address: highperf@artswire.org
Description: A nonprofit organization providing information about the arts community and social issues.
Site Includes: newsletter, program information, links and more.

Arts Foundation of Michigan
Web Address: http://www.tmn.com/Community/afmadams/afmnew.html
E-mail Address: afmadams@tmn.com

Description: Foundation supporting participation and investment in the Michigan arts community.
Site Includes: program information.

Arts Wire
Web Address: http://artswire.org/Artswire/www/awfront.html
E-mail Address: kanter@artswire.org
Description: Arts Wire is a program of the New York Foundation for the Arts and serves as a national on-line arts network.
Site Includes: program, activity, and organization information.

Bethany Christian Services
Web Address: http://www.bethany.org/
E-mail Address: judith@bethany.org
Description: Christian social services organization.
Site Includes: organization and related topic information.

Big Brother/Big Sisters of Monmouth County
Web Address: http://www.texel.com/home/sab/bbbs.html
E-mail Address: scriptunas@att.com
Description: The Web site of the Monmouth County chapter of Big Brothers/Big Sisters, a youth services organization.
Site Includes: program information.

Bionomics Institute
Web Address: http://www.bionomics.org/
E-mail Address: Steve_Gibson@bionomics.org
Description: A nonprofit organization, "dedicated to replacing the traditional, mechanistic view of the economy with economy-as-ecosystem thinking."
Site Includes: resources, archives, publications, and organization information.

Blacksburg Electronic Village
Web Address: http://www.bev.net
E-mail Address: cvmartin@bev.net
Description: A virtual community sponsored by Virginia Tech, Bell Atlantic of Virginia, and the Town of Blacksburg promoting information on and to Blacksburg, Virginia citizens.
Site Includes: organization and activity information.

Brookings Institution
Web Address: http://www.brook.edu/
E-mail Address: jpatterson@brook.edu
Description: A national, nonprofit organization dedicated to research in economics, governmental studies, and the social sciences.
Site Includes: publications, journal, research and organization information.

Center for Civil Society International-(CCSI)
Web Address: http://solar.rtd.utk.edu/~ccsi/ccsihome.html
E-mail Address: ccsi@u.washington.edu
Description: International clearinghouse promoting relations with the former
    Soviet Union.
Site Includes: announcements, newsfiles, and organization information.

City of San Carlos, California
Web Address: http://www.abag.ca.gov/san_carlos/index.html
E-mail Address: scarlos@mail.crl.com
Description: Listing of city information for San Carlos, California.
Site Includes: town information.

Civic Network
Web Address: http://www.civic.net
E-mail Address: mfidelman@civicnet.org
Description: Collection of on-line resources regarding civic life and citizen partici-
    pation.
Site Includes: newsletter, organization and program information.

Digital Gateway Systems
Web Address: http://dgsys.com/
E-mail Address: future@dgsys.com
Description: Internet Service Provider in Metropolitan Washington, D.C. area.
Site Includes: services and organization information.

Duke University School of Engineering
Web Address: http://www.egr.duke.edu/DOHP.home.html
E-mail Address: ptavern@acpub.duke.edu
Description: Official site of the Duke University School of Engineering.
Site Includes: virtual Dean's Office, course information, faculty biographies or con-
    tact information, events information, and engineering-related home pages.

Electronic Frontier Foundation
Web Address: http://www.eff.org
E-mail Address: selena@eff.org
Description: Nonprofit organization promoting unrestricted access to on-line
    resources.
Site Includes: alerts, newsletter, and organization information.

Essential Information
Web Address: http://www.essential.org/EI.html
E-mail Address:
Description: A nonprofit founded by Ralph Nader in 1982 to encourage citizen par-
    ticipation. Offers home pages to nonprofits.

Site Includes: access to Essential publications such as *Multinational Monitor* and *Good Works* and links to over 30 nonprofit sites.

Ethiopian Jewry
Web Address: http://www.cais.com/nacoej/index.html
E-mail Address: andy@cais.com
Description: The home page of the North American Conference on Ethiopian Jewry. The site includes information about Ethiopia, its are, culture and society.
Site Includes: Links to other Ethiopian and Jewish sites.

Free Library of Philadelphia
Web Address: http://www.libertynet.org/~flp/flp_page.html
E-mail Address: inglisj@flp.lib.pa.us
Description: Catalog of one of the largest libraries in the country.
Site Includes: catalog, library information, publications and other announcements.

The Friends of Makerere in Canada Incorporated-(FOMAC)
Web Address: http://www.arch.adelaide.edu.au/~molweny/Uganda/fomac.html
E-mail Address: olweny@mail.cc.umanitoba.ca
Description: Nonprofit supporting educational opportunities in Africa.
Site Includes: program and activity information.

Guide to Internet Resources for Nonprofit Public Service Organizations
Web Address: http://asa.ugl.lib.umich.edu/chdocs/nonprofits/nonprofits.html
E-mail Address: nesbeitt@sils.umich.edu
Description: A very comprehensive downloadable guide to Internet resources for nonprofits.
Site Includes: directory.

Indiana Historical Society
Web Address: http://www.spcc.com/ihsw/ihs.html
E-mail Address: reboomer@indy.net
Description: Nonprofit organization providing information on the Indiana Historical Society's programs, collections, and staff.
Site Includes: publications, grants and fellowships, guides, educational information and more.

Institute for Global Communications
Web Address: http://www.igc.apc.org/
E-mail Address: mstein@igc.apc.org
Description: Institute for Global Communications (IGC) provides full service on-line communication to the progressive community through its networks: PeaceNet, EcoNet, ConflictNet, LaborNet, and WomensNet.
Site Includes: Internet service, program links and membership directory.

International Arid Lands Consortium
Web Address: http://ag.arizona.edu/OALS/IALC/Home.html
E-mail Address: jbanc@ag.arizona.edu
Description: International nonprofit organization concerned with ecological sustainability in arid and semiarid lands worldwide.
Site Includes: newsletter, program, and organization information.

Internet Society
Web Address: http://www.isoc.org/
E-mail Address: jay@isoc.org
Description: International non-governmental organization supporting Internet use.
Site Includes: news, papers and presentations, conferences, Internet standards, organization information, and more.

Macronet
Web Address: http://www.macronet.org/macronet
E-mail Address: brockway@macronet.org
Description: A clearinghouse of information and resources for the nonprofit progressive community.
Site Includes: organization information, links, searchable database and more.

MCNC
Web Address: http://www.mcnc.org
E-mail Address: clark@mcnc.org
Description: A corporation providing electronic and information technologies for businesses, government and educational organizations in North Carolina.
Site Includes: activity and organization information.

Mennonite Central Committee
Web Address: http://www.mennonitecc.ca/mcc/
E-mail Address: jdl@mennonitecc.ca
Description: Official site of the North American Mennonite Central Committee.
Site Includes: activity and organization information.

Needham and Associates
Web Address: http://www.needham.com/
E-mail Address: elaine@needham.com
Description: Company site.
Site Includes: organization information and links.

Nonprofit Outreach Network
Web Address: http://www.norn.org/pub/norn/
E-mail Address: gilly@norn.org

Description: Organization provides free services to assist nonprofits in establishing an on-line presence.
Site Includes: organization and resource information.

Nonprofit Prophets
Web Address: http://edweb.sdsu.edu/edfirst/prophets/prophets.html
E-mail Address: Tmarch@mail.sdsu.edu
Description: Project designed to help high school youth become involved with today's social and environmental problems through the development of research projects and creation of Web sites.
Site Includes: information about the project.

Nonprofit Resources Catalogue
Web Address: http://www.clark.net/pub/pwalker/
E-mail Address: pwalker@clark.net
Description: Sponsored and developed by Phillip A. Walker, it is a comprehensive guide to on-line nonprofit activity and resources.
Site Includes: directory.

Odyssey of the Mind
Web Address: http://www.odyssey.org/odyssey
E-mail Address: cr8vkids@netcom.com
Description: Nonprofit educational organization that promotes a creative team-based problem solving program for students from kindergarten through college.
Site Includes: program and organization information.

One Earth
Web Address: htp//www.1earth.com/1e/
E-mail Address: gfaber@1earth.com
Description: Company which provides on-line services to nonprofits, including page design, hosting and address advertisement.
Site includes: services provided, company profile, packages and pricing.

Ozone Action
Web Address: http://www.essential.org/orgs/Ozone_Action/Ozone_Action.html
E-mail Address: not available
Description: Watchdog organization on the issue of ozone depletion
Site Includes: information about ozone depletion, UV-B radiation, corporations responsible, alternatives and solutions, programs and resources, and related sites.

PagOne
Web Address: http://www.PagOne.com
E-mail Address: karen@pagone.com

Description: Company provides on-line advertising services.
Site Includes: organization information.

PBS Online
Web Address: http://www.pbs.org
E-mail Address: cjohanson@pbs.org
Description: The official Public Broadcasting System site.
Site Includes: what's on, what's new, documentary information and more.

Putnam Barber's Resources for Nonprofits
Web Address: http://www.eskimo.com/~pbarber/
E-mail Address: pbarber@eskimo.com
Description: Contains news and hyperlinks to nonprofit resources on the Internet.
Site Includes: directory.

SOHO America
Web Address: http://www.soho.org/sohoamerica
E-mail Address: jdoctor@fergus.cfa.org
Description: Association supporting small office and home office professionals.
Site Includes: newsletter, program, and membership information.

Stop Prisoner Rape
Web Address: http://www.igc.apc.org/spr/
E-mail Address: ellens@ai.mit.edu
Description: National nonprofit providing assistance and information on prisoner
    rape.
Site Includes: articles, documents and sites related to prisoner rape issues.

Taxpayers Against Fraud
Web Address: http://www.taf.org
E-mail Address: rbt@taf.org
Description: Nonprofit organization combatting tax fraud.
Site Includes: news releases, organization information and publications.

Telecom Information Resources Directory
Web Address: http://www.spp.umich.edu/telecom-info.html
E-mail Address: jmm@umich.edu
Description: Provides 900 links to resources on the Internet.
Site Includes: searchable database.

UK Fundraising
Web Address: http://www.city.ac.uk/~bh543/fundraising.html
E-mail Address: HLAKE@ai-uk.gn.apc.org
Description: Resources for fundraisers and fundraising in the United Kingdom.
Site Includes: resource links.

Universities Space Research Association-(USRA)
Web Address: http://www.usra.edu/
E-mail Address: Bradley@usra.edu
Description: An association which promotes cooperation between universities, research institutions and the U.S. Government in space science and technology.
Site Includes: programs and organization information.

University of Konstanz
Web Address: http://www.uni-konstanz.de/
E-mail Address: Jens-Erik.Weber@uni-konstanz.de
Description: University of Konstanz's official Web home page.
Site Includes: written in German.

WebActive
Web Address: http://www.webactive.com
E-mail Address: webactive@prognet.com
Description: An organization that highlights the on-line activity of national and international activists.
Site Includes: links to activist sites.

Selected Reference Material

BOOKS

Battle, Stafford L. and Harris, Rey O. 1995. *The African American Resource Guide to the Internet.* Columbia, MD: On Demand Press. A cultural and technical guide to the Internet. Offers philosophical perspective on the uses of the Internet, including on-line resources, as well as basic and easy to follow guidelines for going on-line.

December, John and Ginsburg, Mark. 1995. *HTML & CGI Unleashed.* Indianapolis, IN: Sams.Net Publishing. Covers the complete life cycle of Web development: planning, analysis, implementation, and gateway programming using Perl, REXX, and C.

December, John. 1995. *Presenting Java.* Indianapolis, IN: Sams.Net Publishing. Introduction to and programming in Java.

December, John and Randall, Neil. 1995. *The World Wide Web Unleashed.* Indianapolis, IN: Sams.Net Publishing. Overview and guide for a general audience.

Eager, Bill et al. 1995. *net.search.* Que Corporation. Detailed analysis and instruction of how to perform searches on-line. Offers both a quick and easy and more thorough, scientific approach.

Ellsworth, Jill H. and Ellsworth, Matthew V. 1996. *The New Internet Business Book.* New York: John Wiley & Sons. Includes basic Internet information and specifics for businesses including: establishing a presence, finding business resources, doing business on-line and more.

Gilster, Paul. 1994. *Finding It on the Internet.* New York: John Wiley & Sons. Slightly outdated, but still very useful for gaining an understanding of the older model Internet, pre-WWW. Includes, Veronica, WAIS, WWW, Archie and Gopher searches.

Gilster, Paul. 1993. *The Internet Navigator.* New York: John Wiley & Sons. One of the originals, it contains all the basics necessary to operate on the Internet as well as explanation of more complex operations.

Graham, Ian S. 1995. *The HTML Sourcebook.* New York: John Wiley & Sons. Programming guide for HTML. More complex, but offers instruction on Web page construction and linking.

Hoffman, Paul E. 1995. *Netscape and the WWW for Dummies.* Foster City, CA: IDG Books Worldwide, Inc. Best-selling series of computer know-how books for beginners. Tips for browser and Web use with easy to follow instruction.

Lichty, Tom. 1994. *The Official America Online for Windows Tour Guide.* Second Edition. Research Triangle Park, NC: Ventana Press, Inc. Comprehensive guide to using America Online. Includes discussion of Internet connectivity via the service. Approved by AOL.

Swadley, Richards K., publ. 1995. *The Internet Unleashed,* rev 2d ed. Indianapolis, IN: Sams.Net Publishing. Expansive collection of information for home, business, and educational use. Includes information on the Web and is helpful for beginners and experts.

PERIODICALS

ComputerLife Magazine. General computer users' magazine. Includes on-line information as well as that concerning home/office, family, and business use. Subscriptions: P.O. Box 55880, Boulder, Colorado 80322-5880 (http://www.ziff.com/~computerlife).

HomeOffice Computing. Dedicated to small business which makes it distinct from other on-line focused magazines. Also includes general coverage of Internet activity and growth. Subscriptions: 411 Lafayette St., New York, NY 10003, (800) 288-7812.

InfoActive. Telecommunications monthly for nonprofits. Easy to read and understand and dedicated to the nonprofit community. Published by the Center for Media Education. Subscriptions: InfoActive, 1511 K Street, NW, Suite 518, Washington, DC 20005, (202) 628-2620 (cme@access.digex.net).

Information Week. For business and technology managers. Dedicated to communications and information in the business community, also covers general computing and Internet topics. Subscriptions: Information Week, P.O. Box 1093, Skokie, IL 60076, (800) 292-3642 (http:// techweb.cmp.com / iwk).

Internet Connection. Guide to Government Resources available on-line. Comprehensive guide to all the government has to offer. Subscriptions: (800) 274-4447.

Internet World Magazine. Dedicated to Internet use. It offers informative articles for Internet users, both personal and professional. Subscriptions: P.O. Box 713, Mt. Morris, Illinois 61054, (800) 573-3062 (http:// www.mecklerweb.com).

NetGuide Magazine. Periodical that serves as a monthly guide to what is new on the WWW. Subscriptions: 600 Community Dr., Manhasset, New York 11030, (800) 829-0421, (http:// techweb.cmp.com / net).

Online Access Magazine. Devoted to on-line services, bulletin boards, and the Internet. More general information for all types of on-line users. Subscriptions: 5615 W. Cermak Rd., Cicero, Illinois 60650-2290 (e-mail 70324.343@compuserve. com).

PC Computing. General computer user's magazine describing hardware, software and special feature articles. Subscriptions: P.O. Box 58229, Boulder, CO 80322-8229, (303) 665-8930 (72241.1724@compuserve.com).

Wired. Feature magazine for cyberspace community. Subscriptions: P.O. Box 191826, San Francisco, CA 94119-9866, (800)SO-WIRED (subscriptions@wired. com).

ON-LINE RESOURCES

General Internet

Essential Computing Terms: Important Words and Concepts Every Computer Enthusiast Needs to Know
http:// www.revenue.com / first / basicdef / terms.htm#bbs

John E. Goodwin, *E-Mail 101*, version 0.2.5, July 17, 1993.
ftp:// uiarchive.cso.uiuc.edu / pub / etext / gutenberg / etext93 / email025.txt

Adam Gaffin, *EFF's Guide to the Internet*, version 3.15, October 23, 1995.
http:// www.eff.org / pub / Net_infor / EFF_Net_Guide / netguide.eff

Ed Krol and Ellen Hoffman, *What is the Internet?*, May 1993.
ftp:// nic.merit.edu / documents / fyi / fyi_20.txt

Jean Armour Polly, *Surfing the Internet: an Introduction,* version 2.0.3, Revised May 15, 1993.
ftp://nysernet.org/pub/resources/guides/surfing.2.0.3.txt

Netiquette

Vint Cerf, *Guidelines for Conduct on and Use of Internet,* Internet Society, draft Aug. 14, 1994.
http://info.isoc.org:80/policy/conduct/cerf-Aug-draft.html

Sally Hambridge, *Netiquette Guidelines,* October 1995.
ftp://ftp.merit.edu/documents/fyi/fyi_28.txt

Chuq Von Rospach, *A Primer on How to Work with the Usenet Community,* revised January 29, 1995.
http://www.smartpages.com/faqs/usenet/primer/part1/faq.html

Brad Templeton, *Emily Postnews Answers Your Questions on Netiquette,* Nov. 2, 1994.
http://www.smartpages.com/faqs/emily-postnews/part1/faq.html

FAQ

FAQs about FAQs
http://www.smartpages.com/faqs/faqs/about-faqs/faq.html

Internet History

Certnet Project History
http://www.cerfnet.com/cerfnet/about/cerfhistory.html

Vinton Cerf, as told to Bernard Aboba, *How the Internet Came to Be,* 1993.
This article appears in "The Online User's Encyclopedia," by Bernard Aboba, Addison-Wesley, November 1993.
gopher://gopher.isoc.org:70/00/internet/history/how.internet.came.to.be

Henry Edward Hardy, *The History of the Net,* Master's Thesis, Grand Valley State University, September 28, 1993.
http://www.prz.tu-berlin.de/~derek/internet/sources/net.history.thesis.html

Bruce Sterling, *Short History of the Internet,* Literary Freeware, from The Magazine of Fantasy and Science Fiction, Feb. 1993.
gopher://gopher.isoc.org:70/00/internet/history/short.history.of.internet

Robert H. Zakon, *Hobbes' Internet Timeline,* v2.2, The MITRE Corporation, 1993–5.
http://info.isoc.org/guest/zakon/Internet/History/HIT.html

Web History

A Little History
http://www.w3.org/pub/WWW/History.html

World Wide Web People
http://www.w3.org/pub/WWW/People.html

Ben M. Segal, *A Short History of Internet Protocols at CERN*, April, 1995
http://wwwcn.cern.ch/pdp/ns/ben/TCPHIST.html

Marketing

The Usenet Marketplace FAQ: The How-to of the misc.forsale and biz.marketplace newsgroups
http://www.phoenix.net/~lidan/FAQ/

Robert Raisch, *Postage-Due Marketing,* an Internet Company White Paper
http://www.internet.com:2010/merketing/postage.html

Virus

WWW FAX: Can I catch a virus by looking at a web page?
http://sunsite.unc.edu/boutell/faq/virus.htm

Security Issues

CERT Advisory, Feb. 3, 1994, "Online Network Monitoring Attacks"
http://www.cs.ruu.nl/pub/SECURITY/cert...es/CA-94.01.Network.
Monitoring.Attacks

CERT Advisory, Jan. 23, 1995, "IP Spoofing Attacks and Hijacked Terminal Connections"
http://www.cs.ruu.nl/pub/SECURITY/cert...acks.and.hijacked.terminal.
connections

Cyberspeak

Acronyms
http://www.revenue.com/first/basicdef/acronum.txt

Helwig's Smiley Dictionary
http://www.cg.tuwien.ac.at/~helwig/smileys.html

The Unofficial Smiley Dictionary
   http://www.tu-chemnitz.de/~lpo/smiley_dict.html

Pierre Violet, *The Smiley Dictionary*
   http://www.netsurf.org/~violet/Smileys/

Spam

Spam Warz: or How to Crash a Hundred Thousand Computers in Three Easy Steps
   http://www.tardis.ed.ac.uk/~charlie/nonfiction/journalism/spam.html

Axel Boldt, *Blacklist of Internet Advertisers*, revised Nov. 16, 1995.
   http://math-www.uni-paderborn.de/~axel/BL/blacklist.html

Usenet

Mark Horton, *Rules for Posting to Usenet*, revised March 3, 1995.
   http://www.smartpages.com/faqs/usenet/posting-rules/part1/faq.html

Mark Moraes, *What is Usenet*, revised November 25, 1995.
   http://www.smartpages.com/faqs/usenet/what-is/part1/faq.html

Edward Vielmetti, *What is Usenet? A Second Opinion*, revised, October 26, 1994.
   http://www.smartpages.com/faqs/usenet/what-is/part2/faq.html

Glossary

ASCII. Computer code for text characters. This acronym stands for American Standard Code for Information Interchange.

Archie. An electronic directory service for locating information available at FTP archives.

Archive. Collection of stored material available for retrieval, such as an archive of a mailing list messages.

Baud rate. The unit of measure used to describe the speed at which a *modem* can transmit information to and from the user's computer.

BITNET. An academic computer network that uses a different protocol than the Internet. Many mailing lists are run off of Bitnet because of their tie to the academic community.

Bookmarks. A feature of the Netscape browser that stores the name and location of Web sites for easy return.

Bulletin board. Also known as bulletin board systems (BBS). A single computer or a network of computers that people dial into via a modem to use the service. Some BBSs are on the Internet, but most are free standing entities that are either available at no cost or for an hourly or monthly fee.

Browser. Software which interprets *HTML* and presents it to the viewer as a Web page.

Byte. A measurement for computer file size.

Chat.   Live on-line conversations, usually occurring in chat rooms, conducted over the Internet or on-line service provider.

Cyber-fundraising.   Fundraising that is accomplished utilizing on-line methods. In many cases this involves using an electronic commerce provider. In other cases, the Internet is used to solicit the funds and another method is used to make the financial transaction (phone, mail, etc.).

Cyberspace.   The community of Internet users.

Domain name system (DNS).   A naming system that translates Internet addresses into computer interpretable, IP (Internet protocol), addresses. IP addresses are a series of numbers. The DNS allows the numbers to be replaced with words.

Download.   The copying of files from the *Internet,* or any remote source, to a user's personal computer. This is information retrieval, like bringing a book home from the library. In addition, applications can be downloaded from the Internet to be installed and executed on the user's computer.

E-mail.   Mail sent *on-line* over a *network* from one computer to another as opposed to through the postal service.

Emoticon.   (also known as smileys) ASCII characters that are used in cyberspace communication to denote emotion. The word is short for emotive icon. The icons are variations on a sideways smiley face :-).

Encryption.   A code system applied to a file to insure the security of the transmitted information.

FAQ.   (Frequently Asked Questions) A listing of commonly asked questions and their respective answers.

File.   Information grouped together and stored on a disk.

Flame.   A purposely insulting e-mail message.

Free-Net.   A free, volunteer run, community based computer network.

Freeware.   Software distributed free by the author.

File Transfer Protocol (FTP).   Is a tool that allows the transfer of files from an off-site database or server to a user's computer.

Gateway.   A computer or server that moves data between networks.

Gopher.   An Internet tool that simplifies using networked information by creating menus that point the user toward information. The menu or file is in text only format. Gopher was designed at the Information Technology Laboratory at the University of Minnesota.

Hardware. Computer equipment, such as a monitor, printer, modem, scanner, and so on.

Hit. 1) Refers to a visitor accessing a site as in the number of hits a site has received. 2) When performing a search using a *search tool*, a hit is the number of successful entries found relating to the chosen topic or *keyword*.

Home page. The first and introductory page to a *Web* site. When a user travels to a *Web* site, they most often begin at the home page, which offers explanation, instruction and links to the rest of the site.

Host. A computer directly connected to the Internet or to a network.

Hotlist. A feature of the Mosaic browser that stores the name and location of Web sites for easy return.

HyperText Markup Language (HTML). A computer language, used on the *Web*, which formats text files through the use of special commands. *Browsers* interpret HTML for viewing by the user.

HyperText Transport Protocol (HTTP). The commonly accepted protocol for transporting hypertext documents on the Web.

Hyperlink, Hypertext Link or Link. A connection between two *hypertext* documents. This allows users to travel freely, in any direction, throughout an *HTML* document series or *Web site*. Often, *hyperlinks* appear as different colored, underlined text or as a colored border around an image.

Information Superhighway. An all encompassing title for *on-line* information access. In general terms it is the *Internet* itself.

Internet. At the fundamental level, a global network of computer networks. The Internet has come to mean all activity and interaction which takes place on the network, such as e-mail, the World Wide Web, and Usenet news.

Internet Service Provider (ISP). An organization or business that provides a gateway to the Internet. Many of these are commercial ventures. Check local listings for one in your area. *Commercial on-line services* also provide a gateway to the Internet and Web and may be contacted for additional information.

Keyword. The use of specific words as references (similar to the *Find* command on a word processor) to perform a search. This allows for expansive searches for information in numerous resources.

Kilobyte. (abbr. KB) A thousand bytes.

Link. See hyperlink.

Listproc.   Mailing list software.

LISTSERV.   One of the most popular mailing list software's available run. LISTSERV operates on BITNET.

Mailing List.   (also known as list) An e-mail facilitated group discussion.

Majordomo.   Mailing list software.

Megabyte.   (abbr. MB) A million bytes.

Modem.   Short for *mo*dulated *dem*odule which allows transmitting digital data to analog sounds that can be transmitted over ordinary phone lines, then changed back into digital data.

Netiquette.   The Internet community's informal code of conduct for proper Internet use and behavior.

Netizen.   Citizen of the Internet.

Network.   A series of computers that have been electronically linked or are *on-line.*

Newbie.   A person new to the Internet, especially Usenet discussion groups.

On-line.   A computer which is connected to a *network.* Similar to a printer being on-line through its connection to a computer. Computers that are connected to the *Internet* are said to be *on-line* as are people who are connected through their computers.

Protocol.   An understanding on how to communicate between different computers.

Public domain.   Information that is not copyrighted and freely available for public distribution.

Random Access Memory (RAM).   A volatile form of data storage which the CPU uses to store and retrieve information. Volatile memory electronically disappears when power is shut off.

Root Domain.   The root of a domain that signifies the type of entity. The five main root domains in the USA are .com, .edu, .gov, .org, and .net. Countries also have root domains. The root domain for the United States is .us and the root domain for the United Kingdom is uk. There are 106 country domains.

Search Engine.   A device which searches a database of Web sites, documents and other information available through the *Internet.* The search is usually performed based on *keywords.*

Shareware. Software that is distributed by the author for a trial period. This allows you to test the software before purchasing it. If you decide to use the software, you must send the author payment to license the software.

Standard Line Internet Protocol, Point to Point Internet Protocol (SLIP, PPP). Technology that allows the user to turn a standard telephone line into an access way to a *network* (the *Web*).

Smiley. ASCII characters that are used in cyberspace communication to denote emotion. They are also known as emoticons, which is short for emotive icons.

SMTP. The achronym for Simple Mail Transfer Protocol. This is the standard protocol used on the Internet for moving electronic mail between computers.

Snailmail. Term used by Internet users for mail sent through the U.S. postal service to denote the swiftness of e-mail.

Software. Software is a computer program or an application that is run on a computer. It is the opposite of *hardware*. It is what operates the machine and allows it to perform tasks assigned to it by the user.

Spam. Posting an unrelated message to a newsgroup, usually an advertisement. This act is frowned upon by the netizen community.

Subscriber. A person who submits his/her e-mail address to join a mailing list.

Tag. Text added to an HTML document surrounded by a less-than and greater-than sign.

Telnet. An Internet service which allows a computer to log to a remote computer. In this way, both computers function as one.

UNIX. An operating system for computers acting as hosts on the *Internet.*

Uniform Resource Locator (URL). The name of a Web or other address which is inputted into a *browser* or other software to retrieve files from that location.

Usenet. The Internet's bulletin board system of discussion groups, known as newsgroups.

Virus. Software programming code that adds itself to an existing computer program. A virus requires a host program to run or to be activated.

Veronica. A program for searching Gopher menus using keywords.

Webmaster. The person who manages a web site.

Web site. A location on the *World Wide Web* dedicated to a specific purpose. The Web is composed of thousands of sites all *hyperlinked* together. That is where the name *Web* originates.

World Wide Web. (the Web, W3, or WWW) The Web is an *Internet* service which has grown to dominate information distribution on the *Internet*, because of its combined text, graphics, audio and video capabilities as well as ease of use. It is composed of thousands of individual *Web sites* connected to one another via *hyperlinks*.

Worm. A computer program that can copy itself.

Workstation. A souped-up computer, usually with a large amount of memory and other capabilities. Such a computer is often used to link many computers to the Internet.

Index